T0327340

RESEARCH IN MARITIME HISTORY
NO. 4

SHIPBUILDING IN THE UNITED KINGDOM IN THE NINETEENTH CENTURY: A REGIONAL APPROACH

Edited by
Simon Ville

International Maritime Economic History Association/ Trustees of the National Museums and Galleries on Merseyside

St. John's, Newfoundland
1993

ISSN -1188-3928
ISBN -0-9695885-3-4

Research in Maritime History is available free of charge to members of the International Maritime Economic History Association. The price to others is US$15 per copy.

Back issues of *Research in Maritime History* are available:

No. 1 (1991)	David M. Williams and Andrew P. White (comps.), *A Select Bibliography of British and Irish University Theses about Maritime History, 1792-1990*
No. 2 (1992)	Lewis R. Fischer (ed.), *From Wheel House to Counting House: Essays in Maritime Business History in Honour of Professor Peter Neville Davies*
No. 3 (1992)	Lewis R. Fischer and Walter Minchinton (eds.), *People of the Northern Seas*

Research in Maritime History would like to thank the Friends of the Merseyside Maritime Museum and Memorial University of Newfoundland for their generous financial assistance in support of this volume.

CONTENTS

CONTRIBUTORS

About the Editor

SIMON VILLE is Senior Lecturer in Economic History at the Australian National University. He has published widely on transport and business history including *English Shipowning in the Industrial Revolution, 1770-1830* (Manchester, 1987) and *Transport and the Development of the European Economy, 1750-1918* (London, 1990).

Contributors

MICHAEL S. MOSS is Archivist at the University of Glasgow. He has written widely on shipping and shipbuilding, including *A Business of National Importance--The Royal Mail Shipping Group 1902-1937* (London, 1982, with Edwin Green) and *Shipbuilders to the World--125 Years of Harland and Wolff, Belfast 1861-1986* (Belfast, 1986, with John Hume).

FRANK NEAL is Senior Lecturer in Economic and Social Statistics in the Department of Business and Management Studies at the University of Salford.

SARAH PALMER is Senior Lecturer in History at Queen Mary and Westfield College. Her wide-ranging publications on maritime themes include *Politics, Shipping, and the Repeal of the Navigation Laws* (Manchester, 1990). She is currently examining the Port of London in the nineteenth century.

ANTHONY SLAVEN is Professor of Business History at the University of Glasgow and Director of the Centre for Business History in Scotland. He has published widely on the history of shipbuilding and is currently completing a book on the British industry in the twentieth century.

DAVID J. STARKEY is Leverhulm Research Fellow in British Maritime History at the University of Exeter. The author of *British Privateering Enterprise in the Eighteenth Century* (Exeter, 1990) and a joint editor of *The New Maritime History of Devon* (London, 1992), he is currently studying the development of Britain's maritime economy since 1880.

Introduction: Regional Fluctuations in United Kingdom Shipbuilding in the Nineteenth Century

Simon Ville

The international pre-eminence of United Kingdom shipbuilding in the nineteenth century is well known. Although few comparative figures exist for the early part of the century, British output was already greater than that achieved by most countries by the end of the period. Sheltered ports on large navigable rivers such as the Thames, Tyne and Clyde with long shorelines provided the ideal location for the industry. An abundance of capital and a highly-skilled labour force were further benefits for British shipbuilding, as was the large and growing home market of the leading shipowning nation. The position of shipbuilding leadership was most likely extended during the century. The technological changes which transformed the industry in this period all originated, and were mostly exploited, in the United Kingdom.[1] By the later years of the century, when statistical evidence is more readily available, the extent of British domination can be clearly indicated. In the two decades to World War I, UK shipbuilders accounted for sixty to eighty percent of world tonnage, with twenty-five to thirty percent of output being sold overseas.[2] Its domination was even more overwhelming in the new technologies of steam and steel, with only Germany as a second producer of any significance. In 1918 a Board of Trade report noted that "there are few important industries where the predominance of British manufacture has

---

[1]There is a large literature on this. For example see, S. Ville, "Shipping Industry Technologies" in D.J. Jeremy (ed.), *International Technology Transfer. Europe, Japan and the USA, 1700-1914* (Aldershot, 1991), 74-94. For more detail, see Conway's ongoing multi-volume history of the ship.

[2]S. Pollard and P. Robertson, *The British Shipbuilding Industry, 1870-1914* (Cambridge, MA, 1979), 249; A. Slaven, "The Shipbuilding Industry," in R. Church (ed.), *The Dynamics of Victorian Business* (London, 1980), 39.

been more marked than shipbuilding and marine engineering."[3] Thus, at a time when the relative decline of British industry and its poor international competitiveness were under close scrutiny, shipbuilding proved to be a notable exception.

The details of British shipbuilding hegemony have been effectively related in several important studies. Prominent among these are several scholarly papers by Anthony Slaven and a monographic assessment of the industry, mostly after 1870, by Sidney Pollard and Paul Robertson.[4] However, these studies say comparatively little about the regional dimension. Pollard and Robertson devote just a single chapter to regional comparisons and contrasts. Existing regional studies of the industry are mostly narrative and parochial in nature and make little attempt to draw comparisons with other regions.[5] There is, in fact, an important regional story which has been largely obscured by the dramatic success of the industry nationally and internationally. By disaggregating the national figures, we can see substantial fluctuations in the performance of particular regions. Pollard and Robertson have identified the major trend of increased concentration of output into three major areas: Clydeside, the northeast of England and Belfast, which they attribute to "the availability of cheap and docile labour, ready supplies of raw materials and other inputs, and easy access to markets."[6]

The current study seeks to look much more closely at the regional dimension. While Pollard and Robertson correctly identified the industry's major geographical shift, they told us little about its timing, dimensions or the complex mix of factors which help to explain it. It is also intended to say much more about those regions which went into comparative decline, notably the southeast, southwest and northwest of England, and the intra-regional shifts in production.

---

[3]United Kingdom, Board of Trade, "Report of Departmental Committee on Shipping and Shipbuilding" (Cd. 9092, 1918), 35-36.

[4]See footnote 2.

[5]Typical of this genre is D. Dougan, *The History of North-East Shipbuilding* (London, 1968).

[6]Pollard and Robertson, *British Shipbuilding*, 51.

With these objectives in mind, the editor has recruited a team of six authors, each possessing expertise on the historical dimension of shipbuilding in a particular region of the United Kingdom. Each of the major shipbuilding regions have been investigated: Ireland (Moss); Scotland (Slaven); northwest England (Neal); northeast (Ville); southwest (Starkey); and southeast (Palmer). Each author was asked to establish the quantitative and qualitative nature of output in their region and to seek to explain these trends by assessing individual factors of production, the character of the enterprises and the nature of the market. A common approach has also been fostered by mutual exchange and discussion of the papers among the contributors and by the presentation of all of them to the First International Congress of Maritime History at Liverpool's Merseyside Maritime Museum in August 1992. Some have also been circulated and discussed among economic historians not specialising in maritime history. While the study is given focus by a common approach, the results illustrate a variety of experiences both in terms of the changing nature of output and the underlying explanations of such trends. This is a picture more contextual and complex than implied by Pollard and Robertson's brief generalisations.

National studies of the United Kingdom shipbuilding industry have been aided by the availability of good output figures from parliamentary and customs sources throughout most of the century. Although there are some discrepancies between sources, these are mostly minor and have little or no impact on the main trends. Indeed, compared with most other industries we are highly fortunate at the amount of shipbuilding information which has survived. On a regional level the figures are less complete, with a major break for many ports between 1827 and 1865. For a number of ports, however, this omission has been filled by local evidence, particularly from newspapers. At Sunderland, for example, local and national evidence provides virtually an unbroken run of output figures. This was most likely the result of the interest generated by the remarkable growth of output at the port. Here, as elsewhere, the designation, "built and first registered at the port," used in some early returns, suggests a possible omission.[7] Yet it seems clear that the great

---

[7]R. Craig, "A Note on Shipbuilding in the Port of Sunderland," *International Journal of Maritime History*, III, No. 2 (December 1991), 109-119, discusses some of the problems of shipbuilding statistics.

majority of output was sold locally in the early nineteenth century. This had changed by mid-century and was recognised by changes in the presentation of statistical information. Several contributors have sought different solutions to the omissions of 1827-1865; Starkey, for example, uses the Devon shipping registers and *Lloyd's Registers* to calculate local output. Neal covers the missing years by building up evidence for Liverpool and Birkenhead based upon the shipping registers, company histories, yard books and newspaper reports. Slaven adopts a different approach by using the data on UK shipbuilding compiled as part of a project at the University of Newcastle. While this involves only a twenty percent sample, Slaven is able to produce proportional comparisons between Scotland and the rest of the United Kingdom. Palmer and Moss have for the most part used literary evidence to cover the gap.

It is worth remembering that these figures relate to the building of new ships. Unfortunately, we know much less about ship repair. While statistical information on repair is sparse, the importance of this activity is clear enough. During the era of wood and sail, the longevity of many vessels can be explained by regular minor repairs and periodic major overhauls. Shipbuilders possessed the skills and capital to repair vessels, which was probably a compensating source of income during depressions when owners sought to extend the life of existing vessels as far as possible. Evidence from the regions also confirms the importance of repairs for metal steamers. Hawthorn on Tyneside survived difficult years late in the century through repair work, while in the declining southwest firms like Stephens of Fowey and Cox of Bridport survived for some years in this way. In Ireland, where shipbuilding was increasingly concentrated upon several large Belfast firms, smaller concerns at other ports began to turn to repairing in the final three decades or so of the century; these included Malcolmsen's Neptune Iron Works at Waterford and Robinson at Cork. A similar story can be told of many London builders. But the history of British ship repairing remains to be told.

Despite the statistical omissions mentioned above, the regional trend across the period has been closely measured. The northeast's share of national output grew during the century from around a third to a half; Scotland's from ten or fifteen percent to a third; and Ireland's from a few percent to ten or twelve. By contrast, the southwest's share of tonnage built contracted from eight or ten percent to less than one; that of the southeast and northwest from ten or fifteen percent each to no more than a few percent.[8] These regional trends are accentuated by distinguishing between wooden sailing vessels and metal steamers, the latest technology emanating mostly from the yards of Clydeside, Belfast and the northeast of England. Closely associated with this was the growth in vessel size: again, the region-by-region studies indicate that the largest vessels were mostly being built in the three expanding regions. Clearly, the rapid technological progress in the industry had a major bearing upon its changing spatial location.

In addition to the changes between regions, there were also significant intra-regional shifts. In Scotland, this involved a concentration upon Clydeside and in Ireland, upon Belfast. In the northeast many Yorkshire shipbuilding centres declined, including Scarborough, Whitby and Hull, with the emphasis shifting towards Tyneside, Teeside and Wearside. Intra-regional concentration was less clear in the declining regions. In the northwest Liverpool's share of output expanded in mid-century, but then contracted again by the final decades. The demise of the southwest and southeast meant far fewer centres of production by the end of the period, and none of those that remained survived on a large scale. Increased concentration also took the form of fewer but much larger firms, and again the trend to large-scale production was most notable in the expanding regions. In Belfast, Harland and Wolff and Workman-Clark dominated local output by the later decades of the century. In the northeast giants like Armstrong-Mitchell, Vickers-Beardmore, and Swan Hunter and Wigham Richardson were industry leaders before the First World War. The latter two also were influential on Clydeside, Swan Hunter, for example, acquiring Barclay Curle in 1912, to operate alongside other large firms such as Scott and Fairfield. Thus, there was increased concentration of production in three respects: by region, port and individual builder.

Evidence of increased concentration underlies explanations of the changing spatial location of the industry. Shipbuilding migrated to areas which could best meet its changing technological demands in engineering and metallurgy. By their nature, these industries were concentrated in

---

[8]For both the beginning and the end of the period the sum of the six regions does not add to 100% of UK shipbuilding because although they collectively cover the great majority of UK output there are still some other areas of minor production, such as Wales and some of the English mid-coast ports.

particular areas; with the expansion of shipbuilding the economies of localisation in industrial conurbations held particular advantages. The shipbuilding industry of the northeast, for example, benefitted from the products and skilled labour force of local heavy industries. A similar situation existed on Clydeside, where vertically-integrated metallurgy, engineering and shipbuilding industries emerged. In Belfast the situation was somewhat different, since iron and steel had to be imported. The major Belfast firms, on the other hand, illustrate effective sales policies through "tied" customers who were given discounts in return for loyalty. The large size and favourable cost structures of firms in all three regions enabled them to pursue active marketing and sales policies worldwide, as the market for ships stretched well beyond the local orientation of the early nineteenth century. By contrast, the declining shipbuilding areas, particularly in the south of England, lacked the basic technological requirements to build internal economies of scale within large enterprises and external economies from increased localisation.

Shipbuilding in the Northeast of England in the Nineteenth Century[1]

Simon Ville

Introduction

This essay examines the rate and pattern of growth of shipbuilding output in the major ports of northeast England in the nineteenth century.[2] Competing explanations of performance are assessed in light of extant evidence in an attempt to understand why the region was so successful at shipbuilding during this period.

Performance

The northeast has long been an important centre of shipbuilding. The bulk coal and timber trades generated a high demand for shipping, which was mainly provided by local shipowners whose need for vessels was in turn satisfied largely by local yards.[3] By the end of the eighteenth century about one-third of British shipbuilding came from the region: in 1790 the proportion was thirty-four percent and in 1800 thirty-eight percent. This share grew to an average of fifty-two percent of the UK total by 1911-1913. In both periods--and throughout most of the

[1]I am grateful to Dr. Paul Robertson as well as participants at the First International Congress of Maritime History and at the joint seminar programme at ANU for comments on this paper. I also acknowledge the valuable research assistance of Helen Bridge.

[2]The northeast comprises the eastern counties north of the Wash. Merchant and naval shipbuilding are both discussed in this paper, although most extant statistics relate only to the former, which also accounted for the great bulk of output.

[3]Non-local shipowners involved in northeastern trades also relied heavily on the region's shipyards. See S. Ville, *English Shipowning during the Industrial Revolution. Michael Henley and Son, London Shipowners, 1770-1830* (Manchester, 1987), 40-43.

nineteenth century--the northeast was the most prolific shipbuilding region in the country. Most of its output originated from the banks of two principal rivers, the Tyne and the Wear (see figure 1 and appendix table 1). Tyneside shipbuilding is usually associated with Newcastle and Wearside with Sunderland, the major settlements on their respective rivers. In practice, shipbuilding was also located at smaller settlements further up or downstream. This was particularly true on the Tyne, where as early as the end of the eighteenth century there is evidence of production at North and South Shields and Howdonpans.[4] In the nineteenth century Wallsend also became a significant production point on the Tyne. The two rivers' combined share of the region's total was as dominant in 1913 (sixty-eight percent) as a century earlier (sixty-two percent in 1814). Yet there were cyclical fluctuations during the century: in 1832, for example, they accounted for eighty-seven percent of local output. The ranking of secondary ports shifted spatially from the Yorkshire ports of Hull, Whitby and Scarborough north to the Teeside centres of Hartlepool, Stockton and Middlesborough. While much of the discussion will naturally focus upon the two dominant ports, reference will also be made to secondary ones, not least because their changing rank illuminates some of the issues affecting general competitive advantages within the British shipbuilding industry of the last century.

It will be argued that there were essentially two phases to the progress of the region's shipbuilding industry in the nineteenth century. In the first half, the great success story was Sunderland, where local production rose from less than ten percent of national output to nearly forty percent by the 1840s. Growth in the second half was more dispersed geographically, with Newcastle, Sunderland and the Teeside ports all doing well. Markets, factor costs and entrepreneurship will each be analysed to seek explanations for the region's success in shipbuilding.

It should also be made clear that this essay deals solely with the building of new ships and not the repair or modification of existing vessels. There doubtless has always been a close connection between building and repairing, drawing as they do upon identical skills, capital and materials, and frequently taking place within the same firm. Moreover, there is likely an inverse relationship between the two activities: in shipping depressions, when the demand for new vessels is

---

[4]See S. Ville, "Shipping in the Port of Newcastle, 1780-1800," *Journal of Transport History*, 3rd ser., IX (1988), 66.

low, many owners try to economise by extending the life of their fleet through regular repairs. Unfortunately, ship repair remains a Cinderella activity through its poor documentation: we know little of its nature, magnitude or development. For the sailing ship era, at least, repairs may have been more important than building.[5] For one northeast firm, the lengthening of ships in the 1870s provided important business while profitable repair activities helped cover its building losses in the final two decades of the century.[6]

Rate of Growth

At the beginning of the century Newcastle and Sunderland produced comparable tonnages and together accounted for a fifth of national output.[7] By the end of the French Wars this had already begun to change. During the last four full years of hostilities, Sunderland's output reached 42,000 tons compared with 30,000 at Newcastle. Between 1814 and 1826, Sunderland more than doubled its neighbour's output and led the country in every year except 1820, when it was surpassed by London. Sunderland continued to expand throughout the 1830s, despite a general shipbuilding depression, and its national and international pre-eminence became clear. By the 1840s the port accounted for one-third of UK production. Favourable comparisons with New York in the following decade suggest that the town had probably become the largest shipbuilder in the world, producing over 60,000 tons annually in the early 1850s. Yet Newcastle was also important: between 1814 and 1826 it was the second or third largest producer in all but two years. By contrast, the principal Yorkshire ports declined. This was most severe at

---

[5]This reflects the fact that repair costs were often greater than a vessel's original cost. For example, *Lady Juliana*, owned by Henley for over thirty years, had repairs of £2469 in a six-year period alone, representing approximately two-thirds of its original cost. National Maritime Museum, Greenwich (NMM), Henley Papers (HNL), 77/1, 20.

[6]J.F. Clarke, *Power on Land and Sea: 160 Years of Industrial Enterprise on Tyneside. A History of R&W Hawthorn Leslie and Company Ltd.* (Newcastle, 1978), 33, 61.

[7]In 1801-1805 Sunderland built 41,553 and Newcastle 48,461 out of a UK total of 464,106 tons.

Scarborough, while output at Hull held up best, at least to the mid-1820s.[8]

Shipbuilding in the northeast continued to expand absolutely and relatively in the second half of the century, although the concentration on tramps made output highly cyclical because of the volatile demand for this shipping service.[9] Sunderland remained successful and expansive in the second half of the century, although its relative importance waned somewhat. The two ports produced comparable amounts of tonnage in the 1860s and early 1870s, but by the end of the decade Newcastle had clearly surpassed its neighbour as the dominant regional port, producing an aggregate of 1.8 million tons compared with 1.4 million at Sunderland. Sunderland's national contribution also declined from approximately one-third of UK output in the 1840s to fifteen percent in the four years prior to World War I. The other significant feature is the relative growth of the Teeside ports, particularly from mid-century (figure 2 and table 2). Shipbuilding took place from at least the middle of the eighteenth century at Stockton, and by 1800 the port was sharing in the boom of the French Wars. In the depressed postwar decades its output appears to have contracted substantially.[10] Middlesborough does not appear to have launched its first vessel until 1833 and Hartlepool four years later.[11] By the end of the period, however, the joint output of Middlesborough and Stockton was more than half that of Sunderland.[12]

---

[8]For more detail on northeastern output before 1850, see S. Ville, "Rise to Pre-Eminence: The Development and Growth of the Sunderland Shipbuilding Industry," *International Journal of Maritime History*, I, No. 1 (June 1989), 66-71. I am grateful to David Starkey for bringing to my attention the valuable information contained in "Vessels Built and Registered in the Ports of Great Britain and Ireland, 1814-26," *British Parliamentary Papers (BPP)*, XVIII (1826-1827), 286-287.

[9]S. Pollard and P. Robertson, *The British Shipbuilding Industry, 1870-1914* (Cambridge, MA, 1979), 64. For example, Palmer's shipyard is said to have launched 25,000 tons in 1874, dropping to only 9000 two years later before rising to 61,000 in 1883. D. Dougan, *The History of North-East Shipbuilding* (London, 1968), 85.

[10]"Select Committee on Manufactures, Commerce and Shipping," *BPP*, VI (1833), 718.

[11]Dougan, *History of North-East Shipbuilding*, 30.

[12]Data from *Lloyds Register*, in Dougan, *History of North-East Shipbuilding*, 223.

Figure 1
Sunderland and Newcastle Shipbuilding, 1786-1913

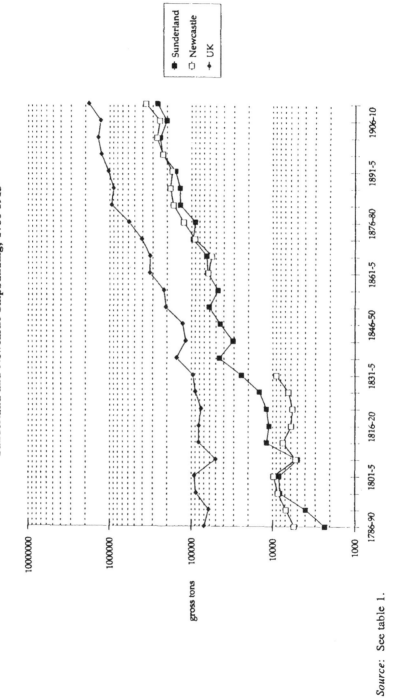

Source: See table 1.

Simon Ville

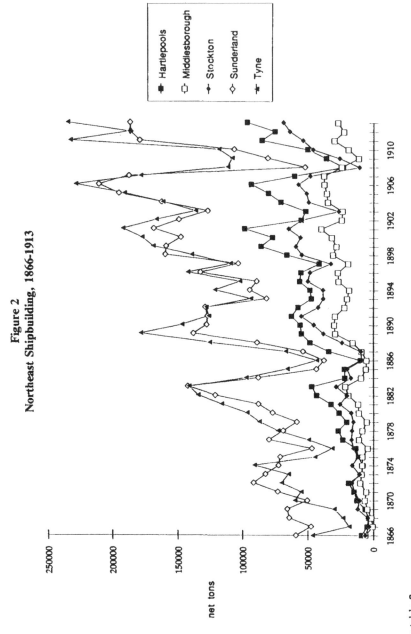

Figure 2
Northeast Shipbuilding, 1866-1913

Source: See table 2.

Pattern of Growth

In the first half of the century Sunderland was a major supplier of medium to large sailing vessels. Its share of national sailing output rose from less than ten percent to half by the mid-1850s, while average size grew from less than 200 to more than 400 tons. Vessels of 200-300 tons were suitable for a range of trades and their adaptability encouraged Sunderland producers to build "on spec" during depressions in the knowledge that they were ultimately more likely to be sold than vessels designed for a specific trade.[13] Vessels from the northeast were generally renowned for capaciousness, often having cargo tonnages fifty percent greater than registered tonnage.[14] Several local yards had reputations for specialist craft, such as East Indiamen and clippers for the Australian trade. Among prominent builders, Austin was known for general cargo vessels while William Pile built a series of clippers.[15]

Increased output appears to have been accompanied by improvements in the quality of Sunderland-built vessels. Local antagonisms may have caused Henry Woodroffe, Secretary to the Seamen's Society at South Shields, to claim that Sunderland ships were the worst in the world.[16] A more impartial observer was George Bayley, a Surveyor of Shipping for Lloyds Register, who noted in the 1830s that "the improvement is most decided and it quite astonished me."[17] This view was repeated in 1851 in *The Times*, which noted that "along with an increase in the number of vessels built on the Wear, we may point with pride to their daily improving character...We have heard of sailing feats of

---

[13]Anon., *A Collection of Interesting Reports and Papers on the Navigation and Trade of Great Britain* (London, 1807), appendix, 137-138, indicates that in 1805-1806 most Sunderland-built vessels were constructed on speculation.

[14]T. Potts, *History of Sunderland* (Sunderland, 1892), 94. See also S. Ville, "The Problem of Tonnage Measurement in the English Shipping Industry, 1780-1830," *International Journal of Maritime History*, I, No. 2 (December 1989), 78.

[15]W.C. Mitchell, *History of Sunderland* (Sunderland, 1919), 132-139; J.F. Clarke, "Shipbuilding on the River Wear, 1780-1870," in R. W. Sturgess (ed.), *The Great Age of Industry in the North-East* (Durham, 1981), 84.

[16]"Select Committee on Shipwrecks," *BPP*, XVII (1836), 27.

[17]*Ibid.*, 194.

Sunderland craft that are equal to anything that has been achieved by the cracks of London or Isle of Wight yards."[18] During this period Sunderland vessels were accorded improved ratings at Lloyd's.[19] It seems likely that a wide range of vessels were built at Sunderland both in terms of type of usage and quality (as reflected in longevity). While builders such as Austin, Pickersgill and Doxford produced to a high standard, smaller yards turned out cheaper, more ephemeral craft.

In the absence of growth as spectacular as on Wearside, less is known about the main features of Tyneside shipbuilding before 1850. From a detailed study of Newcastle shipping registers at the end of the eighteenth century, we can get a good idea of the nature of the local industry at that time.[20] For most of the 1790s at least ninety percent of Newcastle-built vessels were initially registered at the port. Its craft were somewhat larger than those built at Sunderland, averaging over 200 tons throughout the decade. In 1795, ninety-six percent of locally-built tonnage was initially registered at the port, and these vessels averaged 273 tons.[21] Three-masted ships and barques for a range of overseas trades were frequently built at North Shields, while smaller two-masted brigantines and snows for coasting were concentrated at Newcastle.[22]

Evidence on Stockton shipbuilding in the first half of the nineteenth century is patchier, although a couple of examples are well-documented. Thomas Haw was one of the leading builders at the port and launched a number of larger vessels, including the 556-ton *Highland Lass*. The deployment and profitability of the 317-ton *Freedom* have been analysed in detail.[23] Built by Haw in 1791, it was one of the most

---

[18]*The Times*, 4 February 1851. D. MacGregor, *The Tea Clippers* (London, 1952), 73, compares the Sunderland clipper *Kelso* favourably in terms of capacity, stability and speed with *Friar Tuck*, built by William Hall of Aberdeen, a pioneer of this vessel type.

[19]This is explained in more detail in Ville, "Rise to Pre-Eminence," 83-84.

[20]See Ville, "Shipping in the Port of Newcastle."

[21]*Ibid.*, 66.

[22]*Ibid.*, 66-67.

[23]S. Ville, "Wages, Prices and Profitability in the Shipping Industry during the Napoleonic Wars: A Case Study," *Journal of Transport History*, 3rd ser., II, No. 1 (1981).

successful and long-lived vessels of Michael Henley and Son of London, who deployed it in various trades during the following four decades.

An important feature of the Sunderland boom before 1850 was that it was not technologically advanced. Builders were slow to shift from wood to metal and sail to steam compared to Newcastle, Liverpool and Clydeside, causing *The Times* to note that "while the building of timber ships is so active in the Wear, iron shipbuilding is very brisk on the Tyne."[24] Few iron vessels were built before the 1860s, and even then new wooden yards were being established. Table 3 shows that Sunderland did not shift entirely to metal until the late 1870s, several years after the Tyne. The Hartlepools, Middlesborough and Stockton built only metal ships by 1871. M. Pearce and Co. of Stockton built the first steel vessel in the northeast in 1859. Steel building on the Tyne began in 1878 with Charles Mitchell's *Ethel*. Doxford led the way in Sunderland, building three steel ships in 1883. The main transition to mild steel took place in the years immediately following 1885: by 1887 ninety-three percent of Tees output, and by 1888 ninety-five percent of Tyne and ninety-nine percent of Wear tonnage, was also steel.[25]

Steam tugs were built from the 1820s but very few ocean-going steamers were produced at Sunderland before the 1860s. Steam never comprised more than one percent of tonnage before the mid-1850s, compared with a national figure of up to ten percent.[26] Indeed, some sail output persisted until the early 1890s.[27] The Tyne and Tees,

---

[24]*The Times*, 22 December 1852. Although only one northeast firm, T.D. Marshall of South Shields, was among the pioneers of iron shipbuilding in the 1830s. F.M. Walker, "Precision Construction: Iron's Contribution to Modern Shipbuilding," in J. Lang (ed.), *Metals and the Sea* (London, 1990), 25, 27.

[25]J.F. Clarke and F. Storr, "The Introduction of the Use of Mild Steel in the Shipbuilding and Marine Engineering Industries," Newcastle-upon-Tyne Polytechnic *Occasional Papers in the History of Science and Technology*, I (1983), 33, 66-71, also make clear the greater reliability of mild versus Bessemer steel, which was used in the earliest steel vessels.

[26]Clarke, "Shipbuilding on the River Wear," 110; B.R. Mitchell and P. Deane (comps.), *An Abstract of British Historical Statistics* (Cambridge, 1988), 220-221.

[27]Pollard and Robertson, *British Shipbuilding*, 63, inaccurately claim that the transition to steam at Sunderland was completed by 1878 and that few sailing vessels were built on the Tyne or Tees after 1863.

however, were among the earliest districts to concentrate upon steamers. It was a Tyneside firm, Palmer Brothers of Jarrow, which in 1852 built the *John Bowes*, one of the earliest iron screw colliers. At Tyneside, Middlesborough and the Hartlepools the transition was virtually complete by the early 1870s. The situation was somewhat different at Stockton, where significant sail tonnage was built until 1887. One striking feature of the process of technical change was the partial and temporary reversion to sail in the mid-1880s because of low freight rates.[28] This was most noticeable in 1885, when only fifty-two percent of Stockton and sixty-three percent of Sunderland new tonnage was steam-powered. A similar though less marked trend characterised other local ports.

The changes in northeast shipbuilding after 1850 were not restricted to the use of metal as the primary construction material and steam as the principal propulsion. Important developments in the pattern of overseas trade and the character of shipowning led to the increasing division of the merchant marine into "tramps" and "liners." The northeast specialised in tramps. This was clearest on the Wear and Tees, which were at the forefront of design improvements. Doxford of Sunderland played a major role in the development of turret-deckers, building more than 100 by 1904 and experimenting with diesel propulsion. Edward Withy and Co. pioneered the "well-deck" cargo vessel and built more than 350 at its West Hartlepool yard by 1889. Another innovation came from Joseph Isherwood, director of R. Craggs and Son of Middlesborough, who devised a system of longitudinal framing which economised on materials and facilitated the lengthening of vessels.[29]

While most ships built in the northeast before 1850 were general carriers, local firms thereafter began to build craft for specific trades, such as ore and oil. Speculative building became more risky and builders increasingly concentrated on filling their order books.[30] Tyneside yards such as Armstrong and Palmer were among the earliest tanker builders: 147 of the 200 oil tankers built in the northeast in the two decades after

---

[28]See E.A.V. Angier, *Fifty Years of Freights, 1869-1919* (London, 1920), 63.

[29]G.W. Silverwright, "The Development of the Well-Deck Cargo Steamer," *Transactions of the North East Coast Institution of Engineers and Shipbuilders*, V (1888-1889), 153; G.C.V. Holmes, *Ancient and Modern Ships* (London, 1906), 102-130.

[30]Clarke, "River Wear," 89, shows that "on spec" building was still common in 1847-1864, although wooden sailing vessels remained important in these years.

1886 were launched there.[31] Tyneside also built warships, liners and a range of tugs, trawlers and drifters. After the 1883 merger of Armstrong and Mitchell, the new company built all types of warships at Elswick, supplying the navies of Japan, China, USA, Brazil, Argentina, Chile, Norway, Portugal, Italy, Rumania, Spain and the United Kingdom. Swan Hunter, which built a variety of vessels, entered naval production and constructed high-class passenger liners like the *Mauretania* and specialist vessels for the expanding Swedish ore trade of the 1880s and 1890s.[32]

Evidence on vessel prices is fragmentary and ambiguous, although most writers agree they were lower in the northeast, particularly at Sunderland before 1850.[33] Testimony to parliamentary committees in the 1830s and 1840s certainly points in this direction.[34] Given the uncertain reliability of extant shipbuilding prices, most historians have concentrated on costs, as will this author. It is worth noting that the reliance on local markets before 1850 suggests that price differentials were of limited importance in explaining comparative regional performance. Thereafter, as regions began to specialise in particular types of vessels, competition between firms rather than regions was likely more important and stimulated the active sales policies of many enterprises.

Explanations of Performance

To explain the success of northeast shipbuilding in the nineteenth century, a variety of approaches will be used. On the demand side, we will examine not only the size of the local shipowning community but also growing sales elsewhere. On the supply side, neo-classical factors of production will be surveyed to see if the cost and availability of land, labour and capital provided any advantages. Entrepreneurship, which is increasingly recognised as an important influence upon industrial

---

[31]Dougan, *History of North-East Shipbuilding*, 84.

[32]R. Craig, *Steam Tramps and Cargo Liners* (London, 1980), 23.

[33]Clarke, "River Wear," 86; Ville, "Rise to Pre-Eminence," 82.

[34]Ville, "Rise to Pre-Eminence," 82. R. Craig, "A Note on Shipbuilding in the Port of Sunderland," *International Journal of Maritime History*, III, No. 2 (December 1991), 117, argues that prompt delivery was more important in the 1820s and 1830s, a doubtful claim given the large number of unsold vessels available for immediate delivery.

performance, will also be analysed, taking particular account of the structure of firms as well as managerial strategies.

Demand

Pollard and Robertson have argued that "in timber days, the proximity to the markets was alone important, and shipbuilding output was closely proportionate to the trade of the ports."[35] Although they did not attempt to measure it, there was clearly a close tie between building and local shipowners. Between 1786 and 1800 eighty-seven percent of Newcastle-built tonnage was first registered there and most remained, since over the same period more than half of Newcastle-registered tonnage was built there.[36] Local owners remained the principal buyers into the next century, although the reliance diminished: in seven of ten years after 1834/1835 more than half of new Sunderland tonnage was sold to owners from the same port.[37] There was also a strong link between owning and building in the region as a whole: seventy-nine percent of registered tonnage at Newcastle, 1786-1800, was built in the region.[38] While in 1839 fifty-five percent of new Sunderland tonnage was sold locally, sixteen percent went to Newcastle and eight percent to Stockton.[39]

While there is no reason to expect a precise relationship between owning and building, the northeast was the most rapidly growing area for both before 1850. In particular, during the difficult two decades after the French Wars the Tyneside and Wearside shipping industries continued to expand.[40] From especially good data for Sunderland we can see a close cyclical relationship between owning and building in the first half of the nineteenth century (table 4 and figure 3).

---

[35]Pollard and Robertson, *British Shipbuilding*, 56.

[36]Ville, "Shipping in the Port of Newcastle," 65-66.

[37]"Select Committee on British Shipping," *BPP*, VIII (1844), 114.

[38]Ville, "Shipping in the Port of Newcastle," 65.

[39]Tyne and Wear Archives Service (TWAS) 730/2, Notebook of Andrew White.

[40]S. Ville, "Shipping in the Port of Sunderland, 1815-45: A Counter-Cyclical Trend," *Business History*, XXXII, No. 1 (1990), 34-35.

Figure 3

Sunderland Shipowning and Shipbuilding, 1791-1913

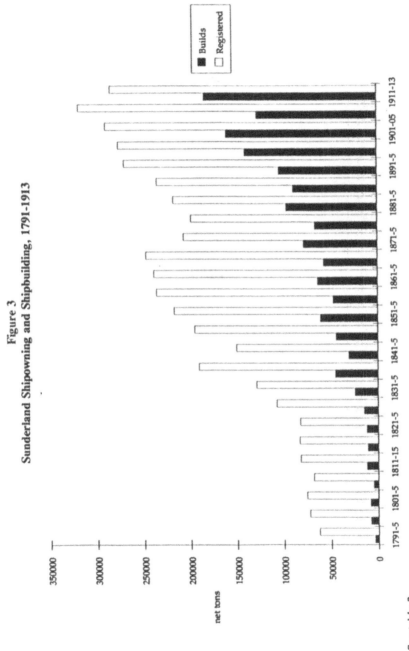

Source: See table 3.

Figure 4: Launch of the *W.S. Lindsay*, iron emigrant ship, at Willington, near Newcastle-upon-Tyne.

Source: *Illustrated London News*, 9 October 1852.

Figure 5: Launch of *La Rogue*, the largest ship ever built in Sunderland.

Source: *Illustrated London News*, 11 August 1855.

There were good reasons why shipowners often preferred local tonnage. With local builders the owner was better placed to supervise construction and guard against extended delivery dates. In an industry that was heavily craft-based before the age of steam and metal, a less standardised product emphasised the importance of supervision. Henley, the London shipowners, stationed one of its masters in Stockton in 1790-1791 to supervise the construction of *Freedom*, but most firms lacked such resources.[41] The owner who bought locally was also able to observe changes in technology and to take advantage of bargains. Personal relationships with local builders through regular orders also led to discounted prices, extended credit and other benefits. An early form of part-exchange of old for new vessels enabled builders to use any remaining good timbers and stores. The Whites were one of the largest Sunderland shipowning families in the first half of the nineteenth century; nearly ninety percent of their fleet was built at the port.[42] By regular patronage of local builders, such as John and William Gales, Partis Oswald, John Brunton and Samson Mills, they secured favourable price, credit and delivery terms on new vessels, including part-exchange.[43]

If shipbuilding were spurred by the buoyancy of shipowning in the first half of the nineteenth century, some explanation of the latter is required. With the growth of iron, engineering and other coal-consuming industries, British coal production increased from less than sixteen million tons at the end of the French Wars to around fifty million by mid-century. While Durham and Northumberland coal fields produced twenty to twenty-five percent of national output, the region's dominance was greatest in seaborne carriage, accounting for two-thirds to four-fifths of movements before the 1850s.[44] Most early railway construction took place in the northeast and initially complemented the seaborne coal trade by improving supply to the ports. The bulk nature of coal suggests important implications for shipping demand. Coastal coal shipments from

---

[41]NMM, HNL 59/1.

[42]TWAS 730/4, Notebook of Andrew White; TWAS 1259, Statutory Shipping Registers for Sunderland.

[43]TWAS 730/4.

[44]B.R. Mitchell, *Economic Development of the British Coal Industry, 1800-1914* (Cambridge, 1984), 16-17.

Tyne, Wear and Tees ports doubled to 5.4 million tons, 1816-1855, while exports rose by a factor of twelve to 2.3 million tons.[45] The very high growth rate of exports is particularly noteworthy given the greater amount of shipping time per voyage on longer hauls. The progress of the coal trade during the difficult years after 1815 was sustained by cost-reducing productivity improvements, including more efficient loading methods. In addition, vertical integration yielded transaction cost savings, in the process encouraging local ownership.[46] Vertical integration also confirmed that the growth of the shipping industry was inextricably linked to the rapid economic expansion of the region.

The growth of coal exports permitted the development of two-way traffic, with timber imports coming back to the northeast. One contemporary believed that timber was "a great part of the shipping trade to the port of Sunderland," while another estimated that 100-140 craft were involved in the trade at the port.[47] This structure gave Sunderland a competitive edge over ports with no staple export. Not a small part of the decline in shipbuilding at the Yorkshire ports of Hull, Whitby and Scarborough was due to the absence of a staple. In addition, the lower inward freight rates resulting from two-way trading reduced the cost of timber for local shipbuilders. "Even from America we can get freights lower than to the west coast of England," noted one local merchant-shipowner.[48] A further advantage for builders at exporting ports was the

---

[45] *Ibid.*, 16-17.

[46] These issues have been discussed in various papers by the current author. On productivity improvements, see "Total Factor Productivity in the English Shipping Industry: The North-East Coal Trade, 1700 to 1850," *Economic History Review*, 2nd ser., XXXIX (1986). On the benefits of vertical integration, see "The Expansion and Development of a Private Business: An Application of Vertical Integration Theory," *Business History*, XXXIII (1991). On increased localisation, see "Patterns of Shipping Investment in the Port of Newcastle, 1750-1850," *Northern History*, XXV (1989).

[47] "Select Committee on Timber Duties," *BPP*, XIX (1835), 297, evidence of John Spence, shipowner, shipbroker and general merchant of Sunderland and Stockton; "Select Committee on Shipwrecks of Timber Ships," *ibid.*, IX (1835), 65, evidence of A.S. Ord, shipowner and merchant of Sunderland.

[48] "Select Committee on the Navigation Laws," *BPP*, XX (1847-1848), part 2, 317, evidence of Joshua Wilson.

avoidance of an initial wasted passage. This was of enduring relevance throughout the century for northeast coal-exporting ports.

In the second half of the century the importance of the local market diminished rapidly. Although local shipowners invested in tramp shipping, this was insufficient to sustain the region's shipbuilding expansion.[49] At Sunderland, for example, there was a progressive convergence of shipbuilding and registered tonnage: the former as a proportion of the latter increased from eleven to fifty-one percent between the first and last quinquennia of the century (figure three and table four). This convergence was not mirrored nationally and reflects the fact that a rising proportion of new tonnage was being sold beyond the port. To begin with, a significant volume of northeast output was sold as far afield as New Zealand.[50] This was particularly the case for Tyneside, where from one-quarter to more than one-third of output was sold abroad between the mid-1880s and World War I (table 5). With the exception of the protectionism of the United States and occasional but mostly ineffective subsidies by several European states, there was free trade in new and second-hand tonnage.[51]

Of particular importance as a foreign market was Japan. Indeed, its late-nineteenth-century merchant and armed navies were largely built on Tyneside. Conte-Helm's study of Japan and the northeast traces close economic relations from the mid-nineteenth century. The symbiosis of Japanese demand and northeast supply, which was reversed in the twentieth century, originated in the simultaneous growth of heavy industry in the region and the Japanese desire to modernise at the end of the Tokugawa shogunate. Conte-Helm notes that "the Japanese...focused their attention on coal, ships and guns. These three elements would form the basis of their continuing dialogue with the North East of England."[52] British success in the conflict with Japan in the Shimoneski Straits in September 1863 confirmed the superiority of British warships

---

[49]Craig, *Steam Tramps*, 40.

[50]S.D. Waters, *Clipper Ship to Motor Liner. The Story of the New Zealand Shipping Company, 1873-1939* (London, 1939), 42, 46-47.

[51]See J.G.B. Hutchins, *The American Maritime Industries and Public Policy, 1789-1914* (Cambridge, MA, 1941), 407-408, 464-467.

[52]M. Conte-Helm, *Japan and the North East of England* (London, 1989), 7.

equipped with Armstrong guns. This was the same year in which Armstrong resigned from the War Department, leaving him free to supply foreign navies. An agreement in 1867 combined Mitchell's shipbuilding capability at Walker with Armstrong's armament technology at Elswick. This was cemented by amalgamation in 1883, putting the combination in a strong position to equip the expanding Japanese navy. The Sino- and Russo-Japanese wars sustained demand for both merchant and naval vessels at the end of the century.[53]

The new Meiji regime was also anxious to expand the merchant marine through government incentives. The dominant shipping companies, such as NYK, OSK and TKK, turned frequently to British yards. Between 1874 and 1912, NYK operated a total of fifty-one northeast-built vessels. Although Japanese yards developed, especially in the 1880s, they could not meet the demand for new ships and were frequently a step behind their British competitors in new technology.[54] With the development of the Japanese railway system, NYK increasingly withdrew from the coastal trade and concentrated upon deep-sea trade. This brought the company into conflict with some European shipping rings, particularly the European-Far Eastern Conference. After negotiating with the conference in 1896, it was agreed that NYK could discharge westbound goods at London but could not load eastbound cargoes. Instead, the company loaded at Middlesborough. From these events a relationship between the port and the company developed and was sustained, even after NYK was granted full London loading rights a few years later. Shipbuilding, repair, iron and steel, and chemical industries, as well as a bunker coal supply, formed the basis of Middlesborough's importance to the company. Table 5 indicates the high proportion of Middlesborough tonnage built for overseas buyers from the mid-1890s.

The oligopolistic structure in Japanese shipping in the final few decades of the century and the simultaneous growth of concentration in the shipbuilding industry of the northeast emphasised the importance of

---

[53]NYK's direct participation in the Sino-Japanese War led to a doubling of its fleet to 128,000, while a decade later 24,000 tons were requisitioned from the company for the Russian war. *Ibid.*, 80, 92.

[54]As well, the 1896 Navigation Encouragement Act enabled Japanese companies to purchase foreign-built ships on favourable terms. Three years later, however, the subsidy was reduced to half the level for domestic yards, causing Britain's supply of merchant ships to diminish. *Ibid.*, 83.

sustained connections to ensure repeat orders. Armstrong was particularly adept at fostering customer loyalty. Inter-company links were encouraged through foreign subsidiaries and joint ventures. In addition, the firm employed S.T. Bridgford as an agent in the Far East from 1885 to seek increased sales. Back in Newcastle, foreign customers were lavishly entertained by Armstrong at his Cragside mansion and Andrew Noble (Managing Director of the Elswick yard) at his Jesmond Dene house. Links with the Japanese were also maintained through such organisations as the North East Coast Institution of Engineers and Shipbuilders, which included Japanese membership and participation.[55]

Other shipbuilders from the northeast encouraged overseas customers, particularly through extended credit. S.M. Kuhnele and Sons of Bergen was allowed eight years at five percent to pay for a vessel built by William Gray of West Hartlepool. Swan Hunter was not alone in accepting as partial payment some fully-paid shares in the shipping company purchasing the vessel. Another firm, Readhead of South Shields, provided a flow of information on the latest ship technology and advice on how such developments might be adapted to the needs of particular shipping firms to attract customers.[56]

Domestically, there was also a strong shift away from the local market in the second half of the nineteenth century. Table 6 indicates that in the four decades prior to World War One output in the region's leading shipbuilding ports exceeded by several-fold investments in new vessels.[57] In other words, there was a substantial net outflow of new tonnage from the area. By far the largest volume of new registrations was to be found in Liverpool and London. These two ports, together with those of the northeast, generally accounted for two-thirds to three-

---

[55]The previous sections are largely taken from Conte-Helm, *Japan*, 21-36, 79-83, 93.

[56]TWAS 1061/1369, Readhead, letter books; R. Craig, "William Gray and Company: A West Hartlepool Shipbuilding Enterprise, 1864-1913," in P.L. Cottrell and D.H. Aldcroft (eds.), *Shipping, Trade and Commerce* (Leicester, 1981), 174-181; TWAS 1826/3/1, Swan Hunter and Wigham Richardson and Co., contract ledgers. Hawthorn-Leslie sold both naval and merchant ships to many countries including Russia, India and Sweden. Clarke, *Power*, 40, 66, 67.

[57]Exceptionally, more new tonnage was registered at Hull than built there during most of the period. However, the figures are quite small and reflect the decline of shipbuilding at the port rather than any expansion of shipowning.

quarters of new registrations in England. Significantly, both Liverpool and London supported only small local shipbuilding industries after 1870, frequently equivalent to less than ten percent of new registrations. Under these circumstances, the large net inflow of new tonnage must have drawn heavily upon the yards of the northeast. As early as the 1850s Brice, Friend and Co. of Liverpool and John Willis of London were buying Sunderland vessels for the southeast Asian and Australasian trades.[58] When the Black Ball Line of Liverpool turned to the purchase of mostly British rather than North American vessels in the 1860s, it drew heavily upon Sunderland yards.[59] Hawthorn-Leslie was a major supplier to Liverpool and London firms. Holt of Liverpool accounted for between twenty-nine and seventy-nine percent of Leslie's output during each year in the period 1863-1877. Rathbone of Liverpool and Hough of London were other major recipients of the firm's output. Only one northeast shipowner, Adamson and Short, was a significant buyer. Thus, similar to the Japanese sales discussed earlier, repeat orders to a small number of buyers was an important feature of their business.[60] The substantial inter-regional flows indicated in table 6 suggest the growth of port, or perhaps regional, specialisation within English maritime industries in the second half of the nineteenth century, with shipbuilding concentrated upon the northeast and shipowning upon London and Liverpool. If this were the case, it provides an agenda for the maritime history of England which stretches beyond the scope of this paper.

A further source of increased demand for northeast-built vessels, both domestically and internationally, was government. John Glover noted in 1869 that since "Thames workmanship can now be equalled both on the Clyde and Mersey, and the Tyne and Wear; our own and other governments...no longer restrict their contracts to the Thames."[61] Although it is not clear whether Glover was talking about mercantile as

---

[58]MacGregor, *Tea Clippers*, 84, 90, 95-96.

[59]M.K. Stammers, *The Passage Makers* (Brighton, 1978), 405. On 428-434, he discusses Sunderland-built ships used by the firm on the Australian route.

[60]Clarke, *Power*, 40. In 1906 three firms accounted for ninety-five percent of Hawthorn-Leslie's output. *Ibid.*, 67.

[61]J. Glover, "On the Decline of Shipbuilding on the Thames," *Journal of the Statistical Society of London*, XXXII (1869), 290.

well as naval vessels, he noted that major shipping companies were looking increasingly to northern yards for the same reason.

Strategy and Structure

Following the decline of the wooden ship, Pollard and Robertson believed that "the availability of cheap and docile labour, ready supplies of raw materials and other inputs" were important in the predominance of the northeast coast, along with Clydeside and Belfast, in British shipbuilding.[62] We will look at each of these factors in relation to the entire nineteenth century. But it is worth remembering that even if the northeast benefited from favourable relative factor costs, it still required entrepreneurship to convert these latent advantages into industrial success. We have seen above the astute sales and marketing policies pursued by Armstrong; we will now look more generally at entrepreneurship in the region's shipbuilding industry in terms of both the structure of the firm and managerial policy. Modern revisions of the classic structure-conduct-performance paradigm tell us that structure and conduct (strategy) interact to shape industrial performance.[63]

For one writer, at least, the success of shipbuilding in the northeast "seems to lie in the handful of brilliant, hardworking men. [From] William Armstrong, Charles Palmer, George Hunter, Andrew Leslie and perhaps another score...around them...sprang the firms and then the industry."[64] Unfortunately, there is little specification of what these entrepreneurs did to make the northeast more successful than other regions. In addition, it is probably an exaggeration to suggest that the industry grew around such individuals. In the first half of the nineteenth century the rapid development of Sunderland shipbuilding lay in the hands of obscure, shadowy entrepreneurs, pursuing short-term, pragmatic policies within small, flimsy business structures.

Prior to 1850 the typical Sunderland shipbuilding firm was small and ephemeral. Between 1800 and 1860 half of all shipyards survived less than two years; as late as the beginning of the 1850s, most built only

---

[62]Pollard and Robertson, *British Shipbuilding*, 51.

[63]See A.D. Chandler, *Strategy and Structure* (Cambridge, MA, 1962), for an important thesis on the relationship between company organisation and policy.

[64]Dougan, *History of North-East Shipbuilding*, 63.

one or two ships a year. Many operated with very informal structures, using minimal fixed capital and consisting of little more than the necessary raw materials, labour and some land on which to put up the stocks. The ending of the French Wars may in fact have reduced the average firm size on Wearside, as a number of established builders were unable to maintain their levels of output or to meet fixed costs as demand fell sharply. The average number of shipwrights per yard declined between 1804 and 1841, a period over which the number of yards trebled.[65] Significantly, some firms in the depressed years after 1815 simply comprised a group of out-of-work shipwrights and carpenters who clubbed their savings together to keep building and therefore receive a wage. Profits were a lesser consideration. The shipwrights' union appears to have commenced building at the depth of the depression in 1819, when many of its members were unemployed, by buying a yard vacated by a bankrupt shipbuilder, Thomas Tiffin.[66] By the 1830s the boom in shipbuilding at Sunderland was such that "working men left their employment to become master shipbuilders, and such energy was put into the trade that the supply of vessels soon overtook and outdistanced demand."[67]

There were several larger yards on Wearside but more particularly on Tyneside before mid-century. Of twenty-four yards mentioned in an Admiralty return for Sunderland in 1804, just two (Laing, fifty-three and Hall, fifty-two) employed more than fifty; the average for the port was twenty-eight. Much larger yards were to be found on Tyneside, including R. Bulmer and Co. (181) and J. Craster (138) at South Shields.[68] In the absence of specific information it is difficult to ascertain whether the larger size of the Tyneside yards caused them to be burdened with higher fixed costs. What does seem clear is that overheads

---

[65]Clarke, "River Wear," 83, 84, 93.

[66]Potts, *Sunderland*, 132. J. Clarke is unable to trace evidence of output by the yard; see "Comments on Simon Ville, 'Rise to Pre-Eminence: the Development and Growth of the Sunderland Shipbuilding Industry, 1800-50,'" *International Journal of Maritime History*, II, No. 2 (December 1990), 188.

[67]Potts, *Sunderland*, 193-194.

[68]Clarke, "River Wear," 82, 108-109. "An Account Shewing the Number of Shipwrights, etc.," *BPP*, VII (1805), 467-491.

were low at Sunderland, and this may go some way toward explaining the more rapid, though erratic, growth of shipbuilding output on Wearside in the first half of the century. Low entry costs also meant firms had few resources on which to rely in hard times. This made for rapid changes in the total number of shipbuilders at Sunderland. From around twenty in the early 1820s the number of builders expanded to over thirty by the mid-1830s. The number then surged to over seventy by the end of the decade, before stabilising at thirty or forty in the 1840s.[69]

Entry was made yet easier by the generous line of credit offered by timber merchants keen to dispose of excess supplies. Sometimes the merchant was prepared to supply the timber and await the final sale of the vessel before claiming payment, "if there was sufficient to pay him with, and if not he takes what he can get."[70] A similar situation existed for other shipbuilding materials, such as tar, pitch, hemp and flax. Credit was also available from banks, which mushroomed in the northeast in the 1830s. Their boards, which included many key figures from the local shipping community, provided builders with finance and credit on unsold vessels.[71] The Sunderland Joint Stock Bank, like many others of the period, became the victim of overlending and the self-interest of its directors when it collapsed in 1851. Allegations of fraud and deception particularly centred upon its financing of the shipping sector.[72]

In an industry characterised by a high degree of perfect competition, the policies of most local builders were quite uniform: to use their skills to build simple, general-purpose vessels at the lowest cost, often on speculation. There were few examples of vertical integration among shipbuilders or other forms of expansion and development designed to improve efficiency or to gain strategic advantages over other firms. Shipwrights, carpenters, "fly-by-night"

---

[69]Ville, "Rise to Pre-Eminence," 66-67.

[70]"Select Committee on Manufactures, Commerce and Shipping," 41, evidence of Henry Tanner.

[71]See examples in Ville, "Rise to Pre-Eminence," 76; Ville, "Expansion and Development," 32-33.

[72]See M. Philips, *A History of Banks, Bankers and Banking in Northumberland, Durham and North Yorkshire* (London, 1894), 319-320, 336-341, 383-384.

operators and most other small builders were attracted into the local industry by the existence of a lower cost structure than at most other ports, supported by a large and easily accessible local market. On the issue of quality, though, policies pursued by specific firms may have been of some significance. It was frequently those firms opting to build to a higher quality which emerged as successful large-scale enterprises by the later decades of the century.

Both firm structure and strategy began to change in the second half of the nineteenth century. With the introduction of steam and metal, ship construction was transformed from a small-scale craft occupation into a technologically advanced business closely linked to heavy industries. These important links with industries such as coal and steel, together with the potential to build much larger vessels, in most cases raised entry costs and the minimum efficient scale of the firm. By the final dozen years of the century, despite a much increased volume of output, there were only thirteen or fourteen shipbuilding firms on the Wear and fifteen to twenty on the Tyne, far fewer than earlier in the century.[73] Although most remained single-yard enterprises, the increased level of activity is apparent. While the average annual output of northeast firms was less than 1000 tons in the early part of the century, by the final decade this figure was well in excess of 10,000 tons and may have been as high as 15,000-20,000. The average number of vessels built also expanded. The Armstrong-Mitchell merger was mentioned above, and the process of amalgamation and concentration continued through to 1914 in both naval and mercantile shipbuilding: Vickers-Beardmore was formed in 1902 and Swan Hunter and Wigham Richardson the following year. These mergers, which were a feature of not only the northeast but also the other dominant shipbuilding regions, aided the provision of finance and the rationalisation of management but did not lead to collusive or monopolistic practices which might have caused inefficiency.

The larger size and frequently greater endurance of most northeast shipbuilding firms by the later years of the century provided scope for developing coherent, enterprise-specific strategies. This was in contrast to the industry-wide policy norms of most small, perfectly competitive shipbuilders before 1850. It was seen earlier that Armstrong had the capacity and resources to devote to sales and marketing strategies

---

[73]Pollard and Robertson, *British Shipbuilding*, 63. The downturn of 1865-1866 had caused a shake-out of many small timber yards.

and was clearly not unique in filling order books with specifically designed vessels rather than building an homogeneous product "on spec." Corporate strategies can also be identified on topics such as production and growth.

The use of metal and steam in shipbuilding, together with the growth of demand, facilitated not only regional but also firm specialisation. Doxford's concentration upon turret-deckers and Withy's on well-deckers were examples. Edward Lorenz has argued that it was yard rather than regional specialisation which was most important in creating high productivity. He goes on to suggest that specialisation was greatest in the production of cargo tramps, the sector in which British shipowners were most dominant.[74] This implies a productivity advantage for the northeast, most likely from a standard basic design requiring similar work practices and capital equipment. But there was no homogeneity of product and components; each vessel was built to somewhat different specifications.

Raw Materials

The northeast shipbuilding industry appears to have benefited from a cheap and plentiful supply of raw materials throughout much of the century. It was noted earlier that staple exports from the region kept freight rates low for timber imports, particularly in Sunderland. This meant cheap wood and a boom in timber merchanting. The result was "great competition among merchants, they [shipbuilders] can purchase timber cheaper than at any of the neighbouring ports."[75] This led to periodic gluts, which explains why timber merchants often offered generous credit terms to builders. A similar situation prevailed for materials such as tar, pitch, hemp and flax, which were often shipped as joint cargoes with timber or loaded as broken stowage. The broadening pattern of foreign trade from the region's ports also meant a wide range

---

[74]E.H. Lorenz, *Economic Decline in Britain. The Shipbuilding Industry, 1890-1970* (Oxford, 1991), 26-27.

[75]"Select Committee on Manufactures, Commerce and Shipping," 417, evidence of John Spence, Sunderland shipowner and timber importer.

of timber, which could be used in different aspects of ship construction.[76]

The region was particularly fortunate in that when coal, iron and engineering products became the major inputs of the industry in the second half of the nineteenth century, it still benefited from a cheap and plentiful supply as one of the growth centres of heavy industry. Coal output continued to be important, which helps explain the development of local metallurgy and engineering. As Pollard and Robertson noted, "it was the cheap supplies of iron and steel plates and bars, of machinery for the yards and coal to drive the steam engines that were ultimately the bases of the location of the industry along the Scottish and northern rivers."[77] This is supported by Glover's evidence for 1869 which compared costs on the Thames, Wear and Clyde. The Wear was cheaper than the others for angle iron and plates, and cheaper than the Thames for rivets. Most revealing were differences in coal prices: fifteen to twenty shillings per ton on the Thames; five to 12 6d on Clydeside; and 2s 6d to four shillings on Wearside.[78]

"Overwhelmingly, in Britain, the men who built the first iron ships were from a mechanical engineering background," one historian has noted.[79] Although no supporting evidence is offered for this assertion, it is clear that the northeast shipbuilding industry drew heavily upon the capital and expertise of local engineering. In particular, this meant the availability of knowledge about the latest technology. The increased concentration of shipbuilding in the area provided for economies of localisation, particularly external economies which facilitated technology transfer. The North East Coast Institution of Engineers and Shipbuilders, founded in 1884, acted as a vehicle to

---

[76]These included oak, beech, pine and elm for the decks and African teak, mahogany and green heart for the cabin and other fittings.

[77]Pollard and Robertson, *British Shipbuilding*, 57.

[78]Glover, "Decline of Shipbuilding," 292.

[79]Clarke, "Wood to Iron," 65. A contrary view was expressed by J. Grantham, who cited three categories of early iron shipbuilder: those with a background in timber shipbuilding, engineers, and "an intermediate class." Grantham, "The Strength of Iron Ships," *Transactions of the Institution of Naval Architects*, I (1860), 59. Pile is a notable example of a northeast builder who made the transition, completing his first iron vessel in 1861 and his last wooden one in 1863.

facilitate the flow of information both within and between these two groups.[80]

The existence of a local engineering industry also enabled transport and transaction cost savings through vertical integration. Thermal economies were achieved by linking up with engineering and metallurgy firms. Palmer is a good example. The firm began building on the Tyne in 1852 and later acquired iron mines at Saltburn and Whitby and an artificial harbour at Port Mulgrave from which ironstone was loaded onto its colliers. Ore was turned into plates and angles at its blast furnace and rolling mill, and a foundry produced iron and brass castings.[81] Vertical integration also came through takeover or merger: the merger of Hawthorn and Leslie in 1885 joined an engineering to a shipbuilding firm. During the 1860s thirty-three of seventy-eight engines purchased by Leslie came from Hawthorn.[82] The recurrent transactions between the two suggests that economies resulted from vertical integration.[83] In addition, there were cost savings to be achieved from supplying engines in batches; vertical integration would have eased the introduction of this technique.[84] Growth strategies, however, were sometimes based upon specialisation: Laing and Bartram, for instance, both remained solely shipbuilders. George Clark and the North East Marine Engineering Company remained independent engineering firms supplying components to shipbuilders. Some followed a mixed strategy:

---

[80]J.F. Clarke, *A Centenary History of the North East Coast Institution of Engineers and Shipbuilders, 1884-1984* (Newcastle, 1984), cites the rapid growth of membership, its spread across several professions and the high quality of the debate. It also included many overseas members and established a library (1889) and a scholarship fund (1907). TWAS 1376/1, General minute books of NECIES, books 2 and 3.

[81]Pollard and Robertson, *British Shipbuilding*, 90.

[82]Clarke, *Power*, 41.

[83]The whole issue of transaction cost economics is best dealt with by O.E. Willamson, *The Economic Institutions of Capitalism* (New York, 1985). A.D. Chandler, *The Visible Hand* (Cambridge, MA, 1977), 8, suggests that administrative coordination within a firm is likely to be more efficient than market coordination when the volume and recurrence of transactions is high.

[84]Clarke suggests that a second or third engine in a batch would have cost only eighty-three to eighty-eight percent of the first. *Power*, 54.

William Gray was successful over several decades as a specialist builder but was able to expand output significantly in 1884 by opening a marine engineering works.[85] The northeast shared with Clydeside the benefits of the localisation of heavy industry, and there is evidence to suggest that many Tyneside engineers came from north of the border.

Labour

Analysing the contribution of labour to the success of an industry involves a variety of considerations, including cost, supply, skill and stability. Pollard and Robertson were sceptical of the importance of regional wage differences to the success of the industry in the early decades of the century; they argued that such differentials would have yielded advantages of no more than five to seven percent in final cost. But there are several problems with accepting this conclusion. First, the methods used in the calculation are far from sound.[86] Second, seven percent is more than a negligible difference, particularly when combined with other savings. Significantly, regional wage differences in the first half of the century seem most marked between Sunderland and ports outside the region. In the mid-1840s shipwrights at the port received only half the weekly wages paid at London and two-thirds of those at Liverpool. In the second half of the century, regional differentials appear to have narrowed, although the wages of shipwrights, joiners and members of the engineering trades remained somewhat lower in the northeast than at Liverpool or London.[87] Despite increased professionalisation and centralisation among trade unions late in the century, local rather than national collective bargaining remained the norm. This was reinforced by

---

[85]Craig, "William Gray."

[86]Pollard and Robertson, *British Shipbuilding*, 52-53. Labour costs are estimated at one-third to one-quarter of the total, although there is no indication of how they derived this figure. Wages are then said to have differed by no more than twenty percent between regions, but this appears to be based upon evidence for the second half of the century. They also talk of the "labour factor" as making no more than a one or two percent cost difference between the Mersey and the Thames compared with Tyneside and Wearside.

[87]S. Pollard, "The Decline of Shipbuilding on the Thames," *Economic History Review*, 2nd series, III, No. 1 (1950-1951), 80. There is also valuable material in Pollard and Robertson, *British Shipbuilding*, 52-53, 246-247.

the unwillingness of shipbuilding firms to negotiate nationally, preferring district agreements on wages and conditions.[88]

The picture is complicated by the fact that wage rates not only varied between geographic areas but also were highly susceptible to fluctuations in economic activity. Variations in wage rates, and particularly in earnings, most likely were greater than for shipbuilding output: employers would often pay above or below the current "list" price for labour. At Hawthorn-Leslie, shipwrights' wages fell from thirty-nine to thirty-one shillings between 1902 and 1903 and the number employed dropped from 1970 to 1346.[89] Actual earnings were also influenced by the nature and amount of work a gang was offered; its effectiveness; and its success in claiming allowances above the basic rate.[90]

The elasticity of the labour supply seems to have been high and was probably helped by the influx of Irish and Scots to the area. In the two decades from 1831 the number of shipwrights, carpenters and shipbuilders at Sunderland soared from 366 to 1372.[91] The vagaries of demand caused high turnover rates, as indicated by the figures for Hawthorn-Leslie. Very few shipyard workers could count upon long-term job security.[92] Yet retention of the workforce may have been as much a problem as recruitment. As migrants with general craft skills, workers could find employment with other local firms or move to another area. We know little of how Sunderland builders overcame this, although some early nineteenth-century businesses appear to have adopted paternalistic

---

[88]J. McGoldrick, "A Profile of the Boilermakers' Union," in A. Slaven and J. Kuuse (eds.), *Scottish and Scandinavian Shipbuilding. Development Problems in Historical Perspective* (Glasgow, 1980), 205.

[89]Clarke, *Power*, 73.

[90]These issues are discussed in S. Price, "Clyde Rivetters' Earnings, 1899-1913," in Slaven & Kuuse (eds.), *Scottish and Scandinavian Shipbuilding*, 175-176, 184.

[91]Clarke, "River Wear," 109.

[92]A.J. Reid, "The Division of Labour in the British Shipbuilding Industry, 1880-1920, With Special Reference to Clydeside" (Unpublished Ph.D thesis, University of Cambridge, 1980), 50. This is a general theme running through the study.

policies by providing educational, religious and financial support.[93] Labour supply problems may have existed in the early years of iron shipbuilding. Most of these workers were recruited not from the ranks of the builders of wooden ships but rather from engineering and boilermaking firms. With the rapid simultaneous expansion of these industries there was doubtless competition for labour. The iron ship- builder Andrew Leslie, for example, experienced problems retaining workers in the 1850s.[94] However, this was in a relatively early phase of iron shipbuilding. Indeed, the existence of other industries requiring similar workforces attracted ever more migrants in the following decades.[95] As shipbuilding became increasingly concentrated upon the northeast and Clydeside towards the end of the century, economies of concentration, as reflected in a pool of skilled labour, benefitted local builders and removed the need for individual firms to offer recruitment and retention incentives, such as paternalistic welfare.

The skill and dexterity of Sunderland shipwrights before 1850 was reflected in the views of William Nicholson, a local shipowner, who believed that they "have acquired an expertness in shipbuilding which surpasses anything I have seen."[96] The productivity of local carpenters was also compared favourably with foreigners and those from other ports. Within the region, Sunderland carpenters were regarded as superior to those of Newcastle. "They are a very different class of men at Sunderland...they are all able-bodied men--and a better class of carpenter," remarked one contemporary.[97] The substantial labour pool by the late nineteenth century permitted extensive specialisation among

---

[93]Such was the approach of local shipowner, John White. W. Brockie, *Sunderland Notables* (Sunderland, 1894), 90-99.

[94]Clarke, "Wood to Iron," 85.

[95]*Ibid.*, 65.

[96]"Select Committee on British Shipping," 127.

[97]"Select Committee on Manufactures, Commerce and Shipping," 504, evidence of Thomas Hedley, shipowner and broker at Newcastle.

what remained a highly skilled workforce.[98] Lorenz contrasts the consequent benefits for the two major British shipbuilding regions with the smaller and dissipated French industry which was incapable of developing local pools of skilled labour and extending labour specialisation.[99] A similar contrast might be made with other British regions in which the economies of localisation were similarly constrained by smaller markets and the absence of a heavy industrial base.

Labour relations seemed generally good on Tyneside and Wearside in the first half of the century. This may have been helped by the predominance of small firms in which worker-manager relations were likely to be less hostile; paternalistic policies were sometimes adopted; and some firms consisted of little more than a group of shipwrights and carpenters. There were few of the disputes which dogged the industry elsewhere: neither the problems of union demarcation at London nor the attempts to limit entry through closed shops at both London and Liverpool. The establishment in 1853 of a Court of Equitable Arbitration at Sunderland to settle grievances suggests a mature approach to industrial relations.[100]

Labour unrest became important in the northeast shipbuilding industry in the later decades of the century. Demarcation disputes arose from the increasingly stratified workforce and the enormous number of labour organisations thus spawned. This was the case particularly from the 1870s, when the increasing complexity of vessel construction necessitated more skilled labour. Labour specialisation was particularly marked in the northeast. It has been estimated that there were 130 general shipbuilding unions in existence between 1892 and 1896, excluding craft societies such as the carpenters. On the Tyne there was

---

[98]Clarke, "Wood to Iron," 79-81, suggests that the changeover to metal construction involved a general de-skilling. Lorenz, *Economic Decline*, 46-47, 53, takes an opposing view, arguing that machinery mostly displaced routine, unskilled tasks in this period and that iron shipbuilding generated a wide range of new skills.

[99]Lorenz, *Economic Decline*, 52-55.

[100]"Select Committee on Manufactures, Commerce and Shipping," 518, evidence of Thomas Brown, retired shipowner and shipbuilder; Pollard, "Thames Shipbuilding," 74-75; Clarke, "River Wear," 87; *The Times*, 8 February 1853; J.F. Clarke, "The Wear Shipwrights and the Arbitration Court of 1853-4," *Bulletin of the North-East Group for the Study of Labour History*, VII (1973), 17-32.

an average of one major strike per month over demarcation issues between 1890 and 1893.[101] Disputes arose from attempts by employers to substitute less skilled workers in some jobs. Evidence is inconclusive as to whether some regions were more prone to disputes than others, although the extensive union and skill fragmentation in the northeast would have made it uncommonly susceptible to conflicts. Evidence from the North East Coast Institution of Engineers and Shipbuilders, however, suggests a cooperative relationship between employers and unions. Many builders advocated conciliation and believed that the best way to achieve it was through direct contact with experienced union leaders. The Sunderland shipbuilder, Robert Thompson, echoed the views of many in arguing that labour and capital had common interests.[102]

The high level of union organisation in the northeast also brought benefits to shipbuilding. The unions provided a range of welfare services, particularly insurance against unemployment and sickness and superannuation pay. This helped foster the local pool of skilled labour by maintaining worker attachment to the district. Union branches served as local labour exchanges, helping to match supply with the skill requirements of firms. Moreover, unions contributed to the coordination of the work process by organising skilled workers into squads or gangs which supervised semi-skilled assistants. This reduced the need for managerial intervention and supervision. Finally, the unions also administered the apprenticeship system.[103]

An interesting hypothesis posited by Pollard and Robertson is that both wage costs and industrial relations most favoured employers in the new and smaller centres of shipbuilding which emerged at mid-century and were often dominated by one industry and sometimes by only one or two firms.[104] As virtual labour market monopsonists and controllers of local government, shipbuilders were in very strong positions in the economic and social life of the town. The experience of

---

[101]Pollard and Robertson, *British Shipbuilding*, 159, 167.

[102]Clarke, *Centenary History*, 41. There may also be something to be said for the growth of shop stewards in highly unionised districts as important links between union membership and leadership. See McGoldrick, "Boilermakers' Union," 206.

[103]These issues are discussed in more detail in Lorenz, *Economic Decline*, 59-60.

[104]Pollard and Robertson, *British Shipbuilding*, 52-56.

these "company towns," including settlements such as Jarrow, West Hartlepool and Wallsend, lends some credence to this argument, which also might be extended back earlier in the century to Sunderland and Shields. It is also worth noting that Armstrong allegedly employed one-third of the population of Newcastle in 1912, suggesting that this kind of dominance could also be a feature of larger settlements.[105] Research on Sunderland at mid-century confirms the weighty political influence of the shipping interest both on the town council and through local representation in Parliament. Although there were no dominant firms, there was significant inter-firm cooperation and joint ownership. The cohesiveness of the shipping interest was further reinforced by the common bonds of Methodism and intermarriage.[106] With the growth of working-class voting rights, however, the direct political influence of major employers may have begun to wane by the later decades of the century.

Land

Pollard and Robertson's discussions of the new shipbuilding centres of the second half of the century may be more pertinent when viewed from the perspective of the availability and cost of waterfront land. Increased cost and reduced supply certainly forced locational changes and a pressure on space which militated against the most efficient organisation of some yards. With at least three major deep-water rivers in the north-east, firms that found an existing site unsuitable or too expensive would probably have been able to find an alternative location. Unfortunately, there are no solid figures on land prices in Britain in this period, although some evidence points to rising rents in London and Liverpool.[107] Nonetheless, German data suggest that land constituted no more than one percent of total production costs in shipbuilding.[108] Related to the land question are port facilities. Dredging and dock

---

[105]*Ibid.*, 54.

[106]Ville, "Shipping in the Port of Sunderland," 47-49. More detail is contained in an unpublished paper presented by the current author at the University of Kent in 1987, "Liberalism, Methodism and the Business Elite in Sunderland, 1800-50."

[107]Pollard and Robertson, *British Shipbuilding*, 57; Clarke, "River Wear," 87.

[108]Pollard and Robertson, *British Shipbuilding*, 57.

construction encouraged shipbuilding indirectly by stimulating local trade and shipowning. Neither would appear to be a particular advantage for the northeast, since these types of improvements were undertaken by harbour boards in most major ports around the country.

Conclusion

The leading contribution of the northeast to the ascendancy of UK shipbuilding in the nineteenth century is unquestionable. A more difficult problem is to explain the area's relative advantage over many other shipbuilding districts. This paper has adopted a standard format of examining the market, firms and factors of production. At the beginning of the century local demand predominated. With the sustained growth of shipowning in the northeast, shipbuilding followed suit. As the century progressed the importance of the local market waned. Before 1850 ship-builders from the northeast had to compete in an increasingly national market for new tonnage. Under these circumstances, price was import-ant. After 1850, with the diffusion of steam and steel throughout the industry, regional specialisation appears to have become an important feature of the English maritime industries, with shipbuilding predominant in the northeast, Clydeside and Belfast and shipowning concentrated to some degree in London and Liverpool. Within the shipbuilding industry there was also product specialisation between major regions, facilitated by a sustained expansion in output, particularly in the form of overseas sales. The focus therefore again became intra- rather than inter-regional competition. The development of regional specialisation, however, was based upon comparative advantage and therefore regional cost structures remained important.

Probably the major cost saving was from raw materials, timber in the first half of the century and heavy industrial products in the second. Cheaper timber resulted from lower inward freight rates and the credit policies of local merchants. The heavy industry input savings after 1850 derived from the localisation of output in the region. The latter produced various other internal and external benefits, such as transaction cost economies through vertical integration and a source of investment for the increasingly capital-intensive industry. Wage costs may also have been lower in the early part of the century, but the differential declined later in the period. Good labour relations in the early years, partly a function of the small, informal nature of many enterprises, gave way to greater industrial unrest towards the end of the century. On the other hand, the growth of unionisation provided benefits in labour recruitment and supervision. In addition, the increasing localisation of shipbuilding and heavy industries built up a pool of skilled labour and extended the process of the division of labour. The predominance of shipbuilding and inter-related industries, especially in the second half of the century, may also have yielded significant social and political leverage to employers. Land cost and availability was more difficult to gauge in the absence of suitable extant evidence, although regional differences were unlikely to have constituted a significant proportion of total costs.

Finally, this paper has also analysed the relevance of the strategy and structure of individual shipbuilding firms to their success. In the first half of the century, the typical firm, particularly at Sunderland, was small with few overheads. This made for low entry costs and therefore a high degree of responsiveness to the vicissitudes which characterised British trade and shipping during this period. With an industrial structure akin to perfect competition, the strategy of most firms was very similar. This shifted later in the century: technological change and continued market expansion led to increased industrial concentration and larger, more permanent structures within which individual strategies were developed. Successful marketing, production and growth policies pursued by leading firms in the area have each been discussed above.

If there is a unifying theme it would be the powerful nature of the economies of localisation in both shipbuilding and heavy industry in terms of labour skills, operating efficiencies and capital investment. Moreover, these gains were cumulative over time, especially in extending specialisation both of product and the factors of production. Thus, the northeast benefited from its long tradition in shipbuilding and the development of heavy industries. The experience of the northeast's shipbuilding industry in the nineteenth century tends to support Porter's notion of competitive advantage based upon clusters of industries linked by various forms of vertical and horizontal integration as an explanation of why some industries in particular countries and regions remain strong over long periods.[109] The industry's decline in the twentieth century may be related to the same general themes, but that is another story.

---

[109]In particular, see his most recent and extensive treatment of the subject: M.E. Porter, *The Competitive Advantage of Nations* (New York, 1990).

Simon Ville

Appendices

Table 1
Sunderland and Newcastle Shipbuilding, 1786-1913

	Sunder-land	Newcastle	UK	S & N % UK	NE % UK
1786-90	2295	5478	70075	11	
1791-95	3983	6907	61700	18	
1796-1800	8133	8617	88420	19	
1801-05	8311	9692	92821	19	
1806-10	4994	5254	50716	20	
1811-15	11924	7477	82245	24	
1816-20	11095	5986	81700	21	
1821-25	12063	5813	77160	23	
1826-30	14725	6446	90460	23	
1831-35	24264	9012	96060	35	
1836-40	45489		153520		
1841-45	30800		118160		
1846-50	44464		129100		
1851-55	61007		208080		
1856-60	47443		220240		
1861-65	63772	63000	330060	38	
1866-70	65555	56400	324700	38	
1871-75	96805	91443	411980	46	
1876-80	90258	125800	588775	37	
1881-85	137577	166562	948000	32	
1886-90	139030	183406	905817	36	
1891-95	157399	172643	1042456	32	52
1896-1900	227238	224612	1267814	36	54
1901-05	244393	267931	1394249	37	53
1906-10	203332	247825	1300027	35	49
1911-13	264175	365648	1821170	35	52

Notes: Quinquennial averages. Gross tonnage except UK before 1876-1880. UK total includes warships, 1878-1891. Missing data: Sunderland, 1833; Newcastle, 1827, 1829-1831, 1833-1863, 1876.

Sources: Public Record Office (PRO), Customs 17, 36/5; "Statistics of the Wear and Port and Harbour of Sunderland," Tyne and Wear Archives Department (TWAS), 202/3255. Income and Expenditure Accounts, 1841-1857; Accounts and Papers, *British Parliamentary Papers* (*BPP*), VII (1814-1815), 160; *BPP*, XVIII (1826-1827), 286-287; *BPP*, LX (1847), 385; "Select Committee on East

India Built Shipping," *BPP*, VIII (1813-1814), 494; "Select Committee on Manufactures, Commerce and Shipping," *BPP*, VI (1833), 718; "Select Committee on British Shipping," *BPP*, VIII (1844), 127; *Sunderland Herald*, 27 December 1833; *The Times*, 9 January 1854; J.F. Clarke, "Shipbuilding on the River Wear, 1780-1870," in R.W. Sturgess (ed.), *The Great Age of Industry in the North-East* (Durham, 1981), 113; B.R. Mitchell and P. Deane (comps.), *Abstract of British Historical Statistics* (2nd ed., Cambridge, 1971), 220-221; S. Pollard and P. Robertson, *The British Shipbuilding Industry, 1870-1914* (Cambridge, MA, 1979), 252-253; D. Dougan, *The History of North-East Shipbuilding* (London, 1968), 221, 223, 230-231.

Table 2
Shipbuilding in the Northeast Ports, 1866-1913

	H'pools	M'boro	Stockton	Sunderland	Tyne
1866	9456	6476	6659	59254	46596
1867	5126	818	3674	47625	19010
1868	3832	1743	4762	64374	23756
1869	6604	4799	12287	65905	30255
1870	12756	6882	11043	50516	59971
1871	15079	5780	14629	73196	55139
1872	19366	10469	16768	91776	70288
1873	9392	9205	11023	82603	64934
1874	8215	8932	16497	72547	91228
1875	11679	8564	12067	71146	44755
1876	13577	4549	15537	47001	31739
1877	23732	11317	17063	79798	49673
1878	27125	8795	16760	69010	73040
1879	20578	5322	15511	58386	87285
1880	26481	11359	17182	77008	96733
1881	32383	11842	25809	87934	116241
1882	43281	19393	20386	121064	134407
1883	47001	21658	28551	142483	141355
1884	21863	9526	17335	87848	97388
1885	22231	5804	20189	43509	65696
1886	9989	5320	9118	37701	43163
1887	34103	9178	9731	53614	66821
1888	48217	15851	24074	88673	125397
1889	54682	29205	38184	137819	178455
1890	55699	30069	45374	127590	146764
1891	62293	29359	54746	127019	126054
1892	57213	22160	42110	128729	127949

	H'pools	M'boro	Stockton	Sunderland	Tyne
1893	47146	20316	38337	81366	93524
1894	48302	18670	38356	94351	121250
1895	56167	26786	50036	89095	102031
1896	55199	27303	48298	132479	142269
1897	41327	19535	32649	103275	109437
1898	65900	30971	54534	159589	139352
1899	85577	28461	58998	158878	169066
1900	76938	31757	55456	147686	177638
1901	98326	39687	64631	168601	191790
1902	54881	24297	54295	149116	166615
1903	51473	23629	26528	126662	136209
1904	70323	34752	49211	162309	161455
1905	79969	35512	50787	194848	190676
1906	93033	37338	56881	210372	228185
1907	60015	37600	47946	187138	178545
1908	23066	24314	10881	51890	111443
1909	35904	11382	25842	80484	108061
1910	50031	19210	45950	106416	118262
1911	84852	29925	53294	179238	232402
1912	74865	22544	63499	186119	186973
1913	96175	27085	68479	186295	234365

Notes: Net tonnage.

Sources: "Return of Number of Vessels Built at Each Port," *BPP* (1867-1871); "Annual
Statement of Navigation and Shipping of UK," *BPP* (1872-1914).

Table 3

Transition to Steam and Metal in Northeast Ports, 1866-1897

	Hartlepools		Middlesborough		Stockton		Sunderland		Tyne Ports	
	Steam %	Metal %	Steam %	Metal %	Steam %	Metal %	Steam %	Metal %	Steam %	Metal %
1866	82	98	81	81	92	100	20	30	91	88
1867	85	100	25	25	100	100	9	26	78	89
1868	69	82	72	83	64	100	21	51	67	88
1869	82	97	46	85	71	100	15	51	84	93
1870	100	100	84	84	87	100	62	64	97	97
1871	100	100	100	100	91	100	85	88	99	97
1872	100	100	100	100	99	100	95	95	98	97
1873	100	100	100	100	98	100	75	87	97	99
1874	100	100	100	100	56	100	40	84	98	99
1875	84	100	91	100	58	100	37	84	83	99
1876	75	100	89	100	32	100	35	89	98	99
1877	89	100	98	100	67	100	58	97	100	100
1878	95	100	100	100	91	100	76	98	100	100
1879	100	100	86	100	99	100	94	97	99	100
1880	100	100	100	100	82	100	93	100	100	100
1881	100	100	100	100	72	100	94	100	100	100
1882	100	100	100	100	100	100	93	99	99	99
1883	100	100	100	100	88	100	97	100	99	100
1884	79	100	96	100	59	100	86	100	94	99

	Hartlepools		Middlesborough		Stockton		Sunderland		Tyne Ports	
	Steam %	Metal %	Steam %	Metal %	Steam %	Metal %	Steam %	Metal %	Steam %	Metal %
1885	84	100	71	100	52	100	63	100	88	100
1886	100	100	100	100	44	100	82	100	99	100
1887	100	100	100	100	100	100	95	100	99	100
1888	100	100	100	100	91	100	98	100	99	100
1889	100	100	100	100	94	100	97	100	100	100
1890	100	100	100	100	95	100	95	100	100	100
1891	100	100	97	100	91	100	76	100	98	100
1892	100	100	100	100	89	100	83	100	94	99
1893	100	100	100	100	98	100	99	100	97	100
1894	100	100	98	100	97	100	100	100	99	100
1895	100	100	96	100	100	100	100	100	94	100
1896	100	100	88	100	97	100	100	100	100	100
1897	100	100	100	100	99	100	100	100	91	100

Notes: Net tonnage. Metal figures exclude foreign sales before 1879.

Sources: See table 2.

Table 4
Sunderland Shipowning and Shipbuilding, 1791-1913

	Built (1)	Registered (2)	1 As % 2
1791-95	3983	62643	6
1796-1800	8133	72694	11
1801-05	8311	75663	11
1806-10	4994	68301	7
1811-15	11924	82099	15
1816-20	11095	83289	13
1821-25	12063	82628	15
1826-30	14725	107628	14
1831-35	24264	129082	19
1836-40	45489	190929	24
1841-45	30800	150527	21
1846-50	44464	195581	23
1851-55	61007	217796	28
1856-60	47443	236484	20
1861-65	63772	239318	27
1866-70	57535	247743	23
1871-75	78254	207321	38
1876-80	66241	199118	33
1881-85	96568	217987	44
1886-90	89079	235465	38
1891-95	104112	270964	38
1896-1900	140381	277133	51
1901-05	160307	290578	55
1906-10	127260	319563	40
1911-13	183884	285321	65

Notes: Shipbuilding in net tonnage from 1866, ownership in net tonnage. Missing data for shipowning: 1809-1812, 1825-1828, 1830-1831, 1833-1839. Shipbuilding totals for vessels of fifty tons and over only: 1866-1870.

Sources: Shipbuilding: See table 1, and "Return of Number of Vessels Built at Each Port," *BPP* (1867-1871); "Annual Statement of Navigation and Shipping of UK," *BPP* (1872-1914). Shipowning: PRO, Customs 17, 36/5; "Select Committee on Manufactures, Commerce and Shipping," *BPP*, VI (1833), 718; *BPP*, XXVII (1830), 35; "Statistics of the Wear and Port and Harbour of Sunderland," TWAS, 202/3255. Income and Expenditure Accounts, 1841-1857; "Return of Vessels Registered at each Port," *BPP* (1867-1871); "Annual Statement of Navigation and Shipping of UK," *BPP* (1872-1914).

Table 5
Shipbuilding for Overseas Markets, 1871-1913

	Hpools	M'boro	Stktn	S'land	Tyne
1871-5	1910(15)	2058(24)	1562(11)	8815(11)	9872(15)
1876-80	285(1)	1482(18)	969(6)	5231(8)	7675(11)
1881-5	570(2)	3624(27)	1063(5)	13194(14)	18756(18)
1886-90	2595(6)	1546(9)	1304(5)	18133(20)	26493(25)
1891-5	3925(7)	6036(26)	10694(24)	12138(12)	32240(34)
1896-1900	13342(21)	12555(46)	9359(19)	29752(21)	52941(36)
1901-05	12825(18)	13080(41)	7763(16)	27516(17)	40667(24)
1906-10	12236(23)	9657(37)	5098(14)	33089(26)	42745(29)
1911-13	17022(21)	7418(28)	4468(7)	46212(25)	51426(24)

Notes: Net tons. Percentage of output in parenthesis. Includes both mercantile and
naval shipping.

Sources: "Annual Statement of Navigation and Shipping of UK," *BPP* (1872-1914).

Table 6
Shipbuilding and New Registrations, 1871-1910

	Dom Shbldg	New Registns	Net Flow	Shbdg%NReg
		Northeast Ports		
1871-75	776187	293515	482672	264
1876-80	826352	316806	509546	261
1881-85	1172745	447310	725435	262
1886-90	1141028	359411	781617	317
1891-95	1375800	452494	923306	304
1896-1900	1552834	437409	1115425	355
1901-05	1896634	509859	1386775	372
1906-10	1446059	429034	1017025	337
		Liverpool		
1871-75	107457	383622	-276165	28
1876-80	118430	385873	-267443	31
1881-85	144540	678954	-534414	21
1886-90	71503	531158	-459655	13
1891-95	45876	667762	-621886	7
1896-1900	5072	834178	-829106	1
1901-05	10103	760337	-750234	1
1906-10	29374	648262	-618888	5
		London		
1871-75	46936	356366	-309430	13
1876-80	17520	333420	-315900	5
1881-85	21826	462978	-441152	5
1886-90	14789	489475	-474686	3
1891-95	20502	592650	-572148	3
1896-1900	64899	578143	-513244	11
1901-05	50066	812822	-762756	6
1906-10	24058	560314	-536256	4

Notes: Net tons. Excludes vessels built for markets outside UK. Northeast ports are taken as the Hartlepools, Middlesborough, Stockton, Sunderland and the Tyne. Net flow is the difference between the volume of shipbuilding and new registrations; a positive figure is thus the net export of new tonnage from the port or region.

Sources: "Annual Statement of Navigation and Shipping of UK," *BPP* (1872-1914).

Shipbuilding in Southeast England, 1800-1913

Sarah Palmer

This essay presents statistical evidence on shipbuilding in the southeast of England during the nineteenth and early twentieth centuries. Based on official data, the series in appendices A and B cover only private shipbuilding, ignoring work in the Royal Dockyards or for the Admiralty. While the gap for individual ports between 1827 and 1865 seriously undermines our understanding of the southeast's performance in the period during which it lost its leading position, an analysis of the output of the various centres both before and after these decades sheds new light on the industry by identifying shipbuilding characteristics in specific ports. Although the statistical record highlights distinct features, an explanation is difficult because shipbuilding in the region has been examined in detail for only two ports, although some studies of shipping in this part of Britain contain relevant incidental detail.[1] The work by Sidney Pollard and Philip Banbury on London, and by Adrian Rance on Southampton, enables us to place the statistical record for these ports in a rewarding comparative context. But for other centres the industry's history remains obscure; for such locales the collation of official figures at least provides a foundation for further study.[2] Yet our understanding of London and Southampton also gains from this data, which has been under-exploited by scholars. Nevertheless, this paper does not claim to do more than provide a firmer basis for further investigation.

---

[1]See, for example, Michael Bouquet, *South Eastern Sail from the Medway to the Solent 1840-1940* (Newton Abbot, 1972); and Edgar March, *Spritsail Barges of the Thames and Medway* (New edition, Newton Abbott, 1970).

[2]Sidney Pollard, "The Decline of Shipbuilding on the Thames," *Economic History Review*, New Series, III (1950); Philip Banbury, *Shipbuilders of the Thames and Medway* (Newton Abbot, 1971); Adrian B. Rance, *Shipbuilding in Victorian Southampton* (Southampton, 1981).

Research in Maritime History, No. 4 (June 1993), 45-74.

For contemporaries, as well as some historians, the most striking change in nineteenth-century British shipbuilding was its relocation to new regions as the introduction of metal in hull construction and the application of steam power shifted comparative advantages northward. Using the evidence for northeast shipbuilding, Simon Ville has shown that this generalization is too crude because it understates the contribution of "new" centres prior to this change.[3] Whether or not Ville overstated the output of Newcastle and Sunderland in the early nineteenth century, his analysis is a reminder that the importance of London shipbuilding requires both more demonstration and explanation than it has been conventionally accorded. London's "success" should not be taken for granted. In a similar vein, the well-documented decline of London shipbuilding after 1866 must not be assumed to be typical of the entire southeast. The experience of Southampton shows that although it too ended up as a fairly minor shipbuilding centre, its path to this ultimate fate was different. Why this was so needs to be considered.

Shipbuilding Centres

The southeast includes London, capital city and great port, together with the Thames and the Medway, and extends west to Portsmouth and Southampton, encompassing the counties of Kent, Sussex and Hampshire. The nineteenth-century southeast cannot be described as a "shipbuilding region" in the same sense as the northeast, since shipbuilding was never a prime focus. In London and on the Thames it was one of a number of industries. Elsewhere, with the exception of Southampton and Portsmouth, it was one element in a coastal agricultural economy.

Yet while from a London perspective shipbuilding was only one of a diverse range of economic activities, the statistics in table 1 show that the city was the leading shipbuilding centre in the first quarter of the century, accounting for almost eight percent of UK tonnage between 1815 and 1825. Given this national significance, it is not surprising that London's output dwarfed the other southern centres, comprising approximately four-fifths of the region's production over the same period. Moreover, as table 2 and figure 1 show, in the early nineteenth century there was no close competitor in the region; the Hampshire ports

---

[3]S. Ville, "Rise to Pre-eminence: the Development and Growth of the Sunderland Shipbuilding Industry," *International Journal of Maritime History*, I, No. 1 (June 1989).

together produced the most tonnage after London, but frequently it was Cowes rather than Southampton which led the way. By 1900, the number and tonnage of vessels built in London and the southeast had dwindled to a small proportion of national output. Within the region, London was still the most significant centre, albeit by a much reduced margin, with Southampton in second place. Nevertheless, consideration of shipbuilding in this part of England cannot be confined to London or extended only to Cowes and Southampton. Throughout the century the listings of "ships built" or "ships built and registered...in the several ports of England" in the *Parliamentary Papers* identify a number of southern ports, testifying to the local significance of small-scale construction in many places.

Table 1
Tonnage Built in London, Other Southeast Ports,
and the United Kingdom, 1806-1826 and 1866-1913
(000 net tons)

	London	Other SE Ports	Southeast Total	United Kingdom	Southeast % Share
1800-1804	58.77	28.83	87.60	528.40	16.58
1805-1809	14.23	18.95	33.17		
1810-1814	28.37	21.56	49.93		
1815-1819	24.96	23.90	48.86	444.70	10.99
1820-1824	27.40	18.30	45.70	330.00	13.85
1825-1826	22.77	14.82	37.59	240.90	15.60
1866-1869	65.97	36.98	102.96	1280.80	8.04
1870-1874	70.68	31.72	102.40	1982.00	5.17
1874-1879	31.48	55.87	87.35	1999.70	4.37
1880-1884	35.05	91.44	126.48	2838.30	4.46
1885-1889	20.31	56.15	76.46	2159.70	3.54
1890-1894	22.44	26.97	49.41	3085.30	1.60
1895-1899	81.01	21.49	102.49	2967.30	3.45
1900-1904	65.68	18.78	84.46	3677.50	2.30
1905-1909	34.41	13.19	47.60	3438.40	1.38
1910-1913	28.02	18.88	46.89	1875.50	2.50

Note: Figures are quinquennial aggregates except for 1825-1826 (two years) and 1866-1869 and 1910-1913 (four years each).

Sources: See text.

Table 2
Tonnage of Vessels Built in Southeast England,
1800-1826, 1866-1913
(annual averages; net tons)

	London	Medway	Kent	Sussex	Hants	Total SE
1800-1804	11754	529	1562	1735	1939	17519
1805-1809	2846	467	1164	999	1159	6635
1810-1814	5673	1329	618	783	1582	9985
1815-1819	4992	705	548	930	2597	9772
1820-1824	5481	893	258	663	1845	9140
1825-1826	11384	1002	527	1880	4004	18796
1866-1829	16494	1526	557	4117	3046	25739
1870-1874	14136	1179	735	2241	2190	20481
1874-1879	6296	1827	383	1886	7078	17471
1800-1884	7009	1252	104	1183	15749	25296
1885-1889	4062	845	33	630	9723	15292
1890-1894	4488	1229	106	518	3541	9882
1895-1899	16201	1638	74	318	2268	20498
1900-1904	13136	1702	80	268	1705	16892
1905-1909	6882	613	37	253	1737	9521
1910-1913	7004	781	7	250	3782	11724

Sources: See text.

In 1800 a tour of the sites at which merchant vessels were built would have included London, Rochester, Faversham, Ramsgate, Sandwich, Deal, Dover, Rye, Newhaven, Shoreham, Chichester, Arundel, Portsmouth, Cowes and Southampton. In the 1870s a similar itinerary would have embraced Littlehampton, but excluded Arundel, Chichester and Sandwich. Thirty years later building had also ceased at Deal and Newhaven. But what is most striking is the long-term persistence. The dramatic reversal in London's status, or the equally notable rise and subsequent fall of Southampton, had few counterparts in a region that continued to produce customary products--the wooden sailing vessels and barges for which there continued to be local markets.

The Statistical Series on Shipbuilding Output

The data presented in appendices 1 and 2 are derived from "official" manuscript series in the Public Record Office (PRO) or published material in the *Parliamentary Papers*, covering the periods 1800-1826 and after 1866. For the earlier years the returns list numbers and tonnage, sometimes (but not generally) naming individual vessels. For the later era they provide considerable detail, categorising vessels by construction material and distinguishing sail from steam. No information has been found on the intervening period, despite the fact that aggregate national figures, which must have been based upon local returns, were published. While it is possible that a systematic search of the Customs or Board of Trade holdings in the PRO might unearth some information on individual ports, nothing has yet been found.

Figure 1
Tonnage of Vessels Built in the Southeast, 1800-1826 and 1866-1913
(annual averages; net tons)

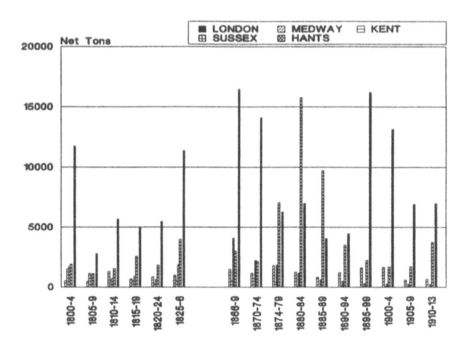

Source: See text.

"Unofficial" returns in the press might help to fill this infuriating gap, but comparisons between such statistics and the published Board of Trade series after 1866 raise further difficulties. David Pollock, writing in 1884, commented on the differences between various sets of statistics:

in comparing...the statistics given by various Journals...
innumerable disparities have been met with...Such being
the case, it may be asked, could not...more reliable
sources be consulted? The obvious alternative of using
the authoritative returns of the Board of Trade, or of
Lloyd's Registry, at once suggests itself, but objections
to this are even more serious than to using the press
statistics. The returns issued annually by the Board of
Trade only relate to "merchant shipping," registered as
such, whereas it is well known that in the returns fur-
nished by the shipbuilders all sorts of vessels built by
them are included, and that a very considerable tonnage
in...vessels for military purposes, also in light draught
river craft both for their own and other countries is
annually turned out from merchant shipyards.[4]

In fact Board of Trade figures do identify vessels built in various ports
for sale overseas, both for military and mercantile use, but not those sold
to the British government. Sidney Pollard has estimated the number of
vessels constructed for the government; these are reproduced in appendix
C.[5] Further research on craft acquired by the government would make
it possible to check the accuracy of these estimates.

Allowing for underestimation in Board of Trade statistics of the
output of private yards in London, Cowes and Southampton, which we
know built for the government, the information on post-1865 output
appears fairly accurate. But the situation is rather less clear for the early
nineteenth century. The eight surviving returns for London are depicted
in table 3. The disparities between the various series in the *Parliamentary Papers*, and between these and the two manuscript series in Customs
17 and Customs 36/5, are not reassuring.[6]

---

[4]David Pollock, *Modern Shipbuilding and the Men Engaged in It* (London, 1884),
186.

[5]Sidney Pollard, "The Economic History of British Shipbuilding" (Unpublished PhD
thesis, University of London, 1950).

[6]The following statistical sources are available for southeast shipbuilding, 1800-1826:
Public Record Office (PRO), Customs 17 and 36/5; Great Britain, Parliament, House of
Commons, *Parliamentary Papers [BPP]*, VII (1802-1803), "Account of Number of

The reasons for the variations remain obscure. Their random nature removes the possibility that they resulted from different definitions. Some discrepancies are very marked and not easily explained as transcription errors. Indeed, the returns in Customs 17 identify individual tonnages and several Parliamentary series also distinguish vessels by name, so it appears that some care was taken in their compilation. The obvious way to proceed would be to use the statutory register for London to rework the figures, but the Customs House fire in 1814 destroyed them. Moreover, when this has been done for other ports it has tended to confirm rather than eliminate the anomalies.[7] Only an examination of the registers for all ports would help, but the enormity of such a task, apart from the problem of missing registers, makes this impossible.

As with the post-1866 statistics, these figures do not accurately reflect building activity because they exclude craft built for government in private yards (it is possible that misidentification of some vessels "for the merchant service" may have led to some disparities). The *Parliamentary Papers* include a number of returns on warshipbuilding in merchant yards during the Napoleonic War, but a desire for consistency, together with some problems of interpretation, has led me to exclude them from table 3 or appendix A. Still, they are an important additional source for those interested in the history of particular centres.[8]

Vessels Built and Registered in Great Britain 1790-92 and 1799-1802, Distinguishing Each Year and Distinguishing the Ports of London, Liverpool, Hull, Bristol, Newcastle, Sunderland, Glasgow and Leith," 167; *BPP*, "Account of Number of Ships built in G.B. from 5th January 1790 to 5th January 1806 Distinguishing Each Year and the Tonnage of Each Ship or Vessel and also the Ports or Places Where They Were Respectively Built," XIII (1806), 741; *BPP*, "Return of Ships Launched in River Thames for E. India Co., 1770-1812," VIII (1812-1813), 59; *BPP*, "Return of All Ships (Not East Indiamen) Launched in the Thames for the Merchants Service, 1786-1812," IX (1812-1813), 451; *BPP*, "Account of Number of Vessels with their Tonnage that Have Been Built and Registered in the Ports of Great Britain and Ireland 1814-1826," XVIII (1826-1827), 271; *BPP*, "Account of Ships and Vessels Built and Registered in the Port of London from 1st January 1810 to the 21 March 1815," VII (1814-1815), 159.

[7]See Robin Craig's useful discussion in "A Note on Shipbuilding in the Port of Sunderland," *International Journal of Maritime History*, III, No. 2 (December 1991), 109-119.

[8]*BPP*, VIII (1805), 467-491; VIII (1813-1814), 498-506, 515, 554-557, 615-617; XI (1813-1814), 357-358. I am grateful to David J. Starkey for drawing my attention to these returns.

Table 3
Shipbuilding at London: Comparative Returns 1800-1826

	Customs 17	Parl. Papers	Customs 36
1800	56-19975	53-10714	63-15277
1801	50-5845	54-11026	59-12845
1802	41-15129	55-17681	50-13653
1803	97-15994	49-5893	64-11563
1804	46-5884	32-6086	31-5430
1805	53-6694	28-3039	29-3979
1806	25-3113	23-2597	24-2750
1807	n/a	24-989	26-1531
1808	27-4602	21-3964	21-4154
1809		16-1628	20-1815
1810		31-5832	31-5901
1811		30-9584	33-10537
1812		25-7991	31-9357
1813			10-1725
1814		15-845	
1815		18-879	
1816		22-2607	
1817		15-8122	
1818		39-5817	
1819		34-7533	
1820		36-11209	
1821		20-4510	
1822		31-2896	
1823		37-3342	
1824		61-5446	
1825		78-15966	
1826		72-6801	

Notes: The first number in each column indicates the number of vessels built; the second denotes total net tons.

Sources: Customs 17, 1800-1808: PRO, Customs 17; Parliamentary Papers (column 1), 1800-1802: *BPP*, VII (1802-1803), 167; 1804-1806: *BPP*, XIII (1806), 741; Parliamentary Papers (column 2), 1800-1812: *BPP*, IX (1812-1813), 451; 1814-1826: *BPP*, XVIII (1826-1827), 271; Parliamentary Papers (column 3), 1810-1814: *BPP*, VII (1814-1815), 159; Customs 36, 1800-1813: PRO, Customs 36/5.

    The tonnage measurements in this paper are "net register tons,"
excluding space unusable for cargo or passengers, such as that occupied
by engines, boilers or crew. Unfortunately, "net tonnage" is a poor
indicator of shipbuilding activity or demand. Nonetheless, it is the best
we have, since gross tonnages were not recorded in official returns until
1886 and then only for steamers. There were in fact four principal
measures used in Britain in the late nineteenth century: gross, net,
deadweight and builder's measurement; at the beginning of the century
official measurement was unsystematic. Unofficial returns in the press
were often based on inflated tonnages reported by builders, which helps
to explain the inconsistency between series.[9]

Characteristics of Output

Aggregate shipbuilding statistics for the southeast show the fluctuations
typical of the industry.[10] The annual time series for 1800-1826 reveals
a classic seven to nine-year cycle, with troughs in 1807, 1814 and 1822
and peaks in 1802, 1811, 1820 and 1825. Since the figures are for
mercantile output only and exclude naval tonnage, the downturns may
have been more apparent than real for some yards. But the depth of the
1813-1816 recession and the weak recovery thereafter was probably
associated with earlier wartime demand for new tonnage and a peacetime
glut of second-hand vessels caused by naval sales. The swings in London
were more pronounced than elsewhere in the southeast: the capital tended
to decline earlier and to recover more quickly. This probably reflected
the more direct connection between overseas trade and demand for new
vessels in London. The sailing barges and small coasters constructed on
the lower Thames, the Medway and along the south coast met less volatile local needs, although these too were affected by foreign trade. The
post-1866 series also exhibits similar characteristics, with three cycles
apparent. It should be understood that this overall pattern reflects not
only the supply of vessels to British owners but, in contrast to the earlier

---

[9]The best discussion of these measurements is in Sidney Pollard and Paul Robertson,
The British Shipbuilding Industry 1870-1914 (Cambridge, MA, 1979).

[10]See A. Slaven, "The British Shipbuilding Industry," in Roy Church (ed.), *The
Dynamics of Victorian Business* (London, 1979); Pollard and Robertson, *British
Shipbuilding*, 26-30; Leslie Jones, *Shipbuilding in Britain Mainly between the Two World
Wars* (Cardiff, 1957), 32-34.

series, also includes sales to foreigners (mercantile and governmental)--a market effectively closed by protective legislation until 1850.

Table 4
Steam Construction in the Southeast, 1866-1913
(000 net tons)

	Steam	Total	% Share
1866-1869	55.46	102.96	53.87
1870-1874	67.32	102.40	65.74
1874-1879	34.55	87.35	39.55
1880-1884	47.49	126.48	37.55
1885-1889	23.10	76.46	30.21
1890-1894	10.68	49.41	21.61
1895-1899	26.43	102.49	25.79
1900-1904	8.30	84.46	9.83
1905-1909	14.20	47.60	29.83
1910-1913	9.87	46.89	21.05

Note: Figures are quinquennial aggregates, except for 1866-1859 and 1910-1913, which include only four years each.

Source: See text.

Table 5
Southeast Shipbuilding: Construction Materials
(000 net tons)

	Iron	Steel	Wood	Composite	Total	% Wood
1866-1869	.00		72.88	3.92	102.96	70.78
1870-1874	41.19		58.29	2.94	102.40	56.92
1875-1879	46.25	5.13	40.19	.39	87.35	46.02
1880-1884	91.70	11.02	22.55	1.20	126.48	17.83
1885-1889	41.15	22.42	12.87		76.46	16.84
1890-1894	7.96	26.11	15.32		49.41	31.02
1895-1899	19.39	45.77	37.33		102.49	36.43
1900-1904	10.54	41.96	31.95		84.46	37.83
1905-1909	2.98	34.43	10.18		47.60	21.39
1910-1913	.81	31.58	14.50		46.89	30.93

Note: Figures are quinquennial aggregates, except for 1866-1869 and 1910-1913, which include only four years each.

Source: See text.

Figure 2
Average Vessel Size Built in Selected Ports,
1800-1804, 1820-1824, 1870-1874 and 1895-1899

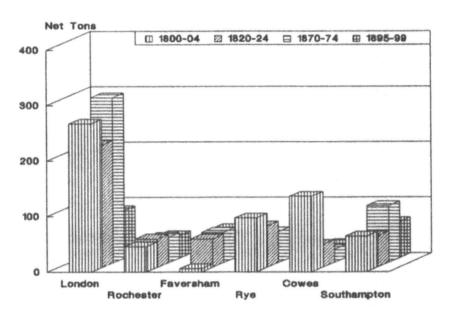

Source: See text.

Taking advantage of the detail in the official statistics for the later period, table 4 shows the share of steam tonnage constructed in the southeast, while table 5 depicts the material used for hulls. Contrary to expectations, steam construction was highest early in the period. More predictably, the commitment to wood diminished (with a particularly sharp drop after 1880) but thereafter recovered to account for approximately one-third of tonnage towards the end of the period. These characteristics reflect the fact that by the early twentieth century "shipbuilding" had become a misnomer for southeast activity; the region had become primarily a producer of boats and small leisure craft.

Aggregating the tonnage produced in the various southeast shipbuilding centres enables a comparison of the region's output with other parts of the country, although it implies a greater homogeneity than was in fact the case. London, Southampton and Cowes were different not only because of their greater volumes of tonnage but also because they produced steam as well as sail and used iron and steel in hull construction. Elsewhere in the region the wooden sailing vessel remained the typical product throughout the century. The inter-port differences in average vessel size (see figure 2) further highlight this distinction. By 1900, however, London and Southampton conformed to the general regional pattern of building small vessels. Nonetheless, each displayed distinctive features. It thus makes sense to examine them in more detail.

London

In the first quarter of the nineteenth century London continued its long-established role as the major producer of vessels. In *Shipbuilders of the Thames and Medway* (1971), Philip Banbury provides a valuable description of individual shipbuilding and engineering firms, showing how particular yards passed from one owner to another over the century and identifying where possible the vessels produced. By 1825 it appears that London had established a lead in the production of steamships, although the statistical series did not distinguish between sail and steam or wood and iron. Unfortunately, Banbury's information does not permit the construction of an output series beyond 1825 because he was concerned principally with better-known firms. In any year many vessels were built by small-scale firms which have escaped the attention of contemporaries and historians. In 1824, for example, William Hutton, secretary of the short-lived Society of Shipbuilders, told the Select Committee on the Combination Laws that he did not know how many shipbuilders were in London but that he corresponded with thirty-two.[11]

How are we to explain the size of London's shipbuilding industry in the early nineteenth century? In the age of wood and sail, London had no special comparative advantage in basic raw materials. While capital was abundant, there is no evidence of a shortage elsewhere. Although the presence of the Royal Dockyards guaranteed a stock of skilled labour, naval demand in peak periods could engross most of the supply. London's waterfront--the "land" of the standard Cobb-Douglas production function--was well suited for shipbuilding, but the number of potential alternative uses increased as the city grew. The answer, however, is not a mystery: as with less exalted centres, London's shipbuilding output reflected the size and nature of the local market. With the capital accounting for about one-third of all UK port entries, and with a large, locally-based shipowning community and a suitable

---

[11]"Select Committee on the Combination Laws," *BPP*, IV (1825), 404.

waterfront for building and launching vessels, shipbuilding was a logical enterprise. The particular character of London's trade further boosted demand: the East and West India business demanded large vessels and encouraged specialisation by certain yards in this type of product.[12]

While it is true that London-built shipping enjoyed a national reputation, it did not serve a national market. We lack reliable information on where London vessels were sold, but studies of registries in other ports reveal only a few London-built craft. Since the city's renown was based on the production of top-quality merchant vessels, its shipbuilders could command higher prices, according to a variety of witnesses to various Select Committees between 1820 and 1849, but information to confirm this is fragmentary and sometimes difficult to interpret.[13] What is clear is that these expensive vessels met an essentially local demand.

The statistical evidence suggests the need to be wary of the standard wisdom about London production. The series in Customs 17 sorts vessels by tonnage and would permit a detailed, if laborious, analysis of output. Some of the printed parliamentary returns which also do this are the basis for the analysis of output between 1803 and 1805 in table 6. While this confirms London's capacity to build large vessels, the range of sizes shows the importance of smaller craft. With London wages generally higher than elsewhere, these must have been overpriced in national terms and vulnerable to competition. Whether higher quality and better classifications at Lloyds' were sufficient counterweights is unclear.

As already noted, London yards were among the first to combine the skills of the shipwright and the engineer to produce steamers. While there is no consistent data prior to 1866 to analyze this aspect of London's performance, a return of the 868 steam vessels on the register in 1845, which gives place of build, suggests that London yards built for local demand. Of the 194 London-built steamers, only twenty-six were registered elsewhere. The picture that emerges of London shipbuilding in the first half of the century is of dependence upon local shipowners.[14]

---

[12]See "Select Committee on Petitions Relating to East India Built Shipping," *BPP*, VIII (1813-1814).

[13]See, for example, the evidence of Nickels, Gray and Woolcome to the "Select Committee on Manufactures, Commerce and Shipping," *BPP*, XII (1833), q. 3615, 5734, and 5849.

[14]*BPP*, XLVII (1845), 548.

Table 6
Size Distribution of London-built Vessels, 1804-1806

Tons	1804	1805	1806
Under 20	8	7	2
20-39	9	9	6
40-59	16	25	9
60-79	2	1	4
80-99	0	0	0
100-199	2	3	1
200-299	3	0	1
300-399	1	1	0
400-499	2	0	1
500-599	0	0	0
600-699	1	0	0
700-799	0	0	0
Over 800	2	5	1
Total	46	51	25

Source: *BPP*, XIII (1806), 741.

According to contemporaries, by mid-century London produced fewer vessels for the low end of the market but increased its dependence on experimental craft--the *Great Eastern* was an extreme example--and government orders, British and foreign. This trend continued for a decade and a half, as the Crimean and US Civil Wars boosted business and encouraged the creation of new yards to build iron steamers. Sidney Pollard, in his seminal article on the decline of Thames shipbuilding, suggests that most private work was for luxury trades, with the Thames acting "as a reservoir, drawn upon when other yards were overloaded with work, but left first when depression set in." According to Tony Slaven's data on shipbuilding employment, by 1841 the northeast had displaced the Thames as the largest centre; in 1867 the London industry, "reliant on marginal, speculative and foreign orders," collapsed in the wake of the Overend Gurney banking crisis and many yards closed.[15] The following year a leading shipbuilder, Samuda, who built for P&O, told the Royal Commission on Trade Unions that:

---

[15]Pollard, "The Decline of Shipbuilding," 78; Slaven, "The British Shipbuilding Industry," 107.

taking the period since I began business as a shipbuilder in 1851, every single establishment that was in existence as an iron shipbuilding establishment on the Thames at the time I began business in 1851, with the exception of my own, had either failed or discontinued work as a shipbuilding establishment.[16]

By 1871 employment had shrunk to 9000, two-thirds of the workforce just six years earlier.

Contemporary commentators like John Glover laid the blame for this catastrophe on high wages and the resistance of unions to any reductions, but Pollard argues that although labour costs were a factor, London's key disadvantage in the age of steam was its location, distant from supplies of coal, iron and steel. While there is no reason to quarrel with this conclusion, the main point is that factor costs were much more important in the second half of the century. Pollard's contention that "the Thames managed to hold its own in the first half of the century, when wage differences were just as great" is misleading because it implies that the market remained the same as sail gave way to steam. Steam was distinct from sail, involving new forms of ownership, investors and managers.[17] The new London shipbuilding firms of the early 1850s lacked the advantage of established connections with particular trades or individuals. Competition was no longer with neighbouring yards but with more distant centres in a nationwide market. Only on government orders did London continue to enjoy the edge of proximity to market, but this too faded in due course. By the end of the century Admiralty orders placed with Thames yards reflected a commitment to spreading government business as widely as possible rather than a preference for London.[18]

We can examine London's decline in some detail, since the official series for shipbuilding output resumed just when the local industry began to decay. The figures for 1866 and 1867 show the

---

[16]"Royal Commission on Trade Unions," *BPP*, XXXIX (1867-1868), q. 16746.

[17]John Glover, "On the Decline of Shipbuilding on the Thames," *Journal of the Royal Statistical Society* (1869), 291; Pollard, "The Decline of Shipbuilding," 81.

[18]Sarah Palmer, "Yarrow of Poplar: The Engineer as Businessman" (Unpublished paper presented to the Queen Mary College Centenary Series, 1985).

importance of steam to London yards, while those for succeeding years reveal the extent of the collapse (see figure 3). What deserves emphasis is that London's decline was not a consequence of a failure to recognise or act on the opportunities offered by new technology. On the contrary, the creation of firms such as Dudgeon and the Thames and the Millwall Ironworks testifies both to substantial entrepreneurial initiative and a level of technical achievement in the early 1860s which, in Pollard's estimation, had no equal in the country but was rapidly to become obsolete. The ease with which capital was raised for what proved in some instances to be short-lived enterprises possibly owed something to a metropolitan location. Indeed, the availability of capital may have been detrimental, inducing firms to invest in modern technology and burdening them with debts not justified by market prospects.

Figure 3
Tonnage of London-Built Vessels, Sail and Steam, 1866-1913

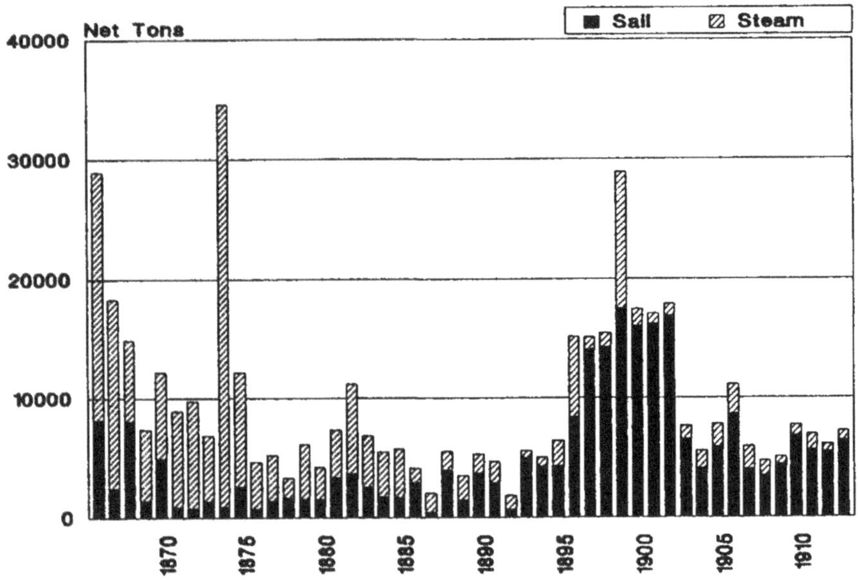

Source: See text.

If there was no real recovery after the 1867 crisis, neither was there a precipitous slide. Several firms that survived were able to continue for a number of years on naval contracts, overseas orders and ship repair (see figure 4). Samuda Brothers and Dudgeon closed in 1885 and Wigram and Sons in 1893, but the Thames Ironworks survived until 1912, even launching the 22,500-ton dreadnought HMS *Thunderer* a year before its demise. Yet for two firms founded in the late 1860s, the last quarter of the century was a period of prosperity and expansion. Yarrow, on the Isle of Dogs, and Thornycroft, upriver at Chiswick, initially specialised in fast steam launches and shallow-draft river steamers, then developed productive lines in torpedo-boats before moving on to destroyers. Both firms, complaining of high labour costs but probably more concerned to introduce new labour practices, left the Thames in the 1900s, Thornycroft for Southampton and Yarrow for Glasgow.[19]

Figure 4
Tonnage of London-Built Vessels Sold at Home and Overseas, 1866-1913

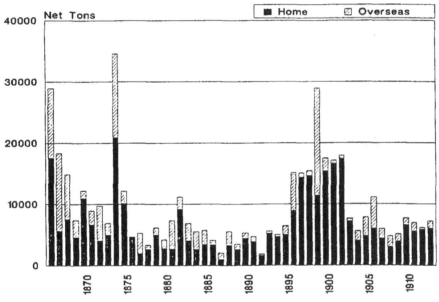

Source: See text.

Southampton

Southampton, a thriving entrepot in the Middle Ages, had by the early nineteenth century declined to a small, fashionable seaside resort. It had a number of shipyards, producing both naval and merchant vessels, but

---

[19]*Ibid.* See also Banbury, *Shipbuilders of the Thames and Medway.*

most were small and served only local needs. By the 1820s the port was expanding, as the need for passage across the Solent to the Isle of Wight encouraged the introduction of steam ferries. This created an opportunity for local shipbuilders; the first Southampton-built steamer went into service in 1830. Iron shipbuilding was introduced a few years later by the innovative engineer William Summers, and Summers and Day earned a reputation for paddle steamers. In 1838 new dock construction gave the port a further impetus. By mid-century, the use of the port by Royal Mail and P&O generated contracts for mail steamers for the yards owned by the London shipbuilder Money Wigram and Summers and Day. The Union Line also had Southampton connections. In the 1860s Southampton produced mainly steamers, but by the time of the launch of the *Hindostan* in 1869 the competitive advantage was shifting to the Clyde, Tyne and Wear. Thereafter Summers and Day shifted into small steamers, from the mid-1880s developing an expertise in yachts and torpedo boats somewhat similar to Yarrow and Thornycroft on the Thames.[20]

Figure 5
Tonnage of Southampton-Built Vessels, Sail and Steam, 1866-1913

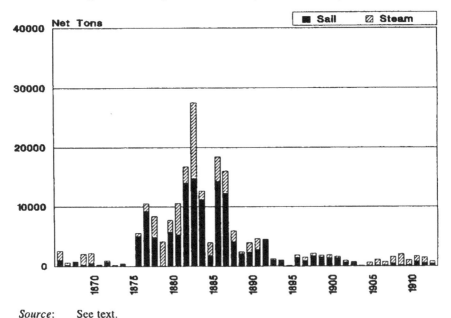

Source: See text.

---

[20]This section is based largely on Rance, *Shipbuilding in Victorian Southampton.*

Figure 6
Tonnage of Southampton-Built Vessels Sold at Home and Overseas, 1866-1913

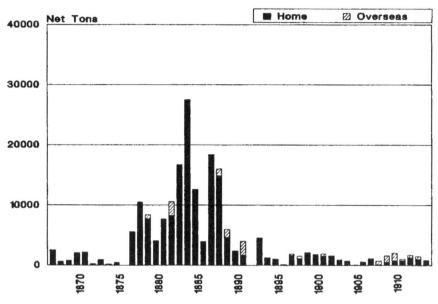

Source: See text.

As spectacular as the 1850s and 1860s were, the real Southampton boom was yet to come. As figure 5 shows, in the late 1870s and 1880s there was a marked expansion based on iron and sail. From the late 1870s Oswald Mordaunt and Co., which specialised in iron sailing vessels, took advantage of demand for large sailing vessels. Southampton's best customers were not overseas but in the UK, especially in Liverpool (see figure 6). Much of its output was accounted for by Mordaunt, which built 104 vessels between 1878 and 1889, and in August 1882 had eleven vessels (25,767 tons) on the stocks.[21] Financial problems forced Mordaunt into liquidation early in 1889; with contracts no longer plentiful similar difficulties afflicted the succession of firms which subsequently occupied its Woolston yard until Thornycroft arrived from Chiswick in 1904. Southampton was committed to iron construction after 1875, although some wooden building continued until about 1900. Steel construction began in earnest in 1887 and iron building ceased by

---

[21]J. Silvester Davies, *A History of Southampton, Partly from the Work of Dr. Speed* (Southampton, 1883), 283-284.

1890. The low average tonnages of steel vessels in the 1890s reflected a trend to the kind of small craft produced by Summers and Day.

Figure 7: Launch of the Screw Steamship *Himalaya* at Blackwall.

Source: *Illustrated London News*, 28 May 1853.

Figure 8: The *Great Eastern*, the largest ship in the world prior to 1897, built on the Thames, 1858.

Source: Courtesy of the Trustees of the National Museums and Galleries on Merseyside.

Conclusion

The limitations of the statistical record force any discussion of southeast shipbuilding to focus on the period of decline. But even a fairly superficial analysis of the southeast demonstrates that a shipbuilding region in decline is worth as much attention as more successful areas.

It is instructive to compare the history of Southampton shipbuilding in the late nineteenth century with London. Both ports had early experience in building in wood and iron, sail and steam; both were in the south and at a competitive disadvantage against northern centres as steam developed. By 1900 both were in similarly reduced states. But while London's decline appeared a foregone conclusion after 1867, staved off only in the medium-term by sales to overseas customers and the Admiralty, Southampton, selling primarily domestically, prospered in the 1880s. The key factor was the ability to switch back to sail, achieved through the initiative of Oswald Mordaunt, a newcomer to Southampton. In Southampton, it would seem, there was not the acute separation between the two sectors of the industry as in London. Until the mid-1880s London stayed with steam. Of the London firms that survived the 1867 crisis, arguably only Wigram, a firm with experience both in sail and steam, might have played a similar role to Mordaunt, but it did not. It is true that after 1895 London constructed more sail than steam tonnage, but this reflected a move toward smaller craft rather than the iron or steel-hulled sailing giants of Southampton. Although London yards used steel, iron barges were still built at the end of the century.

The contrasting experiences of London and Southampton in turn have to be distinguished from other ports in the region. Shipbuilding in places such as Cowes and Portsmouth, which receive some useful but brief attention in Michael Bouquet's *South Eastern Sail* (1972), deserves further investigation. Other southern centres, such as Faversham, seemingly remained unaffected by the transition from sail to steam. Deal and Dover lost out to Rye, but the other ports continued to produce wooden sailing barges and small inshore craft into the twentieth century.

Within a wider economic history perspective, this study warns of the danger of assuming that technological superiority is a precondition for the survival of an economic activity. Failure, like success, is a complex phenomenon.

Appendix A
Output of Southeast Ports, 1800-1826

	London		Rochester		Faversham		Ramsgate		Sandwich	
1800	63	15277	8	366	1	10			9	625
1801	59	12845	9	623	2	125			6	286
1802	50	13653	10	553	3	172			9	278
1803	64	11563	10	391	0	0			5	364
1804	31	5430	9	404	0	0			4	404
1800-04	267	58768	46	2337	6	307	0	0	33	1957
1805	29	3979	7	366	1	78			0	0
1806	24	2750	6	233	1	9			4	238
1807	26	1531	8	399	3	157			2	175
1808	21	4154	8	401	0	0			7	437
1809	20	1815	11	622	2	68			7	685
1805-9	120	14229	40	2021	7	312	0	0	20	1535
1810	31	5901	13	1738	0	0			9	588
1811	33	10537	19	2099	1	56			8	514
1812	31	9357	18	1301	0	0			4	170
1813	10	1725	12	617	4	137			4	163
1814	15	845	7	591	7	106	0	0	5	344
1810-14	120	28365	69	6346	12	299	0	0	30	1779
1815	19	879	13	617	3	41	0	0	3	246
1816	22	2607	9	304	2	38	0	0	3	241
1817	15	3122	10	692	7	106	0	0	2	134
1818	39	5817	17	850	6	238	0	0	5	485
1819	34	7533	9	455	10	184	0	0	5	397
1815-19	129	24958	58	2918	28	607	0	0	18	1503
1820	36	11209	8	348	3	99	0	0	2	131
1821	20	4510	8	2049	7	163	0	0	1	43
1822	31	2896	9	562	9	281	0	0	0	0
1823	37	3342	7	260	4	49	2	199	0	0
1824	61	5446	4	522	5	130	3	281	0	0
1820-24	185	27403	36	3741	28	722	5	480	3	174
1825	78	15966	12	730	5	153	2	43	0	0
1826	72	6801	16	953	5	168	4	150	0	0
1825-6	150	22767	28	1683	10	321	6	193	0	0

	Deal		Dover		Rye		Newhaven		Shoreham	
1800	4	102	26	1271	6	313	1	34	10	1040
1801	3	88	16	1052	8	431	2	187	7	733
1802	4	121	25	1209	7	218	0	0	5	587
1803	4	155	15	745	10	805	0	0	2	106
1804	7	232	15	880	6	325	0	0	1	115
1800-4	22	698	97	5157	37	2092	3	221	25	2581
1805	7	228	14	644	1	90	0	0	2	459
1806	4	85	23	1071	7	559	0	0	0	0
1807	3	100	20	998	6	383	0	0	1	44
1808	5	81	17	805	4	98	0	0	1	15
1809	8	191	4	83	1	102	1	78	1	39
1805-9	27	685	78	3601	19	1232	1	78	5	557
1810	9	173	3	84	3	130	0	0	1	18
1811	4	73	10	269	5	171	1	80	1	33
1812	5	107	4	153	5	286	0	0	3	163
1813	5	99	3	235	9	747	1	18	2	34
1814	3	50	3	68	5	311	1	157	1	70
1810-14	26	502	23	809	27	1645	3	255	8	318
1815	1	22	11	500	10	544	0	0	1	106
1816	1	15	6	455	13	413	1	71	3	146
1817	1	27	3	75	4	285	0	0	2	118
1818	1	15	2	27	12	303	0	0	1	107
1819	0	0	3	101	10	339	0	0	3	579
1815-19	4	79	25	1158	49	1884	1	71	10	1056
1820	0	0	4	220	10	118	0	0	1	71
1821	0	0	1	31	4	98	0	0	1	107
1822	0	0	3	139	9	85	0	0	3	209
1823	1	16	203		4	195	4	503	2	149
1824	1	28	0	0	7	358	9	723	2	167
1820-24	2	44	12	593	34	854	13	1226	9	703
1825	0	0	13	306	7	343	9	801	1	166
1826	2	24	6	530	9	804	10	1193	2	335
1825-6	2	24	19	836	16	1147	19	1994	3	501

	Arundel		Chichester		Portsmouth		Cowes		Southampton	
1800	2	366	1	201	2	191	31	1311	13	674
1801	2	310	2	98	1	60	27	1475	15	902
1802	4	397	7	404	2	236	29	1093	14	703
1803	5	895	4	270	1	16	30	986	16	847
1804	4	557	4	284	0	0	19	761	6	440
1800-4	17	2525	18	1257	6	503	136	5626	64	3566
1805	1	226	0	0	4	276	23	738	9	931
1806	2	318	2	133	2	38	15	601	7	345
1807	2	559	1	40	2	32	14	385	10	546
1808	2	207	4	836	0	0	9	523	5	172
1809	3	786	1	23	0	0	13	464	8	745
1805-9	10	2096	8	1032	8	346	74	2711	39	2739
1810	2	375	2	30	2	79	19	945	9	547
1811	2	293	1	481	0	0	13	492	9	2482
1812	1	149	2	105	1	5	7	272	7	846
1813	0	0	1	14	2	51	9	237	6	381
1814	1	36	4	216	2	477	4	255	9	841
1810-14	6	853	10	846	7	612	52	2201	40	5097
1815	1	136	3	114	8	341	8	902	21	1945
1816	3	326	4	107	2	41	10	547	11	1140
1817	3	503	2	91	3	71	10	593	17	1227
1818	3	183	1	31	2	83	13	1613	13	2173
1819	0	0	5	150	3	68	15	1251	14	988
1815-19	10	1148	15	493	18	604	56	4906	76	7473
1820	2	132	0	0	5	363	10	553	10	701
1821	0	0	3	74	5	122	6	752	9	608
1822	1	23	4	174	2	28	10	407	13	1447
1823	1	25	3	64	5	162	7	610	12	905
1824	2	42	0	0	9	324	4	116	20	2129
1820-24	6	222	10	312	26	999	37	2438	64	5790
1825	1	30	0	0	6	273	14	1263	14	2611
1826	0	0	2	88	4	413	16	1227	17	2220
1825-6	1	30	2	88	10	686	30	2490	31	4831

Sources: Great Britain, Parliament, House of Commons, *Parliamentary Papers* [*BPP*], VII (1802-1803), "Account of Number of Vessels Built and Registered in Great Britain 1790-92 and 1799-1802, Distinguishing Each Year and Distinguishing the Ports of London, Liverpool, Hull, Bristol, Newcastle, Sunderland, Glasgow and Leith," 167; *BPP*, "Account of Number of Ships Built in G.B. from 5th January 1790 to 5th January 1806

Distinguishing Each Year and the Tonnage of Each Ship or Vessel and also the Ports or Places Where They Were Respectively Built," XIII (1806), 741; *BPP*, "Return of Ships Launched in River Thames for E. India Co., 1770-1812," VIII (1812-1813), 59; *BPP*, "Return of All Ships (Not East Indiamen) Launched in the Thames for the Merchants Service, 1786-1812," IX (1812-1813), 451; *BPP*, "Account of Number of Vessels with Their Tonnage that Have Been Built and Registered in the Ports of Great Britain and Ireland 1814-1826," XVIII (1826-1827), 271; *BPP*, "Account of Ships and Vessels Built and Registered in the Port of London from 1st January 1810 to the 21 March 1815," VII (1814-1815), 159.

Appendix B
Output in Southeast Ports, 1866-1913

	London		Rochester		Faversham		Ramsgate		Deal	
1866	129	28957	49	2506	14	571	8	399	1	26
1867	88	15179	41	1646	0	0	7	330	0	0
1868	51	14470	31	1267	2	71	2	87	9	686
1869	68	7368	0	0	1	41	1	45	12	637
1866-9	336	55974	121	5419	17	683	18	861	22	1349
1870	58	11796	20	823	0	0	3	167	11	671
1871	37	8505	16	931	10	534	2	77	16	1061
1872	48	9668	10	419	10	943	2	71	13	720
1873	29	6105	11	475	9	593	1	37	9	510
1874	54	34605	10	436	13	740	0	0	5	300
1870-74	226	70679	67	3084	42	2810	8	352	54	3262
1875	35	12131	12	544	13	513	0	0	8	442
1876	39	4654	20	844	23	1383	1	38	6	364
1877	73	5246	23	1039	24	1092	1	38	4	458
1878	100	3320	20	852	29	1201	0	0	4	199
1879	65	6131	15	633	24	1033	2	74	3	180
1874-79	312	31482	90	3912	113	5222	4	150	25	1643
1880	102	4186	18	780	15	677	2	75		
1881	128	7309	14	590	16	744	1	51		
1882	153	11197	13	591	14	635	2	118		
1883	152	6840	14	650	6	353	2	191		
1884	131	5513	8	400	14	838	1	44		
1880-84	666	35045	67	3011	65	3247	8	479		
1885	59	5172	8	382	7	424	0	0		
1886	62	4099	10	514	6	244	2	73		
1887	41	2039	7	283	7	466	2	68		
1888	68	5528	9	482	8	330	1	23		
1889	55	3472	12	600	9	499	0	0		
1885-89	285	20310	46	2261	37	1963	5	164		
1890	69	5272	15	816	14	1016	2	57		
1891	83	4696	12	628	12	475	3	121		

	London		Rochester		Faversham		Ramsgate		Deal	
1892	47	1829	10	514	8	442	2	105		
1893	99	5609	8	401	7	329	2	121		
1894	109	5035	16	779	12	747	1	24		
1890-94	407	22441	61	3138	53	3009	10	428		
1895	95	6433	17	863	12	721	0	0		
1896	163	15116	15	703	13	678	1	6		
1897	208	15089	13	700	19	891	0	0		
1898	283	15414	0	0	28	1472	0	0		
1899	211	28953	20	960	23	1200	0	0		
1895-99	960	81005	65	3226	95	4962	1	6		
1900	263	17459	22	995	26	1482	0	0		
1901	253	17111	11	519	24	1633	0	0		
1902	273	17897	10	448	16	904	2	56		
1903	122	7674	10	539	16	839	3	89		
1904	88	5540	12	551	12	601	2	51		
1900-04	999	64581	65	3052	94	5459	7	196		
1905	115	7840	6	291	11	1134	2	50		
1906	160	11135	2	98	11	509	2	48		
1907	122	5942	8	397	8	261	2	31		
1908	73	4719	4	193	4	143	2	27		
1909	69	5053	2	28	1	11	1	25		
1905-09	539	34689	22	1007	35	2058	9	181		
1910	97	7711	1	63	6	298	1	24		
1911	104	6952	1	61	6	387	0	0		
1912	115	6143	2	86	12	931	0	0		
1913	106	7210	3	199	9	699	0	0		
1910-13	422	28016	7	409	33	2315	1	24	0	0

	Dover		Rye		Newhaven		Shoreham		Littlehampton	
1866	0	0	24	1954	3	154	11	3194	0	0
1867	0	0	19	1140	1	23	10	3237	0	0
1868	0	0	14	878	0	0	9	2120	0	0
1869	1	17	15	786	1	35	10	2045	3	903
1866-9	1	17	72	4758	5	212	40	10596	3	903
1870	0	0	10	594	0	0	5	954	0	0
1871	0	0	11	572	0	0	5	946	2	694
1872	0	0	12	635	1	212	4	544	3	954
1873	1	45	15	932	3	90	6	377	5	1109
1874	1	14	16	798	1	209	6	833	3	754
1870-74	2	59	64	3531	5	511	26	3654	13	3511
1875	0	0	15	804	2	66	3	166	2	755
1876	0	0	19	872	4	292	4	229	1	544
1877	0	0	22	1151	5	327	2	563	2	617

	Dover		Rye		Newhaven		Shoreham		Littlehampton	
1878	2	84	22	1160	1	76	5	656	2	102
1879	1	39	19	867	1	70	4	115	0	0
1874-79	3	123	97	4854	13	831	18	1729	7	2018
1880	0	0	17	788	0	0	0	0	3	727
1881	1	40	15	898	0	0	2	52	1	189
1882	0	0	14	861	1	73	0	0	2	185
1883	0	0	13	932	1	80	1	21	0	0
1884	0	0	10	714			3	64	2	330
1880-84	1	40	69	4193	2	153	6	137	8	1431
1885	0	0	11	792			2	43	1	70
1886	0	0	7	458			3	51	1	78
1887	0	0	5	322			1	25	2	169
1888	0	0	5	291			2	41	3	280
1889	0	0	3	219			1	13	4	298
1885-89	0	0	31	2082	0	0	9	173	11	895
1890	0	0	2	251			0	0	2	264
1891	0	0	3	242			2	32	3	336
1892	0	0	3	290			0	0	3	279
1893	0	0	3	96			3	40	1	87
1894	2	100	6	326			1	5	3	340
1890-94	2	100	17	1205	0	0	6	77	12	1306
1895	1	56	5	164			2	23	0	0
1896	1	53	7	167			0	0	2	145
1897	1	62	5	129			1	19	4	213
1898	2	126	4	111			2	42	4	277
1899	1	69	1	44			2	29	4	225
1895-99	6	366	22	615	0	0	7	113	14	860
1900	1	64	3	189	0	0	0	0	2	54
1901	2	141	4	165	0	0	0	0	0	0
1902	0	0	3	176	0	0	4	106	1	88
1903	0	0	3	143	0	0	1	29	1	30
1904	0	0	6	248	0	0	0	0	2	113
1900-04	3	205	19	921	0	0	5	135	6	285
1905	1	2	3	143	0	0	1	28	1	35
1906	0	0	4	157	0	0	0	0	1	95
1907	0	0	6	287	0	0	0	0	1	7
1908	0	0	3	138	0	0	1	20	1	93
1909	0	0	4	186	0	0	2	63	1	11
1905-09	1	2	20	911	0	0	4	111	5	241
1910	1	3	2	92	0	0	1	12	1	93
1911	0	0	3	116	0	0	0	0	0	0
1912	0	0	2	160	0	0	1	4	1	92
1913	0	0	3	207	0	0	1	50	4	172

	Dover		Rye		Newhaven		Shoreham		Littlehampton	
1910-13	1	3	10	575	0	0	3	66	6	357
		Portsmouth			Cowes			Southampton		
1866		6	370		10	1510		13	2583	
1867		11	529		10	902		3	626	
1868		12	986		10	1001		7	850	
1869		8	508		9	241		9	2079	
1866-1869		37	2393		39	3654		32	6138	
1870		2	201		10	271		13	2228	
1871		8	595		20	672		4	246	
1872		8	502		51	1091		5	960	
1873		9	631		56	1143		6	190	
1874		7	858		67	911		9	451	
1870-1874		34	2787		204	4088		37	4075	
1875		8	759		38	942		0	0	
1876		12	1100		15	476		15	5558	
1877		9	1278		15	516		17	10540	
1878		6	349		41	640		10	8410	
1879		5	354		14	324		11	4144	
1874-1879		40	3840		123	2898		53	28652	
1880		6	382		39	1196		9	7749	
1881		6	291		18	245		16	10588	
1882		6	275		23	367		20	16765	
1883		2	182		26	259		28	27530	
1884		4	151		6	115		16	12685	
1880-1884		24	1281		112	2182		89	75317	
1885		3	50		7	343		22	3978	
1886		1	32		5	56		20	18447	
1887		4	253		7	257		14	15997	
1888		1	55		3	297		11	5993	
1889		5	200		7	216		9	2440	
1885-1889		14	590		29	1169		76	46855	
1890		6	233		5	77		14	3983	
1891		4	419		5	159		18	4668	
1892		3	70		9	264		7	4574	
1893		5	147		7	156		17	1264	
1894		5	130		13	530		15	1063	
1890-1894		23	999		39	1186		71	15552	
1895		5	182		33	1166		3	138	
1896		8	161		17	407		17	1922	
1897		7	235		12	308		21	1533	
1898		7	324		12	284		38	2166	
1899		7	363		17	316		42	1834	

	Portsmouth		Cowes		Southampton	
1895-1899	34	1265	91	2481	121	7593
1900	8	304	15	545	32	1920
1901	5	322	10	207	18	1607
1902	7	327	8	454	16	953
1903	9	463	5	79	20	725
1904	8	432	6	98	2	88
1900-1904	37	1848	44	1383	88	5293
1905	5	294	10	114	11	637
1906	5	199	6	324	13	1132
1907	6	635	3	22	8	716
1908	9	588	8	136	15	1603
1909	5	133	8	92	16	2058
1905-1909	30	1849	35	688	63	6146
1910	3	246	5	34	23	1021
1911	4	204	5	220	37	1713
1912	4	235	17	1398	19	1458
1913	9	547	9	7210	18	843
1910-1913	20	1232	36	8862	97	5035

Sources: 1866: *BPP*, LXVI (1867), 61, 493-494; 1867: *BPP*, LXVII (1867-1868), 484, 489-490; 1868: *BPP*, LVIII (1868-1869), 485-486, 488; 1869: *BPP*, LXIII (1870), 492, 497-499; 1870: *BPP*, LXIII (1871), 472-476; 1871: *BPP*, LVI (1872), 454-456; 1872: *BPP*, LXIII (1873), 484-486; 1873: *BPP*, LXIX (1874), 536-538; 1874: *BPP*, LXXIII (1875), 234-236; 1875: *BPP*, LXXII (1876), 526-528; 1876: *BPP*, LXXX (1877), 534-536; 1877: *BPP*, LXXI (1878), 536-538; 1878: *BPP*, LXVIII (1878-1879), 544-546; 1879: *BPP*, LXXI (1880), 500-502; 1880: *BPP*, LXXXVII (1881), 496-498; 1881: *BPP*, LXVIII (1882), 500-502; 1882: *BPP*, LXX (1883), 504-506; 1883: *BPP*, LXXVIII (1884), 604-609; 1884: *BPP*, LXXV (1884-1885), 604-607; 1885: *BPP*, LXIV (1886), 656-661; 1886: *BPP*, LXXX (1887), 658-663; 1887: *BPP*, XCVII (1888), 682-687; 1888: *BPP*, LXXV (1889), 694-699; 1889: *BPP*, LXXII (1890), 700-705; 1890: *BPP*, LXXXII (1891), 702-709; 1891: *BPP*, LXXVII (1892), 284-289, 720-725; 1892: *BPP*, LXXXVIII (1893-1894), 760-765; 1893: *BPP*, LXXXIV (1894), 764-767; 1894: *BPP*, XCV (1895), 762-765; 1895: *BPP*, LXXXIII (1896), 825-829; 1896: *BPP*, LXXXVII (1897), 803-847; 1897: *BPP*, XCI (1898), 298-303; 1898: *BPP*, XCVI (1899), 298-303; 1899: *BPP*, LXXXVIII (1900), 290-295; 1900: *BPP*, LXXV (1901), 818-823; 1901: *BPP*, C (1902), 772-776; 1902: *BPP*, LXXXI (1903), 772-776; 1903: *BPP*, XCI (1904), 950-955; 1904: *BPP*, LXXX (1905), 834-839; 1905: *BPP*, XCVII (1906), 834-839; 1906: *BPP*, LXXXIV (1907), 286-290; 1907: *BPP*, CIV (1908), 286-291; 1908: *BPP*, LXXXIV (1909), 368-272; 1909: *BPP*, LXXXVII (1910), 268-273; 1910: *BPP*, LXXIX (1911), 312-317; 1911: *BPP*, LXXXV (1912-1913), 314-319; 1912: *BPP*, LXI (1913), 846-851; 1913: *BPP*, LXXXII (1914), 316-335.

Appendix C
Shipbuilding at London, 1866-1899

Year	Official Statistics		Pollard's Unofficial Statistics for Thames-built British Warships '000 Gross Tons
	Net Tons		
1866	129	28957	
1867	88	15179	
1868	51	14470	
1869	68	7368	
1870	58	11796	
1871	37	8505	
1872	48	9668	
1873	29	6105	
1874	24	34605	
1875	35	12131	
1876	39	4654	
1877	73	5246	
1878	100	3320	
1879	65	6131	
1880	102	4186	
1881	128	7309	
1882	153	11197	
1883	152	6840	22
1884	131	5513	0
1885	59	5172	0
1886	62	4099	0
1887	41	2039	10
1888	68	5528	0
1889	55	3472	8
1890	69	5272	17
1891	73	4696	11
1892	47	1829	+16
1893	99	4609	3
1894	109	5035	3
1895	95	6433	4
1896	163	15116	+17
1897	208	15089	2
1898	283	15414	31
1899	211	28953	3

Sources: *BPP*, Annual Statements Shipping and Navigation; Sidney Pollard, "The Economic History of British Shipbuilding" (Unpublished PhD thesis, University of London, 1950), table A26.

The Shipbuilding Industry of Southwest England, 1790-1913[1]

David J. Starkey

Introduction

Comprising the counties of Cornwall, Devon, Dorset and Somerset, the peninsular region of southwest England was home to a range of maritime activities during the nineteenth century.[2] Shipbuilding was one of the most prominent, in relation to both the local and national economies. During the final quarter of the century, however, shipbuilding contracted to such a degree that on the eve of the First World War only a few yards were left, producing a tiny fraction of the UK's output. The fluctuating fortunes of this regional industry is the concern of this paper. Attention will be focused initially on the scale and character of the southwest's output, and then on the economic forces which conditioned its shipbuilding performance.

Output

The output of the southwest's nineteenth-century shipbuilding industry can be divided into three parts. The first was the construction throughout the era of relatively small wooden merchant sailing vessels. The maintenance and modification of commercial vessels comprised the second facet of the industry's output. Third, warshipbuilding was also undertaken in private shipyards, notably during the Napoleonic Wars.

[1]I am grateful to Simon Ville and the other contributors to this volume, as well as to Stephen Fisher, Basil Greenhill, George Hogg and Tony Pawlyn for commenting on an earlier draft of this paper; to Basil Greenhill and Janet Cusack for their help in locating illustrations; and to Rodney Fry for drawing the graphs.

[2]See Michael Duffy, *et al.* (eds.), *The New Maritime History of Devon* (2 vols., London, 1992), I.

Research in Maritime History, No. 4 (June 1993), 75-110.

The extent and composition of these sectors will be considered separately.

Merchant Shipbuilding

The number and tonnage of commercial vessels built in Britain can be measured with some degree of accuracy for much of the nineteenth century. While Customs returns provide data for the years 1787-1808, various accounts presented to Parliament yield output figures for nearly every year until 1866. From this date, annual port-by-port data are available in the *Annual Statements of Navigation and Shipping*. Yet these sources do not reflect the full range of shipbuilding production, since vessels which were not registered because of size or occupation are excluded. Moreover, the data are primarily quantitative, affording little consideration to the value or quality of the vessels.

Nevertheless, available national output data provide a context in which to place the contribution of a particular port or region. Problems arise, however, in the examination of production at the local level. Comparison with other sources reveals minor discrepancies in Customs returns up to 1808,[3] while the Parliamentary accounts of later periods often conflict, though never very seriously, with detailed analyses of particular ports.[4] That official port-by-port production figures do not exist between 1827 and 1865 presents a more intractable problem. The solution adopted in this essay is to estimate the southwest's output during these years on the basis of the shipping registered in Devon. From 1825 to 1864, 1464 vessels measuring an aggregate 128,456 tons, were built and first registered in the county.[5] This provides only a partial picture of Devon's output, of course, for it takes no account of new tonnage sold

---

[3]Robin Craig, "A Note on Shipbuilding in the Port of Sunderland," *International Journal of Maritime History*, III, No. 2 (December 1991), 109-119.

[4]For instance, the annual totals in Grahame Farr, *Shipbuilding in North Devon* (Greenwich, 1976), differ slightly from the official returns for Barnstaple and Bideford. These divergences reflect the fact that different sources cite different years of build. I am grateful to George Hogg for advice on this matter.

[5]David J. Starkey, "Devon's Shipbuilding Industry, 1786-1970," in Duffy, *et al.* (eds.), *The New Maritime History of Devon*, II. I am grateful to Robin Craig for considerable help in analysing the Devon ship registers.

to ports outside the county. An indication of the extent of this "export" market can be gleaned from *Lloyd's Registers* of the early 1860s, which list the ports of build and first registry of newly-constructed vessels classified by the society. Analysis of this sample reveals that forty-three percent of Devon-built vessels were sold beyond the county's borders.[6] Assuming that this proportion remained constant,[7] it yields an approximation of Devon's annual shipbuilding production between 1825 and 1865. The county's output averaged sixty-five percent of tonnage produced in the southwest in those periods for which port-by-port data are available--1787-1808, 1814-1826 and 1866-1913. Extrapolating from the Devon "total" therefore yields an estimate of tonnage constructed in the southwest from the mid-1820s to the mid-1860s.

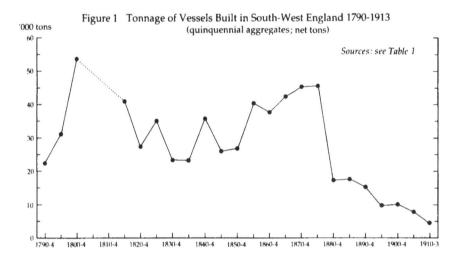

Figure 1   Tonnage of Vessels Built in South-West England 1790-1913
(quinquennial aggregates; net tons)

Sources: see Table 1

---

[6]*Lloyd's Register of Shipping*, 1861-1865.

[7]This assumption is supported by the comprehensive Cornish shipbuilding data assembled by George Hogg.

The results of these calculations are incorporated in table 1 and figures 1 and 2, which places the production of new tonnage in the southwest in the context of national output for much of the 1790-1913 period. Both absolutely and relatively, the region reached its peak in the opening quinquennium of the nineteenth century when 53,700 tons of shipping were launched, over ten percent of the national total. Thereafter, while the volume of new building declined nationally, reaching a nadir of 330,000 tons in 1820-1824, the contraction was more pronounced in the southwest. Accordingly, when the national total in 1835-1839 at last exceeded the 528,400 tons built in the early 1800s, a mere 23,100 tons were launched in the southwest, the lowest five-year total prior to the 1880s. At this point, the region accounted for just 3.4% of new UK construction. Although production in the West Country recovered to 5.3% of national output in the early 1840s, this was the last quinquennium in which the region's shipbuilding grew at a rate significantly faster than the nation as a whole.

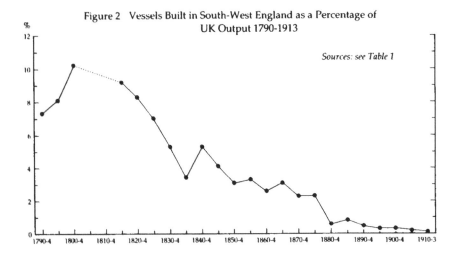

Figure 2   Vessels Built in South-West England as a Percentage of UK Output 1790-1913

Sources: see Table 1

While the volume of new building in the UK accelerated during the third quarter of the nineteenth century, production in the southwest expanded more slowly, reaching a secondary peak of approximately 52,900 tons in 1865-1869, before levelling out at about 45,000 tons in 1870-1874 and 1875-1879. As a proportion of the national total, the West Country's output therefore declined, shrinking from 3.3% in the late 1850s to 2.3% in 1875-1879. There then ensued a sudden collapse in the southwest's production. After five successive quinquennia in which tonnage launched exceeded 37,000 tons, a mere 17,200 tons were constructed in 1880-1884. With a marked increase occurring concurrently in national output, this contraction led to a sharp fall in the southwest's relative standing. Despite a slight recovery in the late 1880s, the region's contribution to UK tonnage not only remained below one percent but also continued to fall in the quarter-century prior to the First World War.

Within the region, the distribution of shipbuilding output remained more-or-less constant during the first half of the nineteenth century. The south coast produced the lion's share, with yards from Poole to Penzance generally launching at least twice as many vessels as those in Somerset, North Devon and North Cornwall. Of the four southwestern counties, Devon was consistently the most important, generally accounting for nearly two-thirds of the region's output, while Cornwall and Dorset together produced most of the residual third, with less than three percent emanating from Somerset. Of the districts engaged in shipbuilding, it is apparent that the South Devon ports of Dartmouth, Exeter and Plymouth were the southwest's pre-eminent centres to the 1820s, though a number of others, notably Weymouth and Poole in Dorset, Falmouth and Fowey in Cornwall, and Bideford and Barnstaple in North Devon, had relatively substantial interests in the industry. This spatially diverse pattern changed during the course of the century. Construction of new tonnage declined at Exeter and its sub-ports from the 1830s, at Fowey from the 1840s, and at Dorset ports in the 1860s. Yet, as table 2 shows, the most pronounced contraction took place in the 1880s. At this stage, new building in Plymouth, Barnstaple, Bridport and a range of lesser locales, chiefly in Cornwall, either ceased or was drastically reduced. As a consequence, by the early twentieth century shipbuilding was much diminished and largely confined to Falmouth, Penzance (chiefly Porthleven), Bideford (chiefly Appledore) and, most notably, Dartmouth and its erstwhile sub-port, Brixham.[8]

Although various types of merchant vessels were launched in the southwest, three basic traits can be discerned about the quality of the

[8]See Starkey, "Devon's Shipbuilding Industry;" Farr, *Shipbuilding in North Devon*; A.E. Cocksedge, *Bridport Harbour: Ships Built 1769-1879* (Bridport, 1992); C.H. Ward-Jackson, *Ships and Shipbuilders of a Westcountry Seaport: Fowey 1786-1939* (Truro, 1986); C.J. Davies, "Shipbuilding in the Isles of Scilly," *Journal of the Royal Institution of Cornwall*, X (1980), 187-220; Peter Ferguson, "Shipbuilding at Bridport," *Maritime South West*, V (1991), 78-116.

region's output. In the first place, as table 3 and figure 3 show, the typical vessel was invariably smaller than the UK average. Moreover, the gap between regional and national means tended to grow over time. The disparity widened in two distinct phases. Between 1800 and 1870, the region conformed to the national pattern: vessel size decreased to 1824 and then rose until the late 1860s. That the decline was steeper than average in the southwest in the first quarter of the century, and the increase more uneven and less pronounced between 1825 and 1869, explains the growing differential in mean tonnage. After 1870, however, southwestern production ran counter to the national trend. Mean vessel size fell from 120.3 tons in 1866-1869 to just thirty-one tons in 1895-1899 and 28.4 tons in 1910-1913, while the national mean increased steadily from 286.5 to 543.5 and finally to 848.4 tons. The contraction of West Country shipbuilding in the late nineteenth century was therefore associated with a marked and steady decline in average vessel size.

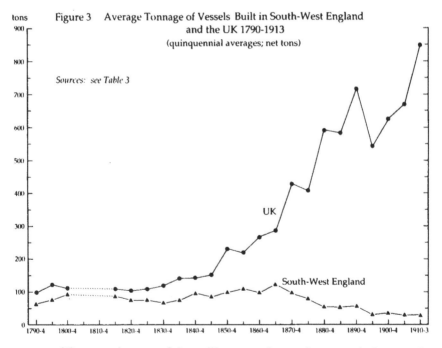

Figure 3   Average Tonnage of Vessels Built in South-West England and the UK 1790-1913
(quinquennial averages; net tons)

Sources: see Table 3

The prominence of the sailing vessel was the second characteristic of shipbuilding output in the nineteenth-century southwest. Only a few steam-propelled tugs or small paddle-steamers were produced in the region before the 1860s, the first being the *Torridge*, launched at

Appledore in 1835.[9] Thereafter, as table 4 indicates, sail remained predominant, despite an increase in steam tonnage built in the region, especially between 1885 and 1895. Moreover, the region's relative contribution to national output was decidedly more pronounced in sail, peaking at 8.8% in the early 1870s and still as high as 4.5% in 1905-1909. In contrast, even at its height during the early 1890s--which in reality was attributable to the completion in Hayle of four screw-steamers of over 1750 gross tons--steam tonnage built in the southwest represented a negligible proportion of national output.[10] Quite clearly, the region's yards played little part in the shift from sail to steam which swept British shipbuilding in the second half of the nineteenth century.

Closely associated with the local predominance of sailing ship production was the third main feature of the southwest's output, the sustained use of wood in hull construction. Again, the region proved increasingly out of step with national developments. As iron superseded wood and then gave way to steel as the principal material in UK ship-building,[11] the majority of southwestern shipyards continued to build wooden hulls, although a few composites were launched in the 1870s, notably the *Silurian* at Topsham and the *Bertha* at Dartmouth, and a number of iron ships were built at Falmouth and Hayle.[12] By 1900, when steel was used in more than ninety-six percent of the UK's sailing and steam tonnage, a comparatively large proportion of the much reduced southwest output used the traditional material, mainly at Bideford, Brixham and Porthleven.[13] Yet this was not true of the region

---

[9]Farr, *Shipbuilding in North Devon*, 15.

[10]Grahame Farr, *The Ship Registers of the Port of Hayle, 1864-1882* (Greenwich, 1975), 115; Stephanie Jones, "Merchant Shipbuilding in the North East and South West of England, 1870-1913," in Stephen Fisher (ed.), *British Shipping and Seamen, 1630-1960: Some Studies* (Exeter, 1984), 68-70.

[11]See Sidney Pollard and Paul Robertson, *The British Shipbuilding Industry, 1870-1914* (Cambridge, MA, 1979), 9-24.

[12]Devon Record Office (DRO), Ship Registers, Dartmouth and Exeter; Cornwall Record Office (CRO), List of Vessels built by Cox and Co., Falmouth; Farr, *Port of Hayle*, 114-115.

[13]B.R. Mitchell (comp.), *An Abstract of British Historical Statistics* (Cambridge, 1971), 224; Jones, "Merchant Shipbuilding," 70-71.

as a whole, for the capacity to build in steel had been established as early as 1885 at Hayle, and only slightly later at Falmouth and Dartmouth.

Overall, West Country shipbuilders concentrated on relatively small wooden sailing vessels. Many were fitted with a single mast and rigged as smacks, barges or, most commonly, sloops. In Devon, for instance, such craft, which rarely exceeded seventy tons, accounted for forty-six percent of the 1759 vessels built and registered between 1825 and 1874. Two-masted vessels were still more important. While the Devon figures reveal that brigs, ketches, snows, and schooners together accounted for over forty-nine percent of locally-built and registered vessels between 1825 and 1874,[14] the significance of such products is clearly apparent in the data for Bridport, Fowey, Scilly and other southwestern ports.[15] The schooner was pre-eminent among these rigs, at least between the 1820s and the 1870s. This was particularly so in South Devon, where this fore-and-aft rig became prominent in the first quarter of the nineteenth century, much earlier than in any other British maritime district. By 1821, Dartmouth, Brixham and Plymouth were the nation's leading schooner-building centres, with Topsham and Teignmouth also exhibiting relatively strong interests.[16] Over the next fifty years, almost 300 of these vessels--forty-two percent of the port's output--were constructed and registered locally in Dartmouth and its sub-ports; 133 were built in Plymouth, most during the 1830s and 1840s; and a further seventy-five were launched in Exeter.[17] Elsewhere in the southwest, schooners dominated from the 1820s. Cornish shipbuilders, notably at Padstow and Fowey, launched at least 360 schooners between 1825 and 1865, approximately fifty-one percent of the county's output,[18] while a similar pattern was evident in Dorset, where schooners

---

[14]DRO, Ship Registers, Devon Ports; Starkey, "Devon's Shipbuilding Industry."

[15]Cocksedge, *Bridport Harbour*; Ward-Jackson, *Ships and Shipbuilders*; Davies, "Shipbuilding in Scilly."

[16]This assertion is based on an analysis of *Lloyd's Register*, 1821. See David J. Starkey, "The Development of the Schooner in Britain, 1775-1900," in Basil Greenhill (ed.), *Sail's Last Century* (London, 1993).

[17]DRO, Ship Registers, Devon Ports.

[18]The figures for Cornwall were kindly provided by Captain George Hogg.

comprised more than forty percent of the vessels launched at Bridport during this period.[19]

Larger vessels, ship- or barque-rigged and equipped with three or more masts, were less commonly constructed in the southwest. That the region possessed the capacity to build such craft had been demonstrated during the Napoleonic Wars when a number of East Indiamen, as well as a range of warships, were completed.[20] Yet it was not until the 1840s that southwestern yards again produced ships and barques in any significant numbers. During the next twenty years or so, vessels like the 1460-ton *Speedy*, the 1220-ton *Sarah Neumann* and the 700-ton *Crystal Palace*--respectively built by Cox of Bridport, Cox of Bideford, and Mansfield of Teignmouth--featured prominently in local output, although nearly all were sold outside the region.[21] At the same time, increases were apparent in the dimensions of schooners. In Fowey, for example, the average schooner increased from seventy-nine to 116 tons between the 1840s and 1870s,[22] while in Brixham the maximum length of the port's schooners, which had been seventy-one feet in the mid-1820s and ninety-one feet in the mid-1850s, rose to over 100 feet in 1867-1869.[23] These twin trends explain the rise in average tonnage of southwest-built vessels to the 1860s. Significantly, they further indicate that regional builders were conforming to national patterns, for in the country as a whole the mid-century decades were marked by appreciable improvements in the size and design of wooden vessels.[24]

Thereafter, the southwest's product mix was increasingly at variance with national trends. The mean tonnage of vessels constructed

---

[19]See Cocksedge, *Bridport Harbour*.

[20]See C.N. Ponsford (ed.), *Shipbuilding on the Exe: The Memoranda Book of Daniel Bishop Davy, 1799-1874, of Topsham, Devon* (Exeter, 1988), xxiv.

[21]Cocksedge, *Bridport Harbour*, 189-191; Ferguson, "Shipbuilding in Bridport," 99-100; Harold J. Trump, *Teignmouth: A Maritime History* (2nd ed., Chichester, 1986), 50.

[22]Ward-Jackson, *Ships and Shipbuilders*, 35.

[23]DRO, Ship Registers, Brixham and Dartmouth.

[24]See David R. MacGregor, *Fast Sailing Ships: Their Design and Construction, 1775-1875* (2nd ed., London, 1988).

in the region declined, symptomatic of the changing composition of output in the last three decades of the century. While the production of relatively large ships and barques, which reached a modest peak in the 1850s and 1860s, largely ceased during the 1870s, demand for the most important product of the region's shipyards, the schooner, also began to contract. Fishing vessels, yachts, cutters and other recreational craft, which had long formed part of the region's output, now assumed a growing prominence, reflecting in part the expansion in local fishing and coastal leisure interests. At the same time, southwestern builders continued to construct merchant vessels, producing a growing number of ketches from the early 1870s. But the fore-and-aft rigged ketch did not compensate fully for the fall in orders for barques, ships and schooners. Ketches were comparatively small, measuring from fifty to ninety-five tons as against the sixty to 200-ton range of the contemporary schooner. Moreover, fewer were built; for instance, only fourteen were completed in Brixham for local owners in 1875-1879, while twenty-six schooners had been built and registered in the port in 1865-1869.[25]

Although steam power and metal hulls had featured occasionally in the southwest's output since the 1830s, in general it was not until the 1890s that the region's shipbuilders combined these twin components of the "modern" steamer. Even then, production was limited in scale and undertaken by just some of the firms which survived the crash of the 1880s. Cox and Co. of Falmouth built a number of barges and launches, as well as various towing vessels and river craft,[26] while the Dartmouth firms of Philip and Son and Simpson Strickland and Co. constructed ferries, paddle boats and luxurious steam yachts, together with a range of engine parts, boilers, tanks and other general engineering goods.[27] But there was one major exception to this pattern. Harvey and Co. of Hayle had first placed steam engines in two iron-hulled tugs in 1848. Thereafter, until its shipyard closed in 1904, the firm built at least

---

[25]DRO, Ship Registers, Brixham; Basil Greenhill, *The Merchant Schooners* (4th ed., London, 1988), 22-24.

[26]CRO, List of Vessels Built by Cox and Co., Falmouth.

[27]*Philip & Son Ltd, Shipbuilders and Engineers, 1858-1958: A Century of Progress* (Dartmouth, 1958), 3, 13; R. Freeman, *Dartmouth: A New History of the Port and its People* (Dartmouth, 1987), 122-123; Brixham Museum, A/SS, Correspondence of Simpson Strickland and Co.

twenty iron or composite-hulled barquentines, brigantines and schooners, as well as a number of wooden sailing craft. At the same time, Harvey launched two paddle steamers, together with thirty-nine screw steamers, twenty-eight with iron hulls and a further eleven, commencing with the *Dartmouth Castle* in 1885, built of steel.[28]

If most Harvey and Co. vessels were relatively small, the largest being the 2660-ton *Ramleh*, the progression from wood to iron to steel, and from sail to paddle to screw propulsion, was broadly in line with general developments in contemporary shipbuilding technology. That such sequences were rare in the West Country underlines the overwhelming predominance of wood and sail in the region's nineteenth-century shipbuilding output.

Maintenance and Modification

A good deal of work undertaken in southwestern shipyards involved the modification or maintenance of existing vessels. Although available sources do not permit precise measurements of the extent or value of this output, qualitative evidence suggests that it formed an important part of production. Three main types of work fall within this category. First there were repairs, which represented an important facet of every shipbuilding enterprise. Ranging from the application of a coat of paint to the total rebuilding of wrecked or decrepit craft, this activity was normally prosecuted concurrently with the building of new tonnage.[29] Since the nature of this work was closely related to the type and scale of the product constructed in the yard, southwestern builders generally concentrated on the repair of small wooden sailing vessels. As the demand for this service owed more to accidents, wear and tear, and the standards set by insurance organisations and the Board of Trade than to market forces, it fluctuated less than demand for new tonnage. Accordingly, repair work, which was often more profitable than building because it yielded swifter returns on smaller capital outlays, might

---

[28]Farr, *Port of Hayle*, 112-115.

[29]The Yard Ledger of John Holman and Sons of Topsham, 1853-1881, provides a good impression of the significance of repair work in the day-to-day operation of a wooden shipyard. DRO, Z 19/65/29.

sustain a yard when orders for new vessels were scarce.[30] This counter-cyclical characteristic was never more apparent than in the 1880s. When demand for new vessels plummeted, firms such as Slade (Polruan), Butson (Bodonnick), Stephens (Fowey), Cox (Bridport) or Westacott (Barnstaple) stayed afloat for some years by fulfilling repair contracts.[31]

Conversions formed a second part of non-building output. As productivity gains assumed a growing importance in ship operation, owners frequently sought to improve efficiency or capacity, or to deploy vessels in new sectors of the tonnage market. Lengthening and re-rigging were therefore commonplace, with the precise form of the conversion reflecting temporal trends. In the early nineteenth century, sloops were often lengthened and fitted with a second mast to accommodate schooner rigging, while in the 1870s large numbers of smacks were upgraded to ketches.[32] Rather less pervasive was the third form of modification work: the practice of fitting-out vessels launched elsewhere and sailed to the southwest using rudimentary rigs. Although sometimes undertaken in ports like Plymouth, this practice was essentially part of the strong family-based ties which linked the maritime economies of North Devon and Prince Edward Island. Central to this relationship was the trans-Atlantic shipbuilding business of James Yeo. Vessels which had been built in Yeo's yard on PEI were despatched, laden with timber, to North Devon for fitting-out at the Richmond drydock in Appledore. Once completed, these vessels were sold, usually by William Yeo, one of the builder's sons. A considerable number of colonial-built barques, ships, brigs and schooners found their way in to the British market via this

---

[30]Basil Greenhill, *The Evolution of the Wooden Ship* (London, 1988), 88.

[31]C.H. Ward-Jackson, *Stephens of Fowey: A Portrait of a Cornish Merchant Fleet, 1867-1939* (Greenwich, 1980), 25; Ferguson, "Shipbuilding in Bridport," 103; Farr, *Shipbuilding in North Devon*, 9.

[32]See W.J. Slade and Basil Greenhill, *Westcountry Coasting Ketches* (Greenwich, 1974).

channel, forming an important part of Appledore's output from the mid-1850s to the late 1870s.[33]

Warshipbuilding

The great majority of vessels launched from shipyards in southwest England in the nineteenth century were for commercial employment. But during the war of 1803-1815, when shipbuilding was at its height in the West Country, an unprecedented number of warships were built in the region's private yards. At least seventy were constructed by merchant shipbuilders in Devon, while a further seventeen were produced by Bools and Good of Bridport Harbour and two more were finished by Symons of Falmouth. Sixth-rates, gun-brigs, sloops-of-war and other lesser vessels formed the bulk of this output, although two ships-of-the-line, the *Armada* and the *Clarence*, both measuring 1749 tons and equipped with seventy-four guns, were built at Turnchapel Dock, Plymouth, by Isaac and Peter Blackburn.[34] This was potentially lucrative work for private builders, since the ships ordered by the Admiralty were generally much larger than the average merchantman and payment was guaranteed. Yet it also entailed substantial financial risk. Competitive tendering encouraged some firms to cut prices unrealistically, while others struggled to complete fixed-price contracts at a time when material and labour costs were rising steeply. Such misjudgments and misfortunes resulted in bankruptcy for shipbuilders like William Record of Appledore, William Good of Bridport and Benjamin Tanner of Dartmouth.[35]

Of course, warshipbuilding took place at Devonport Dockyard after 1815, especially from the 1880s. Yet only a few naval craft were

---

[33]See Basil Greenhill and Ann Giffard, *Westcountrymen in Prince Edward Isle: A Fragment of the Great Migration* (Newton Abbot, 1967). The ship registers of Prince Edward Island indicate that at least 150 colonial-built vessels were completed in North Devon. I am grateful to Basil Greenhill for this information.

[34]"Accounts and Papers," *British Parliamentary Papers (BPP)*, XI (1813-1814), 357, "Accounts Relating to Ships and Shipbuilders'; Accounts and Papers," *BPP*, VIII (1813-1814), 498, "An Account of HM Ships Launched from Private Yards." See Ponsford, *Shipbuilding on the Exe*, xxiv; Ferguson, "Shipbuilding in Bridport," 85-87; Farr, *Shipbuilding in North Devon*, 58.

[35]*Exeter Flying Post (EFP)*, 23 April 1807; see also David J. Starkey, "Shipbuilding in the South West during the Napoleonic War," *Maritime South West*, VI (1993), 5-15.

built in the region's private yards between 1815 and 1913 and most were boats and steam launches for foreign customers in the early 1900s.[36]

Causal Factors

The southwest's shipbuilding output was largely determined by market forces. To explain the changing volume and composition of production, demand and supply factors will be considered in turn.

Demand

The principal source of demand for the products of West Country shipyards, at least until the 1880s, was the region's shipping industry. Typical of the age of wood and sail,[37] the interdependence of local owners and builders is clearly apparent in the shipping registers. In 1800-1809, for instance, over seventy percent of newly-built vessels added to the Bideford and Exeter registers were built in the two ports, while Devon shipbuilders produced 150 of the 171 new craft registered in the county during 1845-1849.[38] Likewise, between 1861 and 1865, over fifty-seven percent of vessels constructed in the southwest and listed in *Lloyd's Register* were purchased by owners resident in the region.[39]

Only a few of these locally-produced and registered vessels were large. While most of the comparatively large ships and barques built in the West Country were sold outside the region, especially to owners in South Wales or Liverpool, local demand was generally satisfied by second-hand vessels purchased from "up country" and by those constructed in British North America, especially Prince Edward Island. The market for steamers in the southwest was also small. Though West Cornwall boasted the impressive fleets of the Hain Steamship Company of St. Ives and R.B. Chellew of Truro (thirty-seven steamers [84,911 tons] and eighteen steamers [56,026 tons], respectively, in 1913), and while a number of small steamship companies were established in Devon,

---

[36]Brixham Museum, A/SS, Correspondence of Simpson Strickland and Co.

[37]Pollard and Robertson, *British Shipbuilding Industry*, 56.

[38]DRO, Ship Registers, Devon Ports.

[39]*Lloyd's Register of Shipping*, 1861-1865.

such enterprises were unusual in the West Country. This perhaps reflected the absence of a major staple export cargo in the region. Significantly, even these modest steamship requirements were largely met by northeast shipyards, with Hain buying nearly all its vessels from Readhead of South Shields, and investors such as R.S. Triplett and J.A. Bellamy of Plymouth, and J. Holman and Sons of Topsham, generally patronising yards on the Tyne, Wear or Tees.[40]

Figure 4   Tonnage of Sailing Vessels Registered in
South-West England   1804-1900
(net tons)

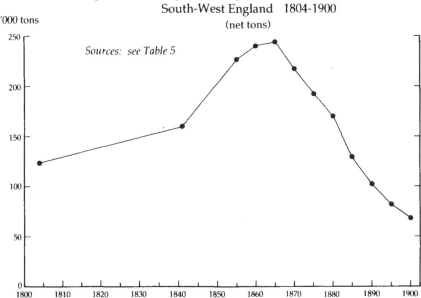

In fact, the close links between the southwest's shipping and shipbuilding industries were founded in the market for one- and two-masted wooden sailing vessels. Essentially, it was local demand for smacks, sloops, brigs and, most particularly, schooners which conditioned the output of the region's shipbuilding industry for much of the 1790-1913 period. Accordingly, as the stock of sailing vessels owned in the southwest increased steadily during the first half of the nineteenth century, rising from 123,400 to 226,400 tons between 1804 and 1855, so demand for the region's shipbuilding output remained generally

---

[40]K.J. O'Donoghue and H.S. Appleyard, *Hain of St Ives* (Kendal, 1986); Robin Craig, "Steamship Enterprise in Devon, 1852-1920," in Duffy *et al.* (eds.), *New Maritime History of Devon*, II.

favourable. However, as table 5 and figure 4 indicate, the volume of shipping owned locally began to contract in the late 1860s, declining from a peak of 244,100 tons in 1865 to 217,500 tons in 1870 and still further to 128,900 tons in 1885. By 1900, the southwest's sailing fleet stood at just 68,600 tons, little more than a quarter its size in the mid-1860s.

Of course, this represented a sharp fall in demand for the southwest's shipbuilders and was chiefly responsible for the decline in vessel construction during the last quarter of the century. Yet this contraction was complex and protracted rather than simple or sudden. It not only shaped the character of output in the late nineteenth century but also underlaid the survival of the region's interest in shipbuilding in the twentieth. It was largely instigated by the encroachment of steamers into the carrying trades in which southwestern shipowners had specialised since the eighteenth century. In particular, the south European fruit trades, long the province of schooners built and owned in the southwest, were penetrated by steamers once the Ponta Delgada harbour facility in the Azores was opened in the early 1860s.[41] Edged out of this carrying business, southwestern owners concentrated on an increasingly narrow range of trades in which they retained a competitive advantage over steamship operators. For the most part, these involved the carriage of cargoes to and from small ports and havens, notably in the home and Newfoundland trades.[42] With cost reduction of the essence, local shipping interests tended to turn from the schooner to the ketch, a smaller, handier vessel which proved adept at expeditiously entering and clearing the small tidal harbours which were staples in Britain's buoyant coastal trade. As the majority of these ketches were local products--some new-built, others converted smacks[43]--they formed an important source of business for shipbuilders, especially during the comparatively prosperous 1870s.

Nevertheless, demand for small wooden sailing craft continued to contract, and a growing number of West Country shipbuilders left the industry during the 1880s. Some retired, others concentrated on

---

[41]Greenhill, *Merchant Schooners*, 14-16, 24.

[42]*Ibid.*, 44; Ward-Jackson, *Stephens of Fowey*.

[43]DRO, Ship Registers, Devon Ports. The shift to ketch production can be seen most clearly in the Dartmouth and Brixham registers.

boatbuilding, while a third group focused on more expansive facets of the maritime economy. Elias Cox, for instance, expended his energies on the creation of the West Bay holiday resort on the site of his former shipyard at Bridport Harbour.[44] Still, a number of enterprises remained viable, principally by moving into markets beyond the region. Such a strategy did not necessarily involve a decisive break with the past. The Brixham firms of Sanders and Co. and Upham, as well as Kitto of Porthleven, continued to construct small wooden sailing trawlers, although from the 1880s more were sold to fishing interests in Ramsgate, Lowestoft, Hull and Grimsby than to local owners.[45] Similarly, the southwest's wooden sailing fleet, despite its contraction, still provided work for local shipyards, as an ageing stock, driven ever harder in a highly competitive environment, required considerable maintenance and modification.[46] Robert Cock and Sons of Appledore was the most successful of the firms catering to this demand, not least because a hard-earned reputation for cheap and speedy repairs encouraged owners from all parts of Britain to send their vessels to the Richmond Yard for repair and renovation.[47] Tapping wider markets, the firm survived and diversified its output with the installation of steel shipbuilding equipment in 1901-1902.[48]

Breaking the constraints imposed by an essentially local market and a product range limited to outmoded wooden sailing vessels was the key to the continuing viability of other southwestern yards. Accordingly, a gradual shift to the production of yachts, launches, ferries and other types of small specialist vessels, often for extra-regional customers,

---

[44]Cocksedge, *Bridport Harbour*, ix; Ferguson, "Shipbuilding in Bridport," 106.

[45]A considerable number of Brixham-registered vessels were transferred to Ramsgate, Lowestoft, Hull and Grimsby at this time, mirroring the migration of the port's fishermen to more productive fishing grounds. DRO, Ship Registers, Brixham.

[46]See W. Slade, *Out of Appledore: The Autobiography of a Coasting Shipmaster and Shipowner in the Last Days of Wooden Sailing Ships* (4th ed., London, 1980); Greenhill, *Merchant Schooners*.

[47]See Tim Latham, *The Ashburner Schooners: The Story of the First Shipbuilders of Barrow-in-Furness* (Manchester, 1991), 103.

[48]Len Harris, *A Two Hundred Year History of Appledore Shipyards* (Combe Martin, 1992), 19-20; Farr, *Shipbuilding in North Devon*, 16.

marked the output of firms like Cox and Co. of Falmouth, and the Dartmouth yards of Philip and Son and Simpson, Strickland and Co. This market was growing not only in size during the late nineteenth century but also in sophistication, with purchasers, whether gentlemen seafarers, harbour authorities or foreign governments, increasingly preferring metal-hulled, steam-driven craft. To meet this demand, in the late 1870s Cox and Co. acquired the capacity to build iron hulls and to fit steam engines. In the early 1890s the firm, like Philip and Son and Simpson, Strickland and Co., installed a steel shipbuilding plant.[49] In so doing, these enterprises adapted to changing demands by embracing the technological advances which transformed British shipbuilding during the second half of the century. Yet supply factors generally meant that such firms were exceptional in the West Country.

Supply

The southwest was probably as well endowed with the productive factors necessary for wooden shipbuilding as any maritime district in Britain during the nineteenth century. With two long, well-indented coastlines, the region offered an abundance of sheltered sites suitable for the construction and launch of wooden ships. Moreover, competition for these spots was seldom intense because port facilities in general, and dock construction in particular, were slow to develop along most of the region's estuaries. Though detailed evidence is lacking, there is nothing to suggest that the supply of shipyard labour was inadequate. Indeed, the 1831 census indicates that more boatbuilders and shipwrights lived in Devon than in any English county except Kent.[50] There are also signs that employers discerned positive attributes in the local workforce. Money Wigram observed that "men from the West Country...are better shipwrights" than their counterparts in the North Country.[51] J.B. Mansfield established a shipyard at Teignmouth in part because of the

---

[49]CRO, List of Vessels built by Cox and Co.; Brixham Museum, A/SS, Specifications of Vessels built by Simpson Strickland and Co.

[50]J. Marshall, *A Digest of all the Accounts...* (London, 1833).

[51]Select Committee on the Navigation Laws, *BPP*, XX, part 2 (1847-1848), 570-571, evidence of Money Wigram.

"existence of a steady and orderly working class."[52] Likewise, capital shortages do not appear to have unduly afflicted southwest shipbuilders. In part, this reflected the comparatively modest capital requirements of the typical production unit for wooden vessels.[53] It can also be inferred that the supply of timber, which accounted for most of the wooden shipyard's physical capital, posed no particular problem, due perhaps to the availability of local stocks[54] and, more significantly, to the vitality of trading links with timber-exporting areas in the Baltic and British North America.

Figure 5: Piles of seasoning timber lie in the shipyard of Samuel Moss at Par, Cornwall, c. 1880. Though the last vessel built in the yard, the *Lizzie Trenberth*, was launched in 1867, repair work was undertaken until the mid-twentieth century.

Source: Private collection of the Gillis family, Newquay, Cornwall.

---

[52]Trump, *Teignmouth*, 50.

[53]See Greenhill, *The Evolution of the Wooden Ship*, 88-90.

[54]For instance, the stock-in-trade of William Record of Appledore included 200 oak trees felled and lying in Bratton Clovelly, Devon. *EFP*, 8 January 1807.

Figure 6: The launch of HMS *Clarence*, 74-guns, at the yard of Isaac Blackburn at Turnchapel, Plymouth, in April 1812.

Source: City of Plymouth Museums and Art Gallery.

Although the presence of a major Royal Dockyard at Devonport may have deflected some resources away from commercial shipbuilding--notably labour and prime waterside sites around Plymouth--there is little evidence to suggest that this seriously impaired the generally favourable supply conditions. With the productive factors readily available, the market was competitive and producers were able to enter and leave according to the level and location of demand. The industry therefore comprised a large number of small-scale units dispersed throughout the coastal areas of the West Country. In 1804, for instance, an Admiralty survey identified ninety-five shipyards in forty-two different ports and havens, the most notable concentrations occurring on the Torridge (with eleven yards), at Brixham and Padstow (seven firms each), and on the banks of the Dart (a further seven concerns). Some units were substantial, at least in terms of labour engaged. Benjamin Tanner of Dartmouth, for example, employed sixty-eight shipwrights and thirteen apprentices, one of the largest workforces in the country, while Richard Symons of Falmouth engaged some fifty-six men. Yet these yards were atypical, for the average West Country firm employed just five shipwrights and an equal number of apprentices, with shipbuilders such as N. Williams of

Padstow and Stephen Richardson of Brixham relying entirely on the latter.[55] Fluidity invariably characterised such a market structure. Thus, between 1824 and 1854 at least forty-three different shipbuilders operated in Plymouth, some constructing only a single vessel, while twenty-four firms built vessels in Brixham during the same period.[56]

While supply factors fostered this high turnover, they did not inhibit the emergence of a number of comparatively large-scale producers in the southwest during mid-century. This trend was closely associated with the increase in vessel size in all tonnage classes. The ships, barques and large schooners constructed from the 1840s to the 1870s were generally the product of firms such as Westacott of Barnstaple, Cox and Evans of Bideford, Cox of Bridport, Holman of Topsham, Mansfield of Teignmouth, and Trethowan of Falmouth. Newspaper reports and advertisements show that these establishments each employed about 100 men and were equipped with facilities far superior to those in the typical southwestern yard of the early nineteenth century. Whereas "a large copper furnace and two pairs of smith's bellows" and "two steam kilns...four pairs of bellows, two anvils and other smith's tools" comprised the jewels of the respective stocks-in-trade of Bass and Bishop of Topsham in 1806 and John Curtis of Dartmouth in 1813, Westacott constructed two barques under cover in 1851 and Holman installed a 400-foot patent slip, a stone-lined drydock able to take vessels up to 1000 tons, and steam-powered machinery at its two Topsham yards in the 1850s and 1860s.[57] Nevertheless, such developments represented a change in degree rather than in kind. Notwithstanding the introduction of comparatively sophisticated equipment, the mode of production remained essentially craft-based, with the eye and experience of the shipbuilder and the skills of the shipwright and blacksmith--each of whom

---

[55]"Accounts and Papers," *BPP*, VII (1805), 467-486, "An Account Shewing the Number of Shipwrights...;" Starkey, "Shipbuilding during the Napoleonic War."

[56]DRO, Ship Registers, Plymouth and Dartmouth.

[57]*EFP*, 6 November 1806, 23 September 1813, 6 July 1848, 8 May 1851; *Western Times*, 21 December 1865.

owned most of his tools[58]--still vital. Critically, the principal product of these yards was still the wooden sailing vessel.

Figure 7: The launch of the ketch *Irene* at Bridgwater, 1907.

Source: Private collection of W. Sharman, Somerset.

The metal-hulled, steam-driven vessel which increasingly dominated British output from the 1850s was in many ways the product of a separate industry which not only entailed rather different production techniques but also required a distinct set of supply conditions. As the late nineteenth century was to prove, the southwest was locationally disadvantaged relative to certain productive factors necessary for this "modern" industry. The land supply imposed no real constraint on steamship building, for even though the Exe, Taw and other relatively shallow estuaries were unsuitable for the production and launch of large metal hulls, there were sufficient sheltered deep-water sites in the region--on the Dart, Fal and Plymouth Sound, for instance--to accommodate substantial yards. Similarly, it is unlikely that either the quantity or

---

[58]As late as 1878, workers at Redway's yard in Dartmouth were deemed to be "great sufferers through losing their tools--one it is said to the extent of £100" in a fire. *EFP*, 18 September 1878.

quality of labour impeded the development of modern shipbuilding. Apart from the probability that any deficiency would have been quickly overcome by in-migration, the fact that up to 14,000 men, largely "platers, rivetters and others engaged in iron ships," were employed at Devonport Dockyard in the years before World War I suggests the existence of a large pool of suitably-skilled labour.[59]

Entrepreneurship, that other human factor of production, was also in evidence. It was apparent, of course, in the adaptive behaviours of firms like Cox and Co. and Philip and Son. Earlier, it had been discernible in the formation in 1865 of the Plymouth Ship Building, Dock and Iron Works Co., an ambitious project to construct and repair iron ships and to manufacture "marine and other engines, armour and other plate, angle iron, and every description of iron work." Attempting to raise £250,000, the company asserted that profitability was assured because "at present there are no iron shipbuilding works at Plymouth, and much inconvenience and expense often results to ship owners in consequence of vessels outward bound having to put back to London for repair."[60] Despite identifying an apparently substantial gap in the market, the company was unable to obtain sufficient finances, a fate which recurred when the proposal was revived in 1870.[61] In the failure of these initiatives, supply factors which inhibited the development of a substantial modern shipbuilding industry in the West Country can be identified. Investment funds were clearly lacking, due in part to the relatively modest scale of shipping and shipbuilding operations in the region, a factor which mitigated against the generation of the large pools of "maritime" capital which fuelled the construction of metal-hulled steamers in other regions.[62] It also implies that potential investors, both within and without the region, preferred to risk their capital in enterprises elsewhere. Significantly, at Devonport Dockyard, where external capital was available--the state invested in excess of £1.3 million to

---

[59]United Kingdom, *Census of the Population, 1911*; K.V. Burns, *The Devonport Dockyard Story* (Liskeard, 1984), 83.

[60]*EFP*, 26 April 1865.

[61]*Shipping and Mercantile Gazette*, 24 November 1870. I am grateful to Robin Craig for bringing this information to my attention.

[62]Pollard and Robertson, *British Shipbuilding Industry*, 92-96.

establish Keyham Steam Yard in the late 1840s, and a colossal £4 million to extend and update the plant between 1897 and 1907[63]--modern techniques were employed on a grand scale.

Figure 8: Work is nearing completion on a wooden sloop in the shipyard of Philip and Son at Sandquay, Dartmouth, in 1870. This firm was one of the few southwestern concerns to acquire a steel shipbuilding capacity in the late nineteenth century.

Source: Courtesy of George Philip.

A paucity of fixed capital was likewise apparent in the failure of the company. The site of the planned development was one of the largest wooden shipbuilding yards in the West Country, possessing a 1200-foot frontage with a stone-built drydock (262 by fifty feet), with steam engine, circular saw gear, smiths' shops, timber sheds and offices. Yet £250,000 was deemed necessary to equip the site with iron-working and engineering capacities. While this highlights the differences in scale between wooden and metal shipbuilding, it also indicates that the transition from wood and sail to iron and steam was not simply a matter of extending or upgrading existing facilities, but required the establish-

---

[63]Burns, *Devonport Dockyard Story*, 43-45, 69-72.

ment of new and expensive plant.[64] Again, the shipbuilding activity of Harvey and Co. of Hayle offered an exception which proved the rule. It was primarily an engineering concern and therefore possessed the capacity to construct iron and steel steamers, an ability it exhibited intermittently between the late 1840s and the early 1890s.[65]

A further factor deficiency was implicit in the prospectus of the Plymouth Ship Building, Dock and Iron Works Co. In emphasising the low level of freights for iron, coal and timber, "added to which much expense will be saved as the materials will be delivered on the quays of the Company free of charge," the proposal pointed to the main obstacle facing steamship building in the southwest. Lacking local coal and iron ore, and therefore a significant ironmaking and engineering capacity, the region relied on imports of necessary capital goods--principally iron and steel plates, and marine engines--from more favourably endowed areas. Naturally, this increased the costs borne by southwestern producers, a competitive disadvantage illustrated by the prices paid for steel steamers by the Cornish shipowning firms of Hain and Chellew in the late 1880s and 1890s. Harvey and Co. of Hayle, which produced its own engines but relied on boiler and ship-plates from Bristol and further afield, charged £13.03 per ton for the 2033-ton *Penpol*, while the 1815-ton *Duke of Cornwall* and the 2042-ton *Trevalgan* were built at West Hartlepool and South Shields at prices of £10.10 and £11.50 per ton, respectively.[66] While such comparisons perhaps explain why Harvey and Co. ceased building vessels in 1893, at a broader level they highlight the locational advantages which led to the gravitation of shipbuilding towards the northeast and other regions endowed with raw materials to facilitate the development of major capital goods industries.

---

[64]The proposal was revived in 1870 largely because "the valuable plant of the Plymouth Foundry & Engine Works Co. Ltd can [now] be purchased and removed to the [shipyard] at great advantage for iron shipbuilding." *Shipping and Mercantile Gazette*, 24 November 1870.

[65]See Edmund Vale, *The Harveys of Hayle: Engine Builders, Shipwrights and Merchants of Cornwall* (Truro, 1966).

[66]CRO, Harvey and Co. Letterbook, R.B. Chellew to Harvey, 19 October 1889, E. Hain to Harvey, 15 July 1889; Robert S. Craig, "Shipowning in the South-West in Its National Context, 1800-1914," in H.E.S. Fisher and W.E. Minchinton (eds.), *Transport and Shipowning in the Westcountry* (Exeter, 1973), 44. I am grateful to George Hogg for advice on this matter.

Thus, by the final quarter of the nineteenth century, when the British shipbuilding industry had become an integral feature of a regionally-skewed process of industrialisation, the southwest, like other "non-industrial" areas, was unable to enter the rapidly expanding market for metal-hulled steamships due largely to major deficiencies in the supply of capital and raw materials. Yet because relatively few supply constraints faced more traditional shipbuilding, the West Country maintained its interest in the construction and repair of wooden sailing vessels. Although this interest declined from the 1870s, it formed the basis for the transition to modern shipbuilding--albeit comparatively late and on a minor scale--by a number of southwestern firms producing small, specialist vessels, generally for extra-regional markets.

Conclusion

Between 1790 and the outbreak of the First World War, the southwest's shipbuilding industry contracted in three principal ways. In absolute terms, output declined from over 4000 tons per annum in 1790-1794 to just over 1400 tons per annum in 1910-1913. The period was also characterised by a sharp fall from 7.3% to 0.1% in the region's contribution to national output. Moreover, its shipbuilding industry was much more concentrated in the early 1900s than in the late eighteenth century, with fewer operational shipyards in fewer districts.

These closely-related contractions did not occur gradually. The volume of new building, for instance, reached its height in the first five years of the nineteenth century, when some 53,700 tons were launched in the West Country. Thereafter, output fluctuated between 20,000 and 40,000 tons per quinquennium before stabilising at a comparatively buoyant level between the mid-1850s and the late 1870s. In relative terms, the region's output also peaked in 1800-1804, when over ten percent of Britain's new tonnage was produced in southwestern yards. A steady decline ensued, as local production failed to keep pace with the expansion in national output, although some stability was apparent in the third quarter of the century, when the southwest accounted for 2.3-3.3% of the UK's newly-constructed tonnage. While evidence relating to the structure of the industry is sparse, newspaper reports suggest that the size of production units tended to increase, with several comparatively large, well-equipped yards in production during the 1850s and 1860s. Each of these various measures plunged in the early 1880s. When output fell to 17,700 tons in 1880-1884, representing just 0.6% of the UK total, shipbuilding ceased at many southwestern ports and a large number of firms withdrew from the industry. This collapse was not all-pervasive, however, and a small core of yards survived and even prospered until the First World War and beyond.

Market forces determined this long-term process. In serving an essentially local demand, southwest shipbuilders were no different than their peers in other regions of Britain during the first two-thirds of the century. With West Country shipowners chiefly engaged in a range of home and North Atlantic trades, this demand was met with relatively small wooden sailing vessels, the merchant schooner being the most prominent. At this juncture, producers of such vessels faced comparatively few supply constraints. But the growing prevalence of metal-hulled, steam-driven vessels disrupted the equilibrium. During the 1860s and 1870s, the increasingly efficient steamer entered and quickly dominated many trades which sustained the region's shipping industry. Although the market for steamers expanded rapidly and assumed a national, and then international character, southwestern England was neither a centre of consumption nor production. Lacking the staple export cargoes which underpinned the substantial steamship enterprises of their rivals in areas like South Wales and the northeast, West Country shipowners tended to disinvest rather than develop locally-based steamer fleets. Accordingly, the demand traditionally served by its shipyards contracted considerably during the final quarter of the century. At the same time, the supply of productive factors, notably capital and raw materials, was not conducive to the establishment of significant modern shipbuilding in the southwest, at least in relation to the factor endowments of other regions.

The southwest shipbuilding industry was therefore depressed by a major fall in demand for its staple product, the wooden sailing vessel, while supply constraints largely inhibited the development of the new mode of shipbuilding production in the region. Yet by tapping wider, more specialist markets and extending product ranges--strategies which chiefly entailed diversification around an existing base--some yards were able to make the transition from wood and sail to steel and steam. Upon the foundations laid a century or so ago in the form of relatively small-scale steel shipbuilding plants at Falmouth, Dartmouth and Appledore, the southwest's current interest in shipbuilding rests.

Appendices

Table 1
Tonnage of Vessels Built in Southwest England
and the United Kingdom, 1790-1913
(quinquennial aggregates; 000 net tons)

	Southwest	United Kingdom	% Southwest
1790-1794	22.3	304.1	7.3
1795-1799	31.6	390.0	8.1
1800-1804	53.7	528.4	10.2
1815-1819	40.9	444.7	9.2
1820-1824	27.4	330.0	8.3
1825-1829	35.1	499.3	7.0
1830-1834	23.2	439.2	5.3
1835-1839	23.1	672.9	3.4
1840-1844	35.7	678.9	5.3
1845-1849	25.9	635.0	4.1
1850-1854	26.8	850.9	3.1
1855-1859	40.4	1212.4	3.3
1860-1864	37.7	1447.1	2.6
1865-1869	42.3	1696.0	3.1
1870-1874	45.2	1982.0	2.3
1875-1879	45.4	1999.7	2.3
1880-1884	17.2	2838.3	0.6
1885-1889	17.6	2159.7	0.8
1890-1894	15.2	3085.3	0.5
1895-1899	9.9	2967.3	0.3
1900-1904	10.1	3677.5	0.3
1905-1909	7.7	3438.4	0.2
1910-1913	4.6	3391.2	0.1

Notes: 1790-1804, United Kingdom refers to vessels built in Britain; 1865-1869, southwest tonnage is averaged from 1866-1869 figures; 1910-1913, data are for four years only.

Sources: 1790-1804: PRO, CUST 17/12-30; 1815-1824: "Accounts and Papers," *BPP*, XVIII (1826-1827), 286-287; 1825-1864: extrapolations based on DRO, Ship Registers, Devon Ports (see text); 1865-1913: *Annual Statements of Navigation and Shipping*; UK figures: B.R. Mitchell (comp.), *Abstract of British Historical Statistics* (Cambridge, 1971) 220-222.

Table 2
Tonnage of Vessels Built in the Ports of
Southwest England, 1866-1913

A. Cornwall

	Fal-mouth	Fowey	Hayle	Pad-stow	Pen-zance	St. Ives	Scilly	Truro
1866	76	579	734	840	69	49	70	205
1867	261	280	451	1069	27	70	0	0
1868	426	781	673	486	115	49	39	347
1869	26	455	155	670	17	67	319	83
1870	493	537	228	456	18	0	256	237
1871	305	219	87	653	493	185	0	135
1872	0	300	451	257	128	311	361	358
1873	247	348	306	415	0	196	139	60
1874	1043 22	481	240	758	0	332	157	95
1875	790	772	521	639	18	390	36	643
1876	847	125	419	766	0	230	0	584
1877	407	739	382	442	125	291	0	495
1878	414	111	734	593	75	0	338	474
1879	257	504	358	807	59	43	0	334
1880	268	75	40	0	315	27	0	80
1881	101	0	289	315	30	0	28	126
1882	191	0	-	0	145	0	0	14
1883	286	0	-	0	76	153	0	4
1884	558	0	-	150	321	36	0	0
1885	353	0	-	0	340	41	0	133
1886	118	0	-	124	87 32	60	0	0
1887	49 69	0	-	0	206 34	0	0	0
1888	21 265	14	-	20	695 78	0	0	0
1889	390	11	-	189	1379 47	0	0	35
1890	33 82	0	-	0	2619	0	0	0
1891	222	0	-	0	2240	0	29	24
1892	181	0	-	0	403	0	0	20
1893	91	0	-	35	291	0	0	40

A. Cornwall

	Fal-mouth	Fowey	Hayle	Pad-stow	Pen-zance	St. Ives	Scilly	Truro
1894	182	13	-	0	12640	0	0	20
1895	4928	0	-	0	188	0	0	0
1896	695	0	-	0	297	0	0	0
1897	135	31	-	0	246	0	0	0
1898	90	7	-	0	39340	0	0	43
1899	130	0	-	0	205	0	0	0
1900	245	0	-	0	41635	0	0	0
1901	836	16	-	0	24745	25	0	0
1902	92	37	-	0	32266	0	0	0
1903	91	0	-	0	524	19	0	0
1904	140	8	-	0	436	0	0	0
1905	50	0	-	0	193	0	0	0
1906	101	40	-	25	346	0	0	0
1907	175	30	-	0	453	0	0	0
1908	166	0	-	0	367	0	0	0
1909	26	13	-	0	157	0	0	0
1910	2811	36	-	0	130	0	0	11
1911	6519	37	-	0	105	0	0	0
1912	90	15	-	0	61	0	0	0
1913	191	19	-	0	88	0	0	0

B. Devon

	Barn-staple	Bide-ford	Brix-ham	Dart-mouth	Exeter	Ply-mouth	Sal-combe	Teign-mouth
1866	449	2029	898	1870	1130	1013	0	78
1867	451	1115	1652	1425	803	949	777	306
1868	15	1168	1461	804	432	1721	779	214
1869	756	1496	971	397	641	1335	1082	103

B. Devon

	Barn-staple	Bide-ford	Brix-ham	Dart-mouth	Exeter	Ply-mouth	Sal-combe	Teign-mouth
1870	258	1020	739	761	497	1983	762	182
1871	624	976	1083	401	50	1067	586	260
1872	505	1803	1203	698	0	838	666	148
						225		
1873	503	1496	1216	1180	80	1309	483	156
1874	468	1461	1071	571	0	621	1168	53
1875	740	1091	892	1335	283	961	606	96
1876	781	1314	1494	1266	80	1272	649	47
1877	459	605	1423	730	75	605	1276	48
1878	378	216	1233	1518	297	672	798	103
1879	238	695	777	1055	89	819	104	27
1880	327	333	453	678	0	1691	212	3
1881	74	189	882	797	0	655	38	0
1882	60	124	722	737	0	319	6	0
1883	66	64	793	537	0	426	128	0
				43				
1884	253	174	1000	573	0	432	76	0
1885	0	392	1513	953	0	352	147	0
				10				
1886	0	254	1369	995	0	292	98	0
1887	0	26	1002	731	0	295	227	0
1888	0	80	948	613	0	184	99	0
				30				
1889	0	0	769	622	0	376	145	0
						120		
1890	0	68	763	552	0	275	97	0
				24				
1891	0	170	170	433	0	302	97	0
				24				
1892	0	99	99	511	0	363	38	15
1893	0	0	735	445	0	230	140	0
				15				
1894	0	93	603	400	0	235	99	0
1895	0	105	589	426	0	188	48	31
1896	0	119	646	321	0	44	95	0
1897	0	363	727	362	0	107	137	1
1898	0	525	554	288	38	220	169	0
				57				

David J. Starkey

B. Devon

	Barn-staple	Bide-ford	Brix-ham	Dart-mouth	Exeter	Ply-mouth	Sal-combe	Teign-mouth
1899	0	0	302	284 18	0	117	39	0
1900	0	0	388	221	0	88	0	0
1901	0	0	507	399	0	36	81	0
1902	0	327	468	583	0	140	30	0
1903	0	194	565	549	0	148	0	3
1904	0	1024	699	553 155	5	70	43	0
1905	0	193	690	397 186	0	0	80	4
1906	0	208	274	696 24	0	82	31	0
1907	0	21	423	485 45	0	123	52	0
1908	0	133	311	321 33	0	1	26	0
1909	0	99	246	273	0	85	25	14
1910	0	210	271	285 10	0	8	25	2
1911	0	91	346	252 45	0	1	36	0
1912	0	378	241	269 28	0	31	32	17
1913	0	280	225	425 26	0	235	0	0

C. Somerset and Dorset

	Bridgwater	Bridport	Poole
1866	194	265	120
1867	249	805	35
1868	386	854	63
1869	102	703	264
1870	180	163	207
1871	109	363	206
1872	304	650	71
1873	418	616	0
1874	617	281	0

C. Somerset and Dorset

	Bridgwater	Bridport	Poole
1875	352	323	105
1876	468	467	116
1877	365	196	92
1878	294	0	0
1879	242	425	0
1880	0	0	16
1881	0	0	272
1882	166	0	9
1883	0	0	5
			21
1884	67	0	36
1885	42	0	0
1886	0	0	26
1887	0	0	0
1888	79	0	7
1889	0	0	11
1890	0	0	17
1891	0	0	86
1892	78	0	0
1893	0	0	0
1894	79	0	120
1895	0	0	186
1896	0	0	48
1897	0	0	19
1898	0	0	80
1899	79	0	355
1900	0	0	168
1901	0	0	60
1902	0	0	34
1903	0	0	0
1904	0	0	0
1905	0	0	192
1906	0	0	0
1907	77	0	9
1908	0	0	13
1909	0	0	12
1910	0	0	11
1911	0	0	15

C. Somerset and Dorset

	Bridgwater	Bridport	Poole
1912	0	0	43
1913	0	0	0

Notes: Net tons. Numbers in bold denote tonnage sold overseas. For registry purposes, Hayle became part of the port of Penzance in 1882. One vessel of twenty net tons was built at Lyme in 1872. Vessels of fifteen, 160 and ninety-two net tons were built at Weymouth in 1879, 1882 and 1893, respectively.

Source: *Annual Statements of Navigation and Shipping*

Table 3
Average Tonnage of Vessels Built in Southwest England
and the United Kingdom, 1790-1913
(quinquennial averages; net tons)

	Southwest	United Kingdom
1790-1794	63.6	99.3
1795-1799	75.5	122.3
1800-1804	93.1	113.9
1815-1819	84.9	109.8
1820-1824	74.0	104.4
1825-1829	74.2	109.9
1830-1834	67.6	118.8
1835-1839	74.4	140.7
1840-1844	95.2	142.0
1845-1849	86.7	152.2
1850-1854	99.7	231.7
1855-1859	109.1	221.8
1860-1864	97.7	266.0
1866-1869	120.3	286.5
1870-1874	97.7	428.8
1875-1879	78.0	407.0
1880-1884	55.2	589.6
1885-1889	54.9	584.3
1890-1894	56.0	717.7
1895-1899	31.0	543.5
1900-1904	36.0	625.9
1905-1909	30.1	669.5
1910-1913	28.4	848.4

Notes: 1790-1804, United Kingdom refers to vessels built in Britain; 1825-1864, Southwest refers to vessels built and first registered in Devon only; 1910-1913, data are for four years only.

Sources: See table 1.

Table 4
Sail and Steam Tonnage Built in Southwest England
and the United Kingdom, 1866-1913
(quinquennial aggregates; 000 net tons)

	Sail			Steam		
	SW	UK	% SW	SW	UK	% SW
1866-1869	42.0	850.7	4.9	0.4	430.1	0.09
1870-1874	44.6	504.3	8.8	0.6	1477.5	0.04
1875-1879	44.1	891.1	4.9	1.3	1108.5	0.1
1880-1884	16.2	604.6	2.7	0.8	2233.8	0.03
1885-1889	15.1	621.3	2.4	2.5	1538.4	0.2
1890-1894	9.1	777.9	1.2	6.0	2307.5	0.3
1895-1899	9.2	265.7	3.5	0.7	2701.6	0.02
1900-1904	7.5	234.4	3.2	2.6	3443.0	0.07
1905-1909	6.3	139.8	4.5	1.4	3298.6	0.04
1910-1913	3.4	115.7	2.9	1.2	3275.4	0.03

Notes: Data for 1866-1869 and 1900-1913 are for four years only.

Sources: Southwest: *Annual Statements of Navigation and Shipping*; UK: Mitchell (comp.), *Abstract of British Historical Statistics*, 220-222.

Table 5
Number and Tonnage of Sailing Vessels Registered
in the Southwest, 1804-1900

	Number	Tonnage (000 net tons)	Average tonnage
1804	1762	123.5	70.1
1841	2153	160.1	74.3
1855	2332	226.4	97.1
1860	2448	239.2	97.7
1865	2406	244.1	101.5
1870	2140	217.5	101.6
1875	2019	192.7	95.4
1880	1899	170.1	89.6
1885	1568	128.9	82.2
1890	1432	102.4	71.5
1895	1329	82.6	62.2
1900	1209	68.6	56.7

Sources: 1804: PRO, CUST 17/26; 1841: "Accounts and Papers," *BPP*, LII (1843), 380-381; 1855-1900: *Annual Statements of Navigation and Shipping*.

Shipbuilding in the Northwest of England in the Nineteenth Century

Frank Neal[1]

I

The central concern of this essay is the performance of the shipbuilding industry in the northwest of England over the period 1814-1913. By "performance" is meant both absolute and relative output. Such a definition is of course limited, ignoring questions about efficiency or innovation. While space limitations make such restrictions necessary, they can be justified on the grounds that a delineation of trends in output is a necessary condition for any more detailed study of the regional industry. The northwest region runs from Chester, Birkenhead and Liverpool up the coast through Lancaster to Barrow, Workington, White-haven and Maryport. Statistics on total output will be examined first, distinguishing between domestic, foreign and government (principally warship) sales. Following this, total output will be disaggregated to identify the contributions of various centres. Then the structure of the industry will be examined and the market for its output analysed, distinguishing between demand and supply factors, with particular attention to Merseyside. Finally, reasons for the region's secular decline in shipbuilding will be suggested.

II

The reality of economic development decreed that the northwest would benefit from facing the Americas. From the beginning of the eighteenth century British trade with the West Indies, South, Central and North America increased rapidly, as did trade with West Africa. Moreover,

---

[1]I would like to thank Michael Stammers and Adrian Jarvis for helpful comments on an earlier draft of this paper.

Research in Maritime History, No. 4 (June 1993), 111-152.

Liverpool's industrial hinterland ensured that it would become a major
port. Chester, Lancaster, Whitehaven and Maryport each enjoyed growth
during the century and all were involved in shipbuilding and ship
repair.[2] Yet in the nineteenth century Liverpool's trade and docks
enjoyed spectacular growth while other regional ports experienced
secular decline. It is useful to remember, however, that shipbuilding and
port activities are separate industries and there is no reason why they
should be directly related.[3]

Before examining the statistical evidence on the region's output,
it is important to make several points. First, there is no continuous
official data for the period 1814-1913. For 1814-1826, there is a
parliamentary return which includes all ports in the northwest. An
appendix to a Select Committee report gives the tonnages built from
1820 through 1832 at principal ports, including Liverpool and Whitehaven. At this time "Liverpool" included Birkenhead while "Whitehaven"
embraced Maryport, Harrington and Workington.[4] A gap exists from
1833 to 1865; thereafter, detailed annual statistics are available for all
ports through the end of our period. In this essay, the gap in official
statistics has been filled for Birkenhead and Liverpool by constructing a
time series based on shipping registers, company histories, yard books,
newspaper reports and various lists in the possession of the Liverpool

---

[2]Standard works on Liverpool include S. Mountfield, *Western Gateway: A History
of the Mersey Docks and Harbour Board* (Liverpool, 1965); F.E. Hyde, *Liverpool and
Merseyside: the Development of a Port 1700-1790* (Newton Abbot, 1971); J.R. Harris
(ed.), *Liverpool and Merseyside: Essays in The Economic History of the Port and Its
Hinterland* (London, 1965); V. Burton (ed.), *Liverpool Shipping, Trade and Industry:
Essays on the Maritime History of Merseyside 1780-1860* (Liverpool, 1989).

[3]On 10 June 1850 Liverpool Borough Council set up a special committee to consider
the state of shipbuilding on the Liverpool side of the Mersey. The committee took
evidence throughout September and produced a report, *The State of the Shipbuilding
Trade in Liverpool*. This is held at the Liverpool City Library, but the evidence and
report in full was covered by the local press. During the enquiry it was authoritatively
claimed that the majority of foreign owners did not repair their vessels at the port and
that Liverpool owners bought most of their vessels from elsewhere. With the move to
iron, the cost advantages of North American yards *vis-a-vis* ship repairs vanished.

[4]Great Britain, Parliament, House of Commons, *Parliamentary Papers*, XVII (1826-
1827); *BPP*, "Select Committee on Manufactures, Commerce and Shipping," XI (1833),
appendix 1.

Nautical Research Society. Thus, we have data for Liverpool covering the entire century to 1913. Second, the basic unit of measurement in my estimates for this period is net tonnage, which was chosen because it was used in official statistics. Finally, it needs to be kept in mind that shipbuilding is a process, while the launch of a vessel is an event. As the year of launch was usually the basis for recording the year of build, annual statistics can be misleading. For example, a vessel may be under construction from March to December and be launched the following January. In this case, economic activity was generated in one year but final output was allocated to another. This is partly why annual statistics show significant fluctuations.

In the context of the official data, we can first consider the output of merchant vessels (see appendix table 1).[5] In 1814, the region contributed 10,996 tons to total UK output, or 13.3%. Ten years later, regional output increased both absolutely and relatively, to 11,245 tons and 17.8% of national output. This was the peak in the region's share of UK production. By 1832, the northwest's contribution to aggregate national tonnage was 10.5%.[6] By 1866, the first year for which detailed national data are available, the northwest's output of merchant shipping was 32,782 tons, or 8.6% of the UK total (see table 2). The data exhibit the fluctuations characteristic of shipbuilding nationally, a major problem for builders who wished to invest in expensive capital equipment. For example, from 46,299 tons in 1869, regional output fell the next year to 26,131 tons, a decrease of forty-four percent. From 22,626 tons in 1872, 1873 output rose to 38,804, a seventy-two percent increase. And 1889 output was 116% larger than the previous year. Some of these fluctuations can be explained partly by the timing of launches. Moreover, a significant change in annual output could be accounted for by two or three ships. In 1889, for example, Liverpool and Birkenhead built nine steamers (9986 tons) for foreign customers, six more than the previous year. In Barrow in the same year, ten vessels were sold to domestic

---

[5]All tables in this paper may be found in the appendices.

[6]Estimated total tonnage for the northwest for 1827-1832 was based on the following calculation. From 1814 to 1826 inclusive, Whitehaven and Liverpool on average contributed eighty percent of the region's total output. From 1827-1832, the aggregative outputs of Liverpool and Whitehaven are given in *BPP*, "Select Committee on Manufactures, Commerce and Shipping," appendix 1. These totals were grossed up to one hundred percent to estimate the northwest's total output for each year.

purchasers, seven (14,491 tons) more than the previous year's output. Despite such fluctuations, the secular trend clearly shows falling absolute and relative output. The years 1893-1903 were particularly lean. Thereafter, there was a slow recovery to the levels of the early 1890s.

Thus far the statistics have referred to merchant vessels. But if warships built for foreign governments are included, the overall trend is not altered significantly (see table 3). In 1901, 1905, 1906 and 1913 such sales were a significant proportion of regional output, particularly for Barrow-in-Furness. Also omitted from regional data are sales of warships to the Royal Navy. While this information is not contained in the "Annual Statements on Navigation" for individual ports, some indication of its relative importance can be illustrated by the case of Laird of Birkenhead (see table 4). From 1892, domestic warship sales were of increasing importance for Birkenhead and Barrow-in-Furness.

Turning from aggregate regional output to individual ports, the location of the principal centres of production reveals a polarisation. In the extreme south are Liverpool and Birkenhead. Nearby are Runcorn and Chester, although they were of marginal significance in most years. For example, the peak output of new ships at Runcorn between 1866 and 1898 was 808 tons in 1878. At Runcorn, Frodsham, Northwich and Winsford, there were flourishing industries building flats for use on rivers, canals and around the Liverpool docks.[7] In the north are Barrow, Workington, Whitehaven and Maryport. In between were small-scale centres, such as Preston, Fleetwood and Lancaster. Although from 1814 to 1832 Liverpool and Whitehaven were of roughly comparable importance, thereafter Liverpool began to pull ahead. By 1832, Liverpool produced 5999 tons compared with 3148 at Whitehaven (including Maryport).

From 1833 to 1865 there is a gap in the official statistics. For Liverpool and Birkenhead, a series covering this period has been constructed for 1815-1865 (see table 5). The official statistics for 1814-1832 differ from my estimates, for which there are a number of possible explanations. Under the heading of "Liverpool" I have included tonnage built at Birkenhead, but it is uncertain if the official statistics included Birkenhead's output. If not, this would account for most of the discrepancies. For 1820, however, my estimate for Liverpool (including Birkenhead) exceeds the official figures by 1794 tons. It is possible that some

---

[7]The standard work on Runcorn is H.F. Starkey, *Schooner Port* (Ormskirk, 1983).

vessels built and sold to foreigners were excluded from the official figures. The other possibility is that clerks made an error.[8]

During the first half of the century the outstanding characteristic of Liverpool output was the lack of expansion. For example, the 6662 tons launched in 1824 were only exceeded next in 1835. Of the following sixteen years, eleven failed to match the 1835 level. From 1856, the output of Liverpool yards grew steadily, reaching 43,844 tons in 1864. It is interesting to note the dip in output in Liverpool from 1846, reaching a low of 2496 tons in 1849. This was the trend which caused the Borough Council to set up a Committee of Enquiry into the local industry. This committee took evidence in September 1850 and produced its report soon after.[9] Growth on the Cheshire bank followed the Liverpool trend, and in 1856 and 1859 output exceeded Liverpool. The industry in Birkenhead was ultimately dominated by Laird.

Table 6 gives a complete breakdown of output for individual ports in the period 1866-1913. In 1866, the combined output of Liverpool and Birkenhead was reported under the heading "Liverpool." The Mersey's output for that year was 23,667 tons compared to a combined 1732 tons for Whitehaven and Workington. Thus, Merseyside still maintained its primacy in the northwest. But a striking feature is the dramatic decline of the Mersey from 1893. The next sign of recovery was rising output from 1906. In the northern part of the region, Barrow emerged as a relatively important producer in the 1870s. In all ports, the endemic problem of sharp fluctuations was prominent (see figure 1).[10]

---

[8]In the case of vessels built at Laird in Birkenhead, a problem of measurement arises because the tonnage of some vessels is recorded as "builder's measurement" rather than net register tons. To convert builder's measurement to net register tons, a regression was run on a sample of forty vessels. The resultant equation gives a conversion which is reasonable for large vessels but less so for small vessels. There is no reason to believe this unduly distorts the aggregates, particularly since Birkenhead production was only part of the total output. Based on a sample of fifty-four vessels, the regression equation is $Y = -246 + 0.778x$, where Y is register tons and x is builder's measurement. $R^2 =$ 93%. The constant suggests that the equation does not work well for small vessels.

[9]See note 3. For detailed reporting of the questioning of witnesses and the final report see, for example, *Liverpool Mercury*, 13, 14, 17, 20 and 24 September 1850.

[10]Gross tonnage is a better indication of the amount of work generated in shipbuilding. However, net register tonnage is an acceptable index of economic *trends*.

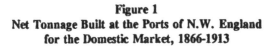

Figure 1
Net Tonnage Built at the Ports of N.W. England
for the Domestic Market, 1866-1913

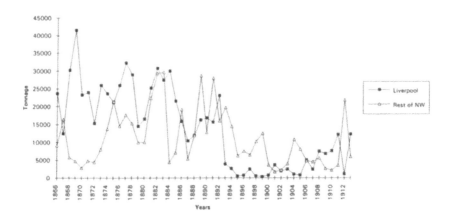

Source: See text.

III

The product of shipbuilding is a vessel which carries people and goods
across water. Such a piece of equipment was not homogeneous throughout the nineteenth century. In the first forty years neither the dimensions
nor construction materials of merchant ships changed greatly from a
century earlier.[11] Vessels were produced in yards in which traditional
craftsmanship and judgement vied with line drawings, half-models and
written specifications. But changing technology, reflecting general
industrial progress, eventually resulted in new types of vessels and hence
product differentiation.

A ship is a capital asset with a relatively long life. Investment
involves an assessment of the flow of revenue likely to be generated. In
our period, this was a function of freight rates or passenger fares. For
example, Liverpool ship carpenters in 1816 were asked by merchants
commissioning new vessels to accept lower wages on the grounds that

---

[11]For a recent survey of issues in the development of the merchant ship, see David
R. MacGregor, *Merchant Sailing Ships 1850-1870* (London, 1984); MacGregor, *Fast
Sailing Ships: Their Design and Construction 1775-1875* (2nd ed., London, 1988).

freight rates were low.[12] Investment decisions are complicated by economic turbulence; a major factor in exacerbating this is technological change, which affects both fixed and variable costs, and hence profits.

Between 1815 and 1885, shipbuilding underwent a technological upheaval, but like the industrial revolution of which it was a reflection, this was a process rather than an event. A large number of improvements were made in materials, propulsion, design, sailmaking, rigging, chainmaking and so on. Merseyside builders and engineers contributed to the pace of technological change which characterised shipbuilding after 1815. While the contribution of Laird at Birkenhead is reasonably well-documented, the efforts of Liverpool builders are less well-known. Probably the most influential was John Grantham, who was particularly interested in iron shipbuilding and wrote influential books on the subject in 1842 and 1858. Others included John Jordan, who in 1839 took out a patent for composite construction. Josiah Jones of the firm of Jones, Quiggin experimented with steel spars for sailing ships and in 1862 built the *Seaforth*, the first sailing vessel with steel masts. In 1840 the local press claimed that the *Roseanne*, launched at Jackson's yard in the South End, was the first to be fitted with iron lower deck beams, adding not only strength but also twelve inches of extra storage space. James Hodgson, well-known for iron ships, was one of the first to build screw-propelled vessels and co-operated in design with John Grantham.[13] Since space does not permit a consideration of all such improvements, attention will be paid to the affects of the major technological transformations, especially from sail to steam and wood to iron and steel.

First, we will examine the response of builders on the Liverpool bank of the Mersey to the introduction of iron (see table 7). Although Liverpool was one of the earliest centres of iron shipbuilding, in the 1830s only three iron vessels were constructed, representing only 484

---

[12]*BPP*, V (1824), 203-204, "Select Committees on Artisans and Machinery," Minutes of Evidence, John Kirwan, 17 March 1824.

[13]I have compiled a database of all vessels built on Merseyside, 1815-1913, from the Liverpool Registers of Merchant Shipping, newspaper reports of launches, various lists held by the Liverpool Nautical Research Society, *Lloyd's Lists* and Laird's Yard Books. I am most grateful to John Taylor of Birkenhead for his help in understanding the Laird material. For a very useful introduction to the issues in the introduction of iron, see E. Corlett, *The Iron Ship* (2nd ed., Bradford-on-Avon, 1990). For John Grantham, see *Iron as a Material for Shipbuilding* (1842) and *Iron Shipbuilding* (1858).

tons or 1.2% of Liverpool output in the decade. The next decade was characterized by the take-off of iron shipbuilding, with 14,032 tons being launched, or 26.2% of total output. In the 1850s, the proportion of iron-built tonnage rose to 55.5%, a figure which was exceeded in the 1860s. By the third quarter of the nineteenth century, iron shipbuilding dominated production.

The aggregates, however, do not tell us much about the size of local output. The statistical profile of these iron vessels exhibits some marked features. First, there was a steady increase in average vessel size between 1840 and 1879. Second, from the 1850s there was a continuous decrease in the variance around the mean; the coefficient of variation fell from eighty-two to fifty-seven percent between the 1850s and 1870s. While this suggests a more standardised product, table 8 includes all iron ships built in Liverpool yards. We need to distinguish between iron steamers and sailing ships.

Figure 2: Laird's yard, Birkenhead, c. 1860.

Source: Courtesy of the Trustees of the National Museums and Galleries on Merseyside.

Figure 3: Laird's shipyard, 1861, with the Irish mail packet *Hibernia* being fitted out.

Source: See figure 2.

For steamships, table 9 shows that the average tonnage of iron-built vessels increased steadily. In the 1850s the maximum size of vessels was 1315 tons, jumping in the 1860s to 3572 tons. Yet the median dipped from 300 to 229 tons, indicating an increasingly skewed distribution. From 1840 to 1869, there was increasing variation; the coefficient of variation peaked in the 1860s at 122%. Significantly, in the 1870s the coefficient fell by almost half, demonstrating increasing standardisation.

In the case of iron sailing vessels, it is noticeable that it exceeded steam in the 1860s (see table 10). Again, there was a steady increase in average tonnage. The most noticeable contrast with steamers was the much smaller variation: in the 1860s, the coefficient of variation was forty-seven percent compared to 122% for steam. In the 1870s, the coefficient plunged to forty-four percent. This implies that iron sailing ships were of a more standard design than steamers. In the case of wooden sailing vessels, average size remained well below the mean for iron, whether steam or sail. There was also greater size variation (see tables 11a and 11b). The average size of wooden steamers increased to mid-century but thereafter began to decline, as did aggregate output. It is noteworthy, however, that in 1842 a composite vessel, the 2017-ton *Hindustan*, was launched at T. Wilson's yard for the Pacific and Orient Steam Navigation Company.[14] Later that year Wilson launched the 1974-ton wooden steamer *Bentinck*. Over the period 1842-1853, the Bank Quay Foundry Company at Warrington built a number of iron sailing ships, including the ill-fated *Tayleur*. This enterprise originated in the experience of Charles Tayleur of the Vulcan Railways works at Newton-le-Willows. A prominent shipowner, he founded a partnership with Robert Stephenson to produce locomotives at the Vulcan, where he and his son, Edward Houlbrooke Tayleur, gained experience with iron and boiler construction. It was the son who was most involved with the Bank Quay Foundry, which closed in 1856.[15]

A reasonable inference from the available evidence is that Liverpool builders eagerly embraced iron in the 1850s, leading rapidly to the demise of wooden vessels. For example, in 1875 only one 237-ton wooden sailing ship was built at Liverpool (including Birkenhead). By contrast, fourteen iron sailing ships and eleven iron steamers were launched (21,020 tons). Steel was beginning to appear as well; by 1879 2.5% of the tonnage built in Liverpool was steel. By 1890, this had reached eighty-one percent. Iron finally disappeared by 1893.[16]

At the yards on the Birkenhead side of the river, iron shipbuilding dominated early. The overall pattern reflected the Liverpool experience. The average size of iron steamers increased steadily from a

---

[14]*Liverpool Mercury*, 29 April 1842. *Hindustan* was a paddle steamer, with 560-hp engines made by the local firm of Fawcett and Preston. *Ibid.*, 29 April 1842. The report states that the *Bentinck* was "laid on the stocks and now in rapid progress."

[15]At the moment little has been published on Warrington's brief experience as a shipbuilding town; this author is working on such a project. For a brief survey of Warrington shipbuilding, see Starkey, *Schooner Port*.

[16]Twenty-five steel vessels (21,054 tons) were built in the UK in 1879, 5.6% of total output. In Liverpool, the *Whinerell* was the sole steel vessel, built by W.H. Potter.

maximum of 452 tons in the 1830s to 2794 tons in the 1860s (see table 12). It is important to remember that during this period Laird built warships for the British government, several exceeding by a good amount the size of large merchant vessels.[17] In the 1860s, the tonnage of iron sailing ships exceeded iron steamers, and sail was on average larger than steam (see table 13). In the same decade, twenty-five percent of all iron sailing vessels in the Birkenhead sample exceeded 1214 register tons, compared to 541 tons for steamers. As in Liverpool, the size variation of iron sail was less than that of steamships.

In Cumberland, builders also turned to the new construction material but concentrated on sail. A comparison of output in the northwest and the northeast is instructive. Total output in the latter in 1866 was 118,979 tons compared with 32,752 in the northwest. Sixty percent of northeast output was iron, while for the northwest it was sixty-nine percent. It is notable that in 1866 the output of wooden ships in Sunderland alone exceeded total production in the northwest.

IV

In its essentials, the market for both new and second-hand vessels is no different than any other market. There are buyers and sellers, and in a competitive market price is determined by the relative level of supply and demand. The ability of an individual producer or buyer to influence price depends on the degree of competition. At an extreme is the model of perfect competition familiar to first-year students of economic theory.

In some of its assumptions, this model describes shipbuilding in the first three-quarters of the nineteenth century. Let us first look at supply in the northwest. We have already noted that northwest shipbuilders contributed 13.3% of UK output in 1814, falling to 10.5% in 1832 and 8.6% by 1866. On Merseyside, Liverpool and Birkenhead output accounted for 3.6% of total UK output in 1815; by 1866, this had risen to 6.2%. When the structure of the local industry is examined, it is clear that the influence of individual suppliers was minimal. For example, over the period 1815-1840 there were thirty-four shipbuilders

---

[17]In 1862, Laird built the 2866-ton (builders measure) troopship *Orontes*; Cammell-Laird, "List of Ships 1829-1910," Cammell-Laird Archives, Birkenhead Town Hall. Laird Yard Book, Job No. 286. In 1865, the 6621-ton (builders measure) *Agincourt* was launched; its engines were 1250-hp. *Ibid.*, Job No. 291.

operating at one time or another. The most common business unit was the individual or partnership. This was not surprising given the state of company law at the time. In 1720, restrictions had been placed on the creation of limited-liability joint-stock companies; not until 1862 were the various statutes codified to produce a comprehensive body of company law. Many of the partnerships split and re-formed in new combinations; many were short-lived and disappeared quickly. Often the firms concentrated on repair work. In this early period the principal builders were Mottershead and Heyes, Jonathan and Roger Fisher, Caleb and James Smith, Bland and Chaloner, Humble and Hurry, F. Wilson and Co., Thomas Royden and Joseph Steel. But the output of each builder was insignificant compared to total UK production. In 1820, for example, the largest producer was Mottershead and Heyes, whose 1698 tons represented 1.9% of UK output. Yet even this is misleading. Shipowners were fully aware of prices elsewhere, particularly in North America. If the output of the British Empire is taken as the base, then Mottershead and Heyes-produced 1.5% In addition, as in the modern car market, the existence of a stock of second-hand vessels influenced the market price for new ships.[18]

Twenty years on, Thomas Royden was the largest producer on the Liverpool shore, with 1510 tons. UK output in that year was 181,301 tons; thus, Royden's contribution was 0.8%. Against Empire production, his share fell to 0.6%. By 1841, some of the early Liverpool builders had ceased operations. Between 1841 and 1865, the number of builders on the Liverpool side of the Mersey fell to twenty. Among the more important newcomers were W.H. Potter; Peter Cato; Thomas Vernon; Jones, Quiggin and Co.; W.C. Miller and R. and J. Evans. This concentration marked a move towards greater capacity. From the earlier period, Thomas Royden and Joseph Steel continued as significant local builders. Yet even though the firms were bigger in absolute terms, they were still relatively small. In 1860, Jones, Quiggin and Co. launched 4022 tons, 1.7% of UK output. In 1864, Thomas Vernon launched 10,000 tons, 2.3% of UK production. R. and J. Evans produced 3646 tons in 1866, one percent of the national aggregate. The 1851 census reveals that fifty-one people in the northwest described themselves as "master shipbuilder." Of these, thirty-seven reported their number of employees--the

---

[18]In February 1855, there were 187 sailing vessels and steamers for sale in Liverpool. Of this number, 102 were colonial-built. *Liverpool Mail*, 3 February 1855.

average was forty-two. Nineteen firms hired fewer than twenty men each, while four employed over a hundred. In the case of the northern counties, sixty master shipbuilders averaged forty-nine employees, while ten employed over 100. In Scotland, eighteen master builders had an average of 135 men, while one employed 447 shipwrights and a second hired 454. Throughout the UK, small firms predominated.[19]

While there can be no doubt that Liverpool builders operated in a competitive market, a model of perfect competition appears less appropriate when we examine market conditions. It is well to remember that a "ship" was not a homogeneous product. Sailing vessels differed from steamers and wood from iron. Similarly, before the advent of standardisation, vessels from various yards showed their idiosyncrasies, further differentiating the products.[20] These factors gave rise to some degree of freedom in pricing. Despite these caveats, competitive forces led to a continual reduction in the size of the industry on Merseyside. By 1874, the only firms left were Laird Brothers (Birkenhead), Thomas Royden and Sons (Liverpool), R. and J. Evans (Liverpool), Bowdler, Chaffer and Company (Seacombe), Clover, Clayton and Company (Birkenhead) and Potter and Hodgkinson (Liverpool). By World War I only Laird survived as a builder of any significance.

The current literature on corporate strategy and marketing suggests that in an era of technological transition, firms which have invested heavily in skills, plant and equipment relevant to the existing technology are rarely able to maintain market share, losing out to new entrants which embrace the more modern technology.[21] The Merseyside experience supports this. An examination of the output of individual firms reveals a degree of target marketing. W.B. Jones produced only

---

[19]1851 Census LXXXVII Pt II Division VII. North West Counties: Occupations of the People, 654. Division X. Northern Counties, 798. Scotland, 1023.

[20]For a full discussion of the change from a craft-based to an "assembly" industry, see S. Pollard and P. Robertson, *The British Shipbuilding Industry 1870-1914* (Cambridge, MA, 1979), especially chapter 6.

[21]For a specific example, see J.O. Rendeiro, "How the Japanese Came to Dominate the Machine Tool Business," *Long Range Planning*, XVIII, No. 3 (1985), 62-67. See also M.E. Porter, *Competitive Strategy* (New York, 1980). For an analysis of the economics of sailing ships in the age of steam and iron, see G.S. Graham, "The Ascendency of the Sailing Ship 1850-85," *Economic History Review*, 2nd ser., IX, No. 1 (August 1956), 74-88.

wooden vessels between 1825 and 1852. From 1856, Jones (later the partnership of Jones, Quiggin and Company) specialised in building iron steamers and sailing vessels. In 1859 it built the steel steamer, *Light of the River*.[22] Entering the market in 1862, Thomas Vernon concentrated entirely on iron steamers and sailing vessels. Another new market entrant, W.H. Potter, which commenced building in 1860, specialised in iron and steel vessels. A notable exception was Thomas Royden. In 1864, the company was the longest-lived of any size, and had successfully made the transition from sail to steam and wood to iron and steel. In 1865 the 1269-ton *Yamuna* was the first iron ship built by Royden.[23]

When studying the market for any product, it is important to recognize that the amount bought and sold is not the same as that which is demanded or supplied. What is sold is identical to what is bought, whereas supply and demand are equal only at an equilibrium price. If demand exceeds supply, prices rise, and *vice versa*. Thus far we have concentrated on supply. Yet aggregate demand for ships in the UK clearly exceeded the northwest's supply capacity. More significant is the fact that demand for new ships by Liverpool owners alone exceeded the capacity of the local industry.

Aside from Liverpool, other ports in the region were insignificant. The major regional demand for new ships came from Liverpool; although its owners bought vessels from a number of centres, the majority of Merseyside-built vessels were sold to local owners. When wooden ships were in demand before about 1860, British North America was an important supplier. In 1850, for example, 41,605 tons of new vessels were added to the Liverpool register, of which only 3474 tons were built locally. Using a definition of new as including "any colonial vessel built within one year of registration at Liverpool," 27,187 tons of new colonial craft were added that year, nearly eight times the Liverpool contribution.[24] In 1852 sixteen colonial-built ships (12,347 tons) were

---

[22]Jones, Quiggin and Company Collection, Merseyside Maritime Museum.

[23]For an account of the growth of Royden, see *Thomas Royden and Sons, Shipbuilders 1818-1893* (Privately printed 1953). This book is not a business history and gives few insights into the economics or strategy of the company. The reference to the *Yamuna* is on p. 24. See also Liverpool Register of Merchant Shipping, No. 15, 1866, Merseyside Maritime Museum Archives.

[24]These data were extracted from the Liverpool Registers of Merchant Shipping.

first registered in Liverpool. This far exceeded the registration of North American-built vessels elsewhere: Glasgow was next with 3778 tons.[25] In 1855, 102 new colonial ships (70,911 tons) arrived in Liverpool.[26]

In general, the purchasers of Liverpool-built vessels were individual merchants for whom shipowning was an adjunct to their trading activities. Similarly, many partnerships combined both functions.[27] Later, joint-stock companies assumed a greater importance but the sole merchant buyer was still common in 1900. Throughout the period, shipbuilders often retained a share of a vessel until a buyer was found. In 1840, the 180-ton steamer *Phlegethon* was launched by John Laird at Birkenhead; Laird was the first registered owner.[28] In the same year, the 350-ton barque *Buenos Ayrian* was built by Joseph Steel, who was the sole registered owner.[29] In 1854 the 482-ton barque *Chilena* was launched at Royden's yard at the Queen's dock and was jointly

---

[25]*BPP*, (H.C.) Accounts and Papers XCVIII (1852-1853).

[26]*European Times*, 5 January 1856.

[27]For a detailed discussion of patterns of ownership at Liverpool up to 1835, see F. Neal, "Liverpool Shipping in the Early Nineteenth Century," in Harris (ed.), *Liverpool and Merseyside*, (London, 1969) 147-181. For an examination of the purchasing policy of specific shipowners, see F.E. Hyde, *Shipping Enterprise and Management: 1830-1939: Harrisons of Liverpool* (Liverpool, 1967), especially chapters 1 and 6. See also C.J. Napier, "Fixed Asset Accounting in the Shipping Industry: P&O 1840-1914," *Accounting, Business and Financial History*, I, No. 1 (1990), 23-50. For investment in steamships, see P.L. Cottrell, "The Steamship on the Mersey, 1815-80, Investment and Ownership," in P.L. Cottrell and D.H. Aldcroft (eds.), *Shipping, Trade and Commerce: Essays in Memory of Ralph Davies* (Leicester, 1981), 135-163.; Cottrell, "Liverpool Shipowners, The Mediterranean and the Transition from Sail To Steam During the Mid-Nineteenth Century," in L.R. Fischer (ed.), *From Wheel House to Counting House: Essays in Maritime Business History in Honour of Professor Peter Neville Davies* (St. John's, 1992), 153-202.

[28]Liverpool Register of Merchant Shipping, 14 August 1840.

[29]Liverpool Register of Merchant Shipping, 24 Sept 1840. For a full account of the company of Joseph Steel, see M. Stammers and J. Kearon, *The Jhelum: A Victorian Merchant Ship* (Stroud, 1992).

owned by Thomas Royden and T.T. Wakeham, a Liverpool shipowner. It was a thirteen-year ship at Lloyds, and Royden retained an interest.[30]

Some builders on the Liverpool shore produced vessels for the foreign market. Before 1866, we have no official statistics on total tonnage sold to foreigners; even later we have only total newly-built foreign sales. There is some evidence of this export trade in the shipping registers, press reports and Laird yard books. More than any builder on Merseyside, Laird targeted the foreign market. In 1855, Laird's Toxteth yard launched the 1200-ton *Jourdain* for the Compagnie des Messageries Imperiale. The same yard soon after launched the *Meandris*, also for a French company. But Laird was not alone in courting foreign buyers. In the same year, Rennie, Johnson and Rankin completed the *Empress Eugenie* for the North-West of France Steam Navigation Company. Similarly, W.C. Miller launched the *Destrelle* for Spanish owners.[31] Despite such examples, available evidence suggests that most output was sold to Liverpool owners.

Even if all Merseyside's output had been sold to local owners, it would still not have met the demand. Yet the decision to buy elsewhere may have been based not only on lack of local output but also on considerations of price, quality, size, or delivery dates. In 1841, a group of Liverpool merchants formed an association to build ships on the Isle of Man to take advantage of lower import duties on timber. The principal builder on the island was John Winram, who supplied a number of vessels to Liverpool owners, in particular James Aiken, a prominent merchant.[32] This price sensitivity ensured that the region's builders could not afford to ignore competition. In 1847, when the British North American Mail Steam Packet Company decided to purchase four large wooden steamers for the Liverpool-New York route, the order went to

---

[30]Liverpool Register of Merchant Shipping, 16 March 1854. Royden owned twenty-four of the sixty-four shares.

[31]*Liverpool Mail*, 21 April and 1 December 1855.

[32]*Liverpool Chronicle*, 17 April 1841. Liverpool and Sunderland shipbuilders had petitioned parliament to equalise timber duties in England and the Isle of Man. For the connection between Aiken, Jonanthan Winram and the Isle of Man, see T. Latham, *The Ashburner Schooners: The Story of the First Shipbuilders of Barrow-in-Furness* (Manchester, 1991), 14-15.

Clydeside.[33] A year later, the Liverpool merchant house, Charles Moore and Company, invested in a new East India vessel, the *Scan Jehan*; this order also went to the Clyde.[34] Loyalty to a particular builder and local patriotism meant little; Liverpool owners would go wherever the best bargain was. In 1850, the Liverpool merchant house John Meluish and Company commissioned the *John Meluish* at Clarke's yard in Jersey. It was 750 tons, classed A1 at Lloyds for thirteen years, and was destined for the East India trade.[35] A further indication of the competitive environment appeared in the *Liverpool Mercury* of 13 March 1863, referring to the launch of the 1953-ton steamer *Southerner* by M. Pearse and Company at Stockton-on-Tees for a Liverpool firm. "It is a noteworthy fact, as indicative of the quality of work turned out of Messrs. Pearse and Company's yard, that almost all of their ships for some time, have been built for Liverpool owners," the paper reported.

In the Birkenhead area, only Laird spanned the whole of our period. It specialised in iron steamers from the outset. In addition to Laird, during the first half of the nineteenth century there were eight other firms in Birkenhead, Tranmere and Seacombe: W. Bird; Daulby and Highton; Lomax and Wilson; Seddon and Leadley; Robert Russell, Thomas Raffield; W. and A. Adamson; and the Liverpool Steam Tug Company. After 1850, most disappeared and Thomas Wilson, Thomas Vernon, Bowdler and Chaffer, and Clover, in addition to Laird, comprised the industry on the Cheshire shore.

From an early date Laird won orders from both foreign buyers and the British government.[36] In 1834 the yard built the *John Randolph*, and in 1838 the *Robert E. Stockton*, both for American owners. In 1834,

---

[33]*Liverpool Telegraph*, 5 February 1847. Three of the ships were to be built by R. Steel of Greenock and one by John Smith of Port Glasgow. All were to be 1000 tons register with engines of 950-hp.

[34]*Glasgow Citizen*, 22 April 1848. It was built by Denny and Rankin and was 800 tons register and classed A1 for ten years at Lloyds.

[35]*Liverpool Mercury*, 23 July 1850.

[36]There is as yet no detailed business history of Laird, although a number of books describe launches and vessels. The most recent of these is D. Hollett, *Men of Iron: The Story of Cammell Laird Shipbuilders, 1828-1991* (Birkenhead, 1992). For a nineteenth-century view of Laird, see "Mr John Laird, MP and the Shipbuilding Trade of Birkenhead," *Practical Magazine*, XVIII, No. 3 (1874), 402-408.

Laird built two vessels for the government, followed in 1840 by four gunboats. As was the case with Liverpool builders, Laird built for local demand, but its markets were much more diversified. For example, the firm sold warships in Latin America, Russia and China. Laird quickly established an international reputation for iron shipbuilding and technical innovation. Perhaps best known was its employee, Ericcson, who contributed to the development of screw-steamers.[37] By the end of the century, Laird was building vessels for the government of a size rarely approached on the Liverpool shore, including the 14,900-ton H.M.S. *Mars*, launched in 1896.[38]

Shipbuilding in Cumberland during the first three-quarters of the century centred on Whitehaven, Workington, Maryport and Harrington.[39] Through 1850, there were about twenty-one builders of note at one time or another. The principal firms were John Peat, Huddleston and Ritson, Kelsick Wood, William Peile, Thomas and James Brocklebank and Isaac Middleton. Although the market was both national and international, in practice Liverpool was a major outlet for Cumberland-built vessels. Thomas and James Brocklebank of Whitehaven also operated out of Liverpool as shipowners and built vessels for themselves and others.[40] The rise of iron and steam initially hit the Cumberland industry badly. The centre of shipbuilding in the area eventually moved

---

[37]C. Dawson, "John Ericcson and Laird's," in H.M. Hignett (ed.), *A Second Merseyside Maritime History* (Liverpool, 1991), 17-19.

[38]Laird's Yard Book, Job No. 603.

[39]There is no comprehensive study of shipbuilding in Cumberland, although there are a number of short books which touch on the subject, including H.M. Jackson, *Holme Shipping Line: Maryport 1873-1913* (Maryport, 1991); this is a popular rather than a business history. See also J.E. Williams, "Whitehaven in the Eighteenth Century," *Economic History Review*, 2nd ser., VIII, No. 3 (1956), 393-404. Harry Fancy and his staff at Whitehaven Museum have produced a number of lists of vessels built at Whitehaven and are constantly updating them. The latest is *Shipping and Whitehaven: A Check List* (1984; reprint, Whitehaven, 1991). Barrow is now in Cumbria but was in Lancashire. The latest study of a shipbuilder in Barrow is Latham, *The Ashburner Schooners*.

[40]Daniel Hay, *The History of Shipbuilding at Whitehaven* (Whitehaven, 1889), contains ship lists. For a detailed history, see J.F. Gibson, *Brocklebanks: 1750-1950* (2 vols., Liverpool, 1953).

south into Barrow-in-Furness in north Lancashire. In 1851, there were only 219 shipwrights and shipbuilders in Whitehaven, compared with 2208 in Liverpool.

No complete list of vessels built in Cumberland yet exists, but the official statistics from 1866 clearly depict the situation.[41] In 1866, Whitehaven builders launched 1935 tons: one iron sailing ship (672 tons), four wooden sailing ships (totalling 706 tons), and a composite sailing vessel. At Workington two wooden sailing vessels were launched (797 tons), while Maryport produced nothing. No steamers were built. Given the absence of detailed information on shipowners' views of Cumberland craft, we can only surmise about the reasons for the area's decline in shipbuilding. In terms of steam and iron, the Cumberland yards did not have the expertise or resources of Merseyside, Clydeside and Tyneside builders. In 1847, the Whitehaven Steam Navigation Company purchased a second iron steamer from Thomas Vernon of Liverpool; it had already taken delivery of another vessel, the *Queen*, from the same builder for use on the Liverpool-Whitehaven route.[42] The rise of iron also had adverse consequences upon sales to Liverpool owners. A search of the Liverpool registers after 1850 reveals that no newly-built Cumberland vessels were registered until 1873. Yet during this period T. and J. Brocklebank built at least sixteen vessels.[43] In 1873 the *Eskdale*, an iron sailing ship, was purchased by Liverpool owners from the Whitehaven Shipbuilding Company.[44] A month later the iron steamer *Maraldi* was registered. Built by the same company, the steamer was purchased by the Liverpool, Brazil and River Plate Steam Navigation Company.[45] Later that year the *Dunmail*, a new 1337-ton iron sailing ship was bought from the same yard by J.B. Walmsley, a

---

[41]*BPP*, Accounts and Papers, "Annual Statement of Navigation and Shipping." From 1866, these statistics distinguish between sail and steam, and iron and wood.

[42]*Cumberland Pacquet*, 23 February 1847.

[43]Hay, *The History of Shipbuilding at Whitehaven.*

[44]Liverpool Register of Merchant Shipping, 26 March 1873.

[45]*Ibid.*, 30 April 1873.

Liverpool shipbroker.[46] This seems to confirm that the new company had some success in winning a share of the lucrative Liverpool market. The importance of the Liverpool market for Cumberland was illustrated by events in 1879. In that year only six vessels (15,531 net registered tons) were built at Whitehaven,[47] of which Liverpool owners bought two: the 929-ton iron sailing schooner *Irene Morris* and the 872-ton iron steamer *Benona*.[48] In tonnage terms, Liverpool owners purchased almost one-third of Whitehaven's output.

V

The causes of the secular decline in shipbuilding on the Liverpool shore cannot be treated in detail here. But if it is viewed in terms of land, labour and capital, some explanation is possible. In the absence of any detailed financial records for shipbuilding firms, it is impossible to reach any firm conclusion about capital availability. Yet on *prima facie* grounds, there is no reason to believe that local builders would have been prevented from raising share capital had they wished. More relevant, firms of the size under discussion could have used undistributed profits as a substitute. Unfortunately, the Liverpool firms do not appear to have been sufficiently profitable to have generated investment funds internally. Why not?

One potential constraint on an industry's growth might be a shortage of labour, skilled or otherwise. On Merseyside this was not a problem. In 1804, there were sixteen shipbuilders in Liverpool, employing 327 shipwrights and 160 apprentices.[49] Table 14 depicts the situation at the time of the 1841 census. Since 1804, the number of ship-

---

[46]*Ibid.*, 7 August 1873.

[47]*BPP*, "Annual Statement of Navigation and Shipping," LXXI (1880), table 24.

[48]Liverpool Register of Merchant Shipping, 17 July 1879 (*Irene Morris*) and 9 October 1879 (*Benona*).

[49]The definitive work on Liverpool shipbuilding before 1814 is R. Stewart-Brown, *Liverpool Ships in the Eighteenth Century* (Liverpool, 1932). The reference to the number of shipwrights in 1804 in on p. 34.

wrights and carpenters had increased by over 1000.[50] Tables 15a-c give a geographic breakdown of those employed in maritime trades. In 1851 there were 2208 shipwrights/shipbuilders in the borough of Liverpool, a total approached only by Sunderland (2025). This was an increase of 713 in a decade during which the local industry stagnated. The appearance of boilermakers in the lexicography of the census is illuminating. The growing use of steam created an increased demand for this new breed of engineers. Boilermakers were crucial for the factories and mines of the industrial revolution. Although there were few factories and no mines in Liverpool, the building of the steam railway accelerated demand for boilermakers, whose skills were transferable to shipbuilding. In addition, the gas industry required their services. It is noteworthy that the number of boilermakers in Liverpool in 1851 was exceeded only by Glasgow. In 1871, there were at least 5048 shipwrights/shipbuilders on Merseyside compared with 152 at Whitehaven (see table 16).

What this suggests is that a shortage of skilled labour was not a constraint on the growth of shipbuilding in Liverpool or Birkenhead. On the contrary, all available contemporary data suggest persistent underemployment except at times of peak demand. For example, in October 1845 the *Liverpool Mercury* reported that the Vernon Company and Peter Cato each turned down orders because of shortages of shipwrights and space.[51] In 1850 the local shipbuilding enquiry was told repeatedly of the underemployment of shipwrights. In Liverpool, the principal engine makers were Fawcett, Preston and Company, Bury and Kennedy and Forresters and Company. Mr. Preston of Fawcett, Preston claimed that in 1850 it employed 400 hands, whereas previously the average had been 900-1000. He claimed that seventy-five percent of the company's work was maritime.[52] Mr. Kennedy of Bury and Kennedy told the enquiry that in 1850 his company employed 170 men, compared to 1200 three years earlier. He also reported that while in 1847 forty

---

[50]In the 1851 census, the term "carpenter" was dropped from the list of occupations and the label used for shipbuilding became shipwright/shipbuilder. The dropping of "carpenter" may have reflected a recognition of the growing importance of iron.

[51]*Liverpool Mercury*, 3 October 1845. In Liverpool there were a number of engineering companies from the 1840s. Most important were three firms: Fawcett, Preston; Forester and Bury; and Curtis and Kennedy.

[52]*The State of the Shipbuilding Trade in Liverpool*, Evidence of Mr. Preston.

percent of the firm's work was marine engineering, in 1850 it had almost none.[53] In the case of unskilled labour, Liverpool and Birkenhead had access to an almost unlimited supply of Irish workers.

Yet despite this regular underemployment, shipwrights' wages were higher on Merseyside than elsewhere. The evidence for this is anecdotal but persistent, and was a major complaint of builders during the 1850 enquiry. Sidney Pollard and Paul Robertson also provide some evidence to substantiate this claim.[54] The ship carpenters in Liverpool had a powerful trade union up to 1835. Their influence arose from the fact that many possessed both parliamentary and municipal votes. This meant that Liverpool power brokers had to stay on good terms with the carpenters, at least near elections. One manifestation of this concern was an unwillingness by the mayors, who were also the chief magistrates, to take action against the carpenters when they used force to stop the use of outside labour or to intimidate master shipwrights. By 1850, this power had been diluted, first by reforms of the voting system in 1832 and 1835 and then more significantly by the move to steam and iron, which rendered their skills obsolete. By 1870, shipbuilding was becoming more of an assembly industry and boilermakers became the new aristocracy.[55] Since no detailed study of the Merseyside labour market exists prior to 1880, we simply do not know why wages were so high relative to other locales.

The most scarce factor of production for shipbuilding in Liverpool was land. The majority opinion of builders giving testimony to the 1850 enquiry was succinctly summarised by J.A. Tobin:

---

[53]*Ibid.*, Evidence of Mr. Kennedy.

[54]Pollard and Robertson, *British Shipbuilding*, table B.

[55]For a detailed examination of the activities of ships' carpenters in Liverpool before 1850, see F. Neal, "Patriots or Bigots? The Political and Religious Allegiances of the Liverpool Ships' Carpenters, 1815-1851," in Fischer (ed.), *From Wheel House to Counting House*, 203-244. I am again grateful to Mike Stammers for pointing out that the surviving firms were based on two sites and that the building industry was extinguished rapidly. Laird was more vertically-integrated than the Liverpool firms, with iron foundry and engine-making facilities on site. In the absence of these, sub-contractors had to deliver the required parts and materials.

What then are the disadvantages which have produced
this state of things? The report of the committee sufficiently points them out: small, incommodious yards,
high rents, and taxes, want of leases, restrictions
imposed by the club [union] and the want of public
graving docks.[56]

While this seems an accurate summary of the voluminous evidence, it
does not weigh the relative importance of each cause. The claim made
by most witnesses--that the Shipwrights' Association was pricing builders
out of the market--was not empirically proven. Instead, we are left with
anecdotal evidence.[57] It does seem that shipwrights' wages were higher
on Merseyside, but this does not prove that wage levels were the
principal cause of high prices.

Of crucial importance is productivity, and here there is stronger
evidence that work practices had a deleterious effect. The principal cause
of upward pressure on costs had its origin in the cramped conditions of
Liverpool yards and the lack of long leases. This latter feature led to an
unwillingness to invest in plant and equipment and adversely affected
productivity. The municipality owned the riverfront land and consistently
refused long leases. Thomas Wilson told the committee that on one
occasion he was given only six months notice to quit his yard. During
that period he received a government order for four 1800-ton steamers.
Another enquiry was received from the Pacific and Orient Company for
up to four 1500-ton steamers. To ensure his ability to fill these orders,
he transferred his business to Birkenhead.[58] The cramped conditions
increased costs. Timber had to be piled up to save space, greatly increas-

---

[56]*Liverpool Mercury*, 1 October 1850. Tobin was the person who actually proposed
the establishment of the Committee of Enquiry.

[57]*Ibid.*, 10 September 1850; *The State of the Shipbuilding Trade in Liverpool*,
Evidence of Peter Chaloner. Joseph Steel told the committee that carpenters' wages in
Cumberland were three shillings and sixpence per day while in Liverpool they were five
shillings. *Warrington Guardian*, 22 October 1853.

[58]*The State of the Shipbuilding Trade in Liverpool*, Evidence of Thomas Wilson.
Wilson, who moved his premises to Birkenhead before the 1850 enquiry, told the
committee that private graving docks were necessary but that ship repairers should not
be allowed to own them. In his view, only such action could save Liverpool shipbuilding.

ing the time it took to find a particular piece. A wooden shipbuilder also needed space for sawpits, blacksmith shops, and perhaps some cottages. An iron builder would need even more buildings for furnaces. The pressure on space along the waterfront was the fundamental cause of the corporation's niggardliness towards making land available for builders. The powerful dock committee represented the interests of merchants and shipowners whose primary concerns were docks and warehouses.[59]

Figure 4: Langton Dry Docks, Liverpool, c. 1880 with American sailing ship under repair.

Source: See figure 3.

---

[59]The work of the Dock Committee has recently come under scrutiny, opening an examination of the Liverpool dock politics. See A. Jarvis, "Harold Littledale: The Man with a Mission," in Hignett (ed.), *Second Merseyside Maritime History*, 5-16; Jarvis, *Liverpool Central Docks, 1799-1905* (Stroud, 1991). I am grateful to Mike Stammers for pointing out that the issue of space in the economics of local building needs further examination. The yards in Sunderland were cramped, as were some in Canadian creeks.

Another adverse influence on shipbuilding profits was the existence of public graving docks. Private docks were prohibited. The public graving docks enabled a journeyman carpenter to tender for a repair job while avoiding the costs of running a yard, thus enabling him to undercut established builders. Most witnesses expressed the view that by cutting into the volume of work available to shipbuilders this practice was a disincentive to invest in equipment. Peter Chaloner claimed that two-thirds of all repair work in Liverpool was undertaken by journeymen carpenters using the graving docks. He also expressed the view that a lease of at least fourteen years was necessary to induce a master shipwright to invest in the necessary fixed plant and equipment for profitable operations. An opinion generally held by builders was that they should be able to build private docks and that the public graving docks should be closed. Despite the fact that after 1850 the output of Liverpool yards increased and the industry enjoyed a revival based on the shift to metal, the space shortage continued to affect the industry adversely. Although the industry soon slimmed down to four firms on the main sites, the demise of Liverpool firms came quickly in the 1890s: Royden (1893), Potter (1894) and R. and J. Evans (1895) all ceased operations.

By contrast Birkenhead, Tranmere and Seacombe on the Wirral bank provided adequate space for shipbuilding. William Laird bought land in Wallasey in 1824 and established a business making boilers about 1829. He commenced shipbuilding and quickly became a specialist iron builder. The absence of a business history makes it impossible to analyse the factors behind its success, but William Laird and Son not only specialised early in iron vessels, particularly steamers, but also targeted the foreign market. The company eventually had its own on-site iron foundry and facilities for making engines. This investment in plant and equipment could only be undertaken because the firm did not have the disincentive of short leases. This degree of vertical integration gave Laird a considerable advantage over its Liverpool competition.

VI

The picture of long-term decline in northwest shipbuilding is unequivocal. The reasons are fairly clear. Merseyside was the centre of the industry and the major constraint on the Liverpool shore was land. From this and the tradition of short leases flowed a number of adverse consequences for costs and profits. In Liverpool, shipbuilding competed for land with powerful shipowners and merchants who wanted docks and warehouses. Unlike Barrow, Birkenhead and other towns, Liverpool was not a "company" town and shipbuilders had little influence on the council or its committees. By comparison with the northeast, Liverpool was not close to iron mines or ironmaking facilities, although it did have coalfields nearby at Prescot, St. Helens and Wigan and a local iron works. But these did not overcome the other disadvantages. While Birkenhead had fewer land constraints, the lack of a local iron and coal industry put builders on the Wirral shore at a cost disadvantage compared with the northeast and Clydeside. Nonetheless, the economics of the local shipbuilding industry has not yet been examined in detail.

This essay has concentrated on the output and the structure of the industry. It will hopefully provide a base for a more detailed examination of northwest shipbuilding. We need to know more about cost of building, the quality of ships, the region's contribution to technological change, and profitability. It is highly likely that the existence of excellent records will soon lead to a business history of Laird, but there is a dearth of information on other Merseyside builders.

One of the barriers to a comprehensive history, however, may be historical romanticism. In retrospect it is clear that the decision to use land on the Liverpool shore for docks and warehouses was correct. Liverpool's trade increased spectacularly during the nineteenth century and shipbuilding had little to do with this. Between 1816 and 1845, there was little relationship between tonnage entering the port and shipbuilding. Indeed, the correlation coefficient was only 0.186. Put simply, Liverpool did not need a local shipbuilding industry to prosper. Yet as the increasing numbers of shipwrights suggests, there was a flourishing ship repair business. It was this that maintained an unbroken link with Liverpool's shipbuilding history.

Appendices

Table 1
Net Tonnage of Vessels Built and Registered
at Various Ports in the Northwest, 1814-1832

Year	Liver-pool	Ches-ter	Pres-ton	Lancas-ter	White-haven	NW Total Output	NW % of UK
1814	3846	953	239	1247	4711	10996	13.3
1815	3847	1549	93	880	6307	12676	14.7
1816	2638	2604	99	699	4735	10775	10.5
1817	2105	807	71	410	3341	6734	8.0
1818	2641	910	135	263	3583	7532	9.3
1819	1940	1535	38	594	3105	7212	8.3
1820	4329	862	-	264	2749	8204	9.2
1821	2583	624	15	738	2142	6102	9.1
1822	3588	422	-	501	2502	7013	12.1
1823	3986	185	-	333	1805	6309	12.4
1824	6440	961	144	721	2979	11245	17.8
1825	5552	1486	-	1241	3502	11781	12.9
1826	5999	1815	133	1071	3148	12166	9.9
1827	2797				3581	7972	6.7
1828	2935				4429	9205	9.9
1829	4479				2151	8288	9.3
1830	3346				3294	8300	10.8
1831	3727				2204	7413	9.8
1832	4553				2552	8801	10.5

Note: Northwest totals for 1827-1832 are estimates.

Source: *BPP*, Accounts and Papers, XVII (1826-1827), 197; *BPP*, "Select Committee on Manufactures, Commerce and Shipping," XI (1833), appendix 1.

Table 2
Tonnage of Merchant Vessels Built in the Northwest, 1866-1913
(Domestic and Foreign Markets)

Year	Tonnage	Northwest Tonnage as % of UK Total	Year	Tonnage	Northwest Tonnage as % of UK Total
1866	32782	8.6	1890	30531	3.8
1867	28958	9.5	1891	44458	5.5
1868	36048	9.9	1892	40798	5.1
1869	46299	11.9	1893	26174	2.8
1870	26131	6.6	1894	18417	2.8
1871	28837	7.3	1895	10454	1.6
1872	22626	4.8	1896	9463	1.3
1873	38804	8.6	1897	11172	1.7
1874	38431	6.3	1898	12954	1.3
1875	42826	9.1	1899	14964	1.6
1876	41392	10.9	1900	14839	1.6
1877	50024	11.1	1901	8009	.8
1878	46201	9.8	1902	4963	.5
1879	31813	7.8	1903	6708	.9
1880	27538	5.8	1904	16640	-
1881	56041	9.2	1905	10399	.9
1882	70914	9.1	1906	11495	1.0
1883	59897	6.7	1907	12047	1.2
1884	57579	9.8	1908	14496	2.4
1885	28800	6.5	1909	14603	2.4
1886	35142	10.7	1910	12129	1.9
1887	18678	5.0	1911	18590	1.7
1888	25563	4.5	1912	31948	2.9
1889	55244	6.5	1913	25970	2.2

Note: All totals include foreign sales from 1872 to 1889.

Source: *BPP*, "Annual Statements of Navigation and Shipping of the United Kingdom," various years.

Table 3
Tonnage Built For Foreigners, Merchant and Naval Vessels, in the Northwest, 1872-1913

Year	Mercan- tile	War- ships	Total	Year	Mercan- tile	War- ships	Total
1872	2845	-	2845	1893	2518	-	2518
1873	4716	-	4716	1894	1289	405	1694
1874	972	-	972	1895	3721	140	3861
1875	70	-	70	1896	1146	256	1402
1876	847	-	847	1897	2225	75	2300
1877	-	-	-	1898	2091	1084	3175
1878	1818	-	1818	1899	2052	-	2052
1879	7380	-	7380	1900	10332	-	10332
1880	933	-	933	1901	2589	5379	7968
1881	8297	-	8297	1902	666	-	666
1882	10650	-	10650	1903	197	-	197
1883	6597	-	6597	1904	5013	-	5013
1884	3102	-	3102	1905	1414	4850	6264
1885	74	-	74	1906	1655	7575	9230
1886	-	246	246	1907	5071	-	5071
1887	2906	-	2906	1908	1398	270	1668
1888	1629	-	1629	1909	5082	-	5082
1889	10136	-	10136	1910	3647	-	3647
1890	321	634	1455	1911	2721	2569	6958
1891	687	-	687	1912	8899	-	8899
1892	1642	821	2463	1913	7687	9013	16679

Source: See appendix table 2.

Table 4
Warships Built For the British Government
by Laird of Birkenhead, 1840-1913

Year	Tonnage	Unit of Measurement	Year	Tonnage	Unit of Measurment
1840	1396	Builders	1894	1160	Draught
1846	1400	Builders	1895	1420	Draught
1847	697	Builders	1896	15965	Draught
1855	5173	Builders	1897	1520	Draught
1856	4291	Builders	1898	320	Draught
1861	165	Builders	1899	14934	Draught
1862	2866	Builders	1900	642	Draught
1865	6621	Builders	1901	14000	Draught
1869	8046	Builders	1903	8200	Draught
1876	1256	Net Tonnage	1904	7800	Draught
1877	1031	Net Tonnage	1905	1200	Draught
1883	481	Net Tonnage	1907	2690	Draught
1886	89	Net Tonnage	1909	2760	Gross Ton
1892	15730	Draught	1911	8830	Draught
1893	410	Draught	1912	23090	Draught
			1913	933	Draught

Source: Cammell-Laird, "List of Ships 1829-1910," Cammell-Laird Archives, Birkenhead Town Hall.

Table 5
Estimated Net Register Tonnage of Vessels Built at Liverpool and Birkenhead, 1815-1865

Year	Liverpool	Birkenhead	Total	Total as % of U.K. Output	Year	Liverpool	Birkenhead	Total	Total as % of U.K. Output
1815	3284	195	3479	3.6	1835	6896	1071	7967	5.0
1816	2929	234	3163	2.5	1836	5341	1672	7013	3.8
1817	2199	100	2299	2.0	1837	2047	2568	4615	3.0
1818	2975	-	2975	2.8	1838	7009	1664	8673	4.2
1819	1529	214	1743	1.7	1839	3992	2551	6543	2.7
1820	5972	155	6127	5.5	1840	7883	2592	10475	4.1
1821	3311	-	3311	3.9	1841	5325	1561	6886	1.9
1822	4004	-	4004	5.3	1842	4084	984	6068	?
1823	3978	-	3978	5.9	1843	7247	1289	8536	4.1
1824	6662	-	6662	7.7	1844	4594	1836	6430	4.6
1825	5908	318	6226	4.3	1845	5175	1628	6803	-
1826	6295	319	6614	3.2	1846	7935	1058	8993	4.2
1827	2281	437	2718	1.3	1847	7726	515	8241	3.4
1828	3020	72	3092	1.9	1848	3717	568	4285	1.4
1829	4886	50	4936	3.5	1849	2496	113	2609	1.1
1830	3315	200	3515	3.0	1850	3499	2029	5528	2.3
1831	2847	85	2932	2.7	1851	5772	2022	7794	3.1
1832	4149	1253	5402	4.5	1852	6949	2332	9281	
1833	2759	599	3358	2.5	1853	9165	6563	15728	
1834	4820	2392	7212	5.5	1854	16773	14660	31443	

Year	Liverpool	Birkenhead	Total	Total as % of U.K. Output	Year	Liverpool	Birkenhead	Total	Total as % of U.K. Output
1855	13253	10366	23619		1861	11989	4495	16484	7.9
1856	9364	10675	20039		1862	23212	2201	25418	9.7
1857	8665	3807	12472		1863	37701	7378	45078	11.9
1858	7382	3527	10909	4.6	1864	43844	14052	57896	12.6
1859	8805	9274	18079	8.5	1865	32520	17550	50070	11.2
1860	10767	9411	20178	8.9					

Note: Laird produced warships for the Royal Navy in 1840, 1846, 1847, 1855, 1856, 1861, 1862 and 1865. These tonnages are not included.

Sources: Liverpool Registers of Merchant Shipping, Merseyside Maritime Museum Archives; Liverpool newspapers; *Lloyd's Lists*; List of John Reece, Archives of the Liverpool Nautical Research Society; "List of Ships," Cammell-Laird Archives.

Table 6

Tonnage of Shipping Built at the Ports in the Northwest for the Domestic Market, 1866-1913 (Net Tons)

Year	Liverpool	Runcorn	Chester	Preston	Barrow	Workington	Whitehaven	Maryport	Rest	Total
1866	23667	308	611	2737	-	797	1935	-	2727	32782
1867	12475	341	10458	1248	-	1111	1406	-	1920	28959
1868	30257	662	-	377	-	1073	2360	-	319	36048
1869	41577	651	-	363	167	832	1682	740	287	46299
1870	23298	444	135	627	348	865	-	-	414	26131
1871	24046	244	74	685	328	1754	1491	-	215	28837

Year	Liverpool	Runcorn	Chester	Preston	Barrow	Workington	Whitehaven	Maryport	Rest	Total
1872	15350	-	95	158	313	1032	2522	-	311	19781
1873	26014	354	-	355	2496	1028	3697	-	144	34088
1874	23707	94	135	343	4941	2049	5691	-	499	37489
1875	21257	159	201	339	10628	2278	7541	-	353	42756
1876	25993	-	140	553	4234	2628	6960	-	37	40545
1877	32347	232	278	433	11435	1817	3312	-	170	50024
1878	29040	808	277	667	7703	2070	3148	388	282	44383
1879	14509	670	-	393	1185	2167	5321	-	188	24433
1880	16541	820	94	448	8295	-	221	-	86	26605
1881	25308	741	158	603	15343	-	4745	707	-	47744
1882	30848	686	-	844	19054	3577	5255	-	-	60264
1883	27517	290	101	339	15069	3800	6184	-	-	53300
1884	30091	150	99	57	14172	3893	5742	-	273	34477
1885	21629	434	200	214	2996	1819	-	1426	-	28726
1886	15917	422	-	1963	9375	3659	2406	1400	-	35142
1887	10417	224	166	139	836	3858	-	-	132	15772
1888	12001	225	80	79	717	1897	7136	1799	-	23934
1889	16297	-	-	115	15208	4256	9157	-	75	45108
1890	16871	80	256	100	7716	2599	94	1994	-	29710
1891	15663	259	-	621	19173	4935	-	3120	-	43771
1892	23122	227	-	1169	8416	4813	-	1268	141	39156
1893	3871	77	91	848	15755	2923	-	-	60	23656
1894	2650	-	82	175	12639	128	115	1291	48	17128
1895	539	120	91	231	2616	2931	-	-	205	6733

Frank Neal

Year	Liverpool	Runcorn	Chester	Preston	Barrow	Workington	Whitehaven	Maryport	Rest	Total
1896	774	73	98	227	5219	329	-	1597	-	8317
1897	2493	-	48	70	1807	2814	-	1715	-	8947
1898	580	387	102	421	7814	1150	-	132	277	10863
1899	338	-	25	25	11429	968	-	92	60	12912
1900	825	790	99	151	-	1516	-	1116	10	4507
1901	3653	165	175	312	-	664	-	402	49	5420
1902	1999	1044	6	9	7	954	-	214	64	4297
1903	2503	324	216	-	2406	668	-	-	394	6511
1904	1041	1330	-	1137	5845	889	-	-	1385	11627
1905	907	530	238	777	5490	288	-	375	380	8985
1906	5044	1086	504	931	65	1716	-	84	410	9840
1907	2432	1409	717	440	1013	383	-	-	582	6976
1908	7489	1047	300	1014	2190	551	-	-	507	13098
1909	6795	694	-	465	930	280	-	46	311	9521
1910	7616	522	133	344	-	383	-	99	385	9482
1911	12211	732	732	671	22	479	-	77	885	15809
1912	1138	647	542	1203	17964	842	-	-	713	23049
1913	12298	1396	1445	2052	59	620	-	106	308	18284

Source: See appendix table 2.

Table 7
Tonnage of Vessels Produced on the Liverpool Shore
of the Mersey, Wood and Iron Vessels, 1815-1879

Period	Wooden Vessels Tons	Iron Vessels Tons	Total Vessels Tons	Iron as % of Total
1815-1819	12760	-	12760	-
1820-1829	42877	-	42877	-
1830-1839	38752	484	39236	1.2
1840-1849	39448	14032	53480	26.2
1850-1859	36920	46035	82955	55.5
1860-1869	15863	184218	200081	92.1
1870-1879	2456	145013	147469	98.3

Note: Data for 1860-1869 and 1870-1879 are incomplete.

Source: Calculated from a data set compiled by the author.

Table 8

Number, Net Tonnage and Size Distribution of Iron Vessels Built on the Liverpool Shore of the Mersey, 1840-1879

Decade	No. of Ships	Total Tonnage	Average Tonnage Per Ship	Median Tonnage	First Quartile	Third Quartile	Maximum Sized Ship	Coefficient of Variation
1840-1849	40	14032	351	333	132	494	931	67
1850-1859	89	46035	517	385	170	879	1629	82
1860-1869	262	184218	703	598	308	1154	3572	69
1870-1879	143	145013	1014	1052	638	1400	2959	57

Note: Data for 1860-1869 and 1870-1879 are incomplete.

Source: See appendix table 7.

Table 9

Number, Net Tonnage and Size Distribution of Iron Steamships Built on the Liverpool Shore of the Mersey, 1840-1879

Decade	No. of Ships	Total Tonnage	Average Tonnage Per Ship	Median Tonnage	First Quartile	Third Quartile	Maximum Sized Ship	Coefficient of Variation
1840-1849	36	12031	334	288	107	473	931	72
1850-1859	50	19992	400	300	113	536	1315	91
1860-1869	90	36541	406	229	100	573	3572	122
1870-1879	78	71599	918	800	534	1303	2959	67

Note: Data for 1860-1869 and 1870-1879 are incomplete.

Source: See appendix table 7.

Table 10

Number, Net Tonnage and Size Distribution of Iron Sailing Vessels Built on the Liverpool Shore of the Mersey, 1840-1879

Decade	No. of Ships	Total Tonnage	Average Tonnage Per Ship	Median Tonnage	First Quartile	Third Quartile	Maximum Sized Ship	Coefficient of Variation
1840-1849	4	2001	500	494	-	-	564	-
1850-1859	39	26043	668	504	283	992	1629	67
1860-1869	172	147677	859	765	548	1200	1873	47
1870-1879	65	73414	1129	1257	779	1435	1877	44

Note: Data for 1860-1869 and 1870-1879 are incomplete.

Source: See appendix table 7.

Table 11a

Number, Net Tonnage and Size of Wooden Sailing Vessels Built on the Liverpool Shore of the Mersey, 1815-1879

Decade	No. of Ships	Total Tonnage	Average Tonnage Per Ship	Median Tonnage	First Quartile	Third Quartile	Maximum Sized Ship	Coefficient of Variation
1815-1819	88	12760	145	129	37	216	455	81
1820-1829	155	34813	225	225	86	327	573	63
1830-1839	140	32340	231	219	98	314	756	68
1840-1849	121	33880	280	184	76	486	765	80
1850-1859	100	35200	352	271	63	518	1469	93
1860-1869	46	14398	313	244	84	468	1117	82
1870-1879	8	2320	290	74	69	95	1794	210

Note: Data for 1860-1869 and 1870-1879 are incomplete.

Source: See appendix table 7.

Table 11b
Number, Net Tonnage and Size of Wooden Steamships Built on the Liverpool Shore of the Mersey, 1820-1879

Decade	No. of Ships	Total Tonnage	Average Tonnage Per Ship	Median Tonnage	First Quartile	Third Quartile	Maximum Sized Ship	Coefficient of Variation
1820-1829	48	8064	168	184	89	207	500	57
1830-1839	28	6412	229	215	82	332	550	63
1840-1849	12	5568	464	288	69	798	1974	122
1850-1859	8	1720	215	213	80	369	403	65
1860-1869	5	1465	293	195	152	483	689	78
1870-1879	2	136	68	-	-	-	88	-

Note: Eleven wooden steamers have been excluded because of lack of information; data for 1860-1869 and 1870-1879 are incomplete.

Source: See appendix table 7.

Table 12
Number, Net Tonnage and Size Distribution of Iron and Steel Sailing Vessels Built on the Wirral Shore of the Mersey, 1830-1879

Decade	No. of Ships	Total Tonnage	Average Tonnage Per Ship	Median Tonnage	First Quartile	Third Quartile	Maximum Sized Ship	Coefficient of Variation
1830-1839	1	61	61	-	-	-	-	-
1840-1849	2	219	110	-	-	-	129	-
1850-1859	11	7689	699	-	66	1293	1444	83
1860-1869	82	65108	794	816	398	1214	1657	58
1870-1879	9	2295	255	219	68	448	595	82

Note: Data for 1860-1869 and 1870-1879 are incomplete.

Source: See appendix table 7.

Table 13

Number, Net Tonnage and Size Distribution of Iron and Steel Steam Vessels Built on the Wirral Shore of the Mersey, 1830-1879

Decade	No. of Ships	Total Tonnage	Average Tonnage Per Ship	Median Tonnage	First Quartile	Third Quartile	Maximum Sized Ship	Coefficient of Variation
1830-1839	17	3570	210	194	117	309	452	57
1840-1849	25	5800	232	213	85	357	630	67
1850-1859	92	45264	492	318	100	734	2524	100
1860-1869	99	40887	413	293	97	541	3509	117
1870-1879	116	69020	595	462	125	829	2794	98

Note: Data for 1860-1869 and 1870-1879 are incomplete.

Source: See appendix table 7.

Table 14
Number of Males Employed in Shipbuilding and Related Trades
in the Borough of Liverpool, 1841

Occupations	Number
Shipbuilders and Carpenter	1495
Sailmaker	439
Ship's Rigger	189
Anchorsmith and Chairmaker	103
Sailcloth Manufacturer	8
Ship's Surveyor	1
Total	2305

Source: Great Britain, Census (1841), XIII, "Population, Occupations County of Lancaster," 90.

Table 15a
Number of Males in Occupational Groups Related to
Shipbuilding Industry in the Northwest, 1851

Occupation	Liverpool (Borough)	Lancaster (Borough)	Chester (City)	Preston (Borough)	Whitehaven (Town)
Shipwright/ Shipbuilder	2208	12	34	23	219
Others engaged in fitting ships	934	5	-	-	19
Anchorsmiths	95	1	44	-	1
Sailcloth Manufacturers	604	7	5	6	56
Ropemakers	683	27	59	100	56
Boilermakers	464	2	11	83	56
Shipowners	82	-	1	3	11

Source: Great Britain, Census (1851), "Occupations of the People," Division VIII, Northwest Counties, 650-651. Whitehaven appears in Division X, Northern Counties, 795.

Table 15b
Shipbuilding Occupations in the Northeast, 1851

Occupation	Newcastle (Borough)	Tynemouth (Borough)	South Shields (Borough)	Sunderland (Borough)
Shipwright/ Shipbuilder	315	319	738	2025
Others engaged in Fitting Ships	40	59	61	248
Anchorsmiths	72	116	15	99
Sailcloth Manufacturers	94	47	90	118
Ropemakers	129	45	54	216
Boilermakers	185	3	58	19
Shipowners	28	359	64	146

Source: Great Britain, Census (1851), "Occupations of the People," Division X, Northern Countries, 795.

Table 15c
Shipbuilding Occupations in Scotland, 1851

Occupations	Greenock (Burgh)	Glasgow (City)	Aberdeen (City)
Shipwright Shipbuilders	425	363	338
Others engaged in Fitting Ships	49	57	12
Anchorsmiths	12	10	-
Sailcloth Manufacturers	27	11	2
Ropemakers	151	560	231
Boilermakers	172	627	37
Shipowners	29	42	30

Source: Great Britain, Census (1851) Census, "Occupations of the People," Scotland, 1018-1019.

Table 16
Number of Shipbuilders and Shipwrights
in the Principal Shipbuilding Areas, 1871

Area	Number
Stepney (18)	823
Poplar	1651
St. Saviour Southwark (22)	689
Greenwich (26)	580
Medway (45)	918
Stepney (60)	384
Portsea Island	913
Southampton (96)	291
Plymouth (277)	351
Stoke Damerel (279)	601
Birkenhead (454)	738
West Derby	2889
Liverpool (455)	1421
Sculcoates (519)	909
Hull (520)	309
Stockton (541)	822
Hartlepool (542)	790
Sunderland (55)	3294
South Shields (551)	2079
Newcastle-on-Tyne	462
Tynemouth (554)	1991
Cardiff (583)	549
Swansea (588)	300
Pembroke (595)	544

Note: Figure in parentheses refer to the registration district.

Source: Great Britain, Census (1871), appendix A.

Shipbuilding in Nineteenth-Century Scotland

Anthony Slaven

At the beginning of the nineteenth century Scotland was not a major shipbuilding region. The Parliamentary returns of ships built and first registered at UK ports suggest that Scotland contributed about fifteen percent of UK tonnage during the Napoleonic Wars. The return for 1790-1791 indicates Scottish output of 18,817 net tons, or 15.3% of the UK total. In 1805 Scotland delivered 23,360 net tons, some 15.4% of national production. To put this in perspective, at the beginning of the century Scotland's entire annual production of merchant tonnage was roughly equivalent to the output of one of the great English shipbuilding rivers. The Thames delivered 16,370 tons in 1791, the Tyne 15,034 tons and the Wear 14,198 tons. By 1820 the position was practically unchanged; Scotland then contributed 11,004 tons, or 16.5% of the UK total (see table 1).[1] There was little at this stage to indicate that Scottish shipbuilding was soon to play a leading role in British industrialisation.

Scottish Shipbuilding in Profile

Scottish shipbuilding and the term "Clyde-built" are commonly held to be synonymous, but this is not an appropriate perspective before 1850. At the beginning of the century the Clyde regularly launched 3000-4000 tons of merchant ships each year, about one-fifth of Scottish production. The remainder were built on the east coast, with Aberdeen, Leith and Dundee leading production in that order. The great estuaries of the Dee, Tay and Forth were home to hundreds of small builders, providing employment for the majority of Scotland's shipwrights. By 1831, when the first usable census employment data are available, the Clyde employed just over one-quarter of Scotland's shipbuilding workforce, the remainder concentrating in the east coast yards (see table 2).

---

[1]Great Britain, Parliament, House of Commons, *Parliamentary Papers* (*BPP*), "Annual Accounts of Vessels and Tonnage Built and First Registered at the Ports of Great Britain and Ireland," 1790-1826.

Research in Maritime History, No. 4 (June 1993), 153-176.

Table 1
UK Shipbuilding by District, 1820-1911 (Net Tons)

District	1820		1871		1911	
	Tons	%UK	Tons	%UK	Tons	%UK
Thames/SE	2574	18.8	13038	3.3	8284	0.8
South Coast	2480	3.7	3903	1.0	2404	0.2
South West	4661	6.9	5524	1.4	906	0.1
Bristol Channel	5358	8.0	4139	1.1	2166	0.2
Wash-Lowestoft	2371	4.1	2491	0.6	2059	0.2
Humber	4055	6.1	28410	7.4	22829	2.3
Tyne	2222	3.3	55398	14.3	237678	23.8
Wear	7560	11.3	73196	18.7	179238	17.9
Tees	3533	5.3	37034	9.5	168071	16.8
Mersey and NW	8222	12.3	28837	7.4	18594	1.9
Wales	618	0.9	833	0.2	-	-
England and Wales	**54014**	**81.0**	**252803**	**64.7**	**642229**	**57.9**
Clyde	3961	5.9	115136	29.5	332220	33.2
Forth	2360	3.5	1557	0.4	5439	0.5
Tay	1794	2.7	6090	1.6	9503	0.9
Aberdeen/NE	2092	3.1	7314	1.9	5203	0.5
W Coast/Island	797	1.2	44	-	4497	0.4
Scotland	**11004**	**16.5**	**130141**	**33.3**	**356862**	**32.2**
Belfast	634	1.0	7842	2.0	107604	9.7
Dublin	240	0.4	412	-	1045	0.2
S W Ireland	810	1.1	-	-	56	-
Ireland	**1684**	**2.5**	**7894**	**2.0**	**108705**	**9.8**
UK	**66702**		**390838**		**1107796**	

Sources: 1820: Great Britain, Parliament, House of Commons, *Parliamentary Papers*
(*BPP*), XVIII (1826-1827); 1871: *BPP*, LIII (1871); 1911: *BPP*, "Annual
Statement of the Navigation and Shipping of the United Kingdom" (1911), Cd.
6398, table 23.

This reflected the historic position of east coast dominance in
Scottish shipbuilding, but thereafter the locus of the industry began to
shift to the Clyde. Between 1831 and 1851 the census returns of
occupations in Great Britain show that adult male employment in
shipbuilding on the Clyde roughly trebled to around 1900 men while the
east coast rivers doubled their workforce to 2500. Twenty years later, in

1871, nearly eighty percent of Scotland's shipbuilding labour found employment on the Clyde (table 2), and the historic positions of the east and west coast yards had been reversed. Clyde leadership and dominance were consolidated swiftly and relentlessly after that, and by 1911 around ninety percent of Scotland's workforce and output in shipbuilding emanated from the Clyde.

Table 2
Adult Male Employment in Shipbuilding
in Great Britain, 1831-1911

District	1831		1871		1911	
	No.	% GB	No.	% GB	No.	% GB
Thames/SE	4453	26.3	8304	13.5	9799	6.3
S Coast	1241	7.3	2208	3.6	10066	6.5
SW/Bristol Channel	2233	13.2	3476	5.6	10241	6.6
Humber	475	2.8				
NE Coast	3016	17.8	14618	23.8	56722	36.5
NW Coast	2834	16.7	7786	12.7	15004	9.6
Wales	635	3.7	2955	4.8	1785	1.1
England/Wales	14884	87.9	45066	73.3	103617	66.7
Clyde	559	3.3	12829	20.8	45314	29.2
Forth	313	1.8	951	1.5	1979	1.3
Tay	239	1.4	1399	2.3	1453	0.9
Aberdeen/NE	451	2.7	1260	2.1	1782	1.1
W Coast/Islands	161	0.9			1219	0.8
Other	332	1.9				
Scotland	2055	12.1	16439	26.7	51747	43.3
GB	16939		61505		155364	

Sources: Great Britain, *Census*, "Occupational Returns," 1831; England and Wales, *Census* 1871 and 1911; Scotland, *Census*, 1871 and 1911.

In the century between the launching of the *Comet* and the onset of the First World War Scottish shipbuilding grew from relative insignificance to world leadership, supplying over one-third of UK tonnage. The Clyde was the dynamic element in the transformation, increasing its output more than 100-fold. By 1914 the Clyde annually launched more tonnage than any other river in Britain. It was also the leading shipbuilding river in the world, contributing over twenty percent of new merchant tonnage each year between 1890 and 1913.[2]

The development of Scottish shipbuilding was, of course, only one major element in the dramatic changes that reshaped the British, and world, industries in the nineteenth century. Few industries were so totally altered as shipbuilding, the industry being completely transformed in scale, product and technology. By the end of the nineteenth century shipbuilding had become a complex engineering and metal assembly trade. Vessels in wood had given way to large hulls in iron and latterly in steel, and the power of wind and sail had largely been replaced by that of steam and the screw propeller. These transitions are well understood and it is not the intention to repeat them in detail here. Rather it is proposed to outline the pace and consequences of these changes for the emergence of modern shipbuilding in Scotland, and to set out the nature of the Scottish contribution to the development of the modern industry.

The Emergence of Steam Shipbuilding in Scotland, 1812-1850

If the engineers and shipbuilders on the Clyde had done nothing more than build and launch the *Comet* in 1812, their fame would have been assured. But the Scottish contribution to the development of steamship building did not stop there. The data, however, are not easy to interpret.

The returns of tonnage built and first registered in the UK in the *Parliamentary Papers* indicate that between 1814 and 1849 no fewer than 1544 steamships of 202,500 tons were built and first registered in the UK. Porter's breakdown of these data indicates that Scotland contributed 412 (27.5%) of the vessels and 84,800 (41.2%) of the tonnage. By either measure Scottish shipbuilders made a leading contribution.[3]

However, it is not clear how accurate these data are. In a separate compilation of the number and tonnage of steam vessels built and launched on the Clyde, John Strang's data indicate that the Clyde built 309 vessels of 87,700 tons between 1814 and 1849. This is a larger

---

[2]Between 1909 and 1913 the Clyde launched 2.845 million gross tons of merchant vessels, or an average of 569,000 tons per year. At the same time launches of world merchant tonnage totalled 12.455 million tons, or 2.48 million tons annually. The Clyde's contribution averaged 22.8%. Derived from *Lloyds Register of Shipping*, Annual Returns.

[3]G.R. Porter, *The Progress of the Nation* (London, 1851), 316.

tonnage than that indicated for all Scotland in the Parliamentary returns, but over 100 fewer vessels. Since we know that very few steamboats were built outside the Clyde in Scotland, Strang's data, while not dissimilar in tonnage, leaves a large gap in vessels registered. The Parliamentary returns may well reflect tonnage and vessels first registered in Scotland, but not necessarily all constructed there, while Strang's figures are more likely to reflect accurately the actual scale of output on the Clyde. On Strang's data the Clyde delivered 43.3% of UK steam tonnage built to 1849, and twenty percent of the vessels.[4]

Table 3
Place of Build, Wood Steamships, 1810-1849

Percent Share of Tonnage Built and Registered

District	1810-19	1820-29	1830-39	1840-49	1810-49
Thames	14.5	36.9	48.8	31.4	37.5
S Coast	-	3.7	1.2	19.4	11.7
S West	13.1	8.1	1.5	6.4	5.8
N West	4.9	23.1	10.9	7.5	10.2
N East	-	0.8	0.5	-	-
Clyde	67.5	21.0	22.1	29.2	26.4

Source: R.J. Raper, "Register" File, British Shipbuilding History Project, University of Newcastle-upon-Tyne.

We can now go further, however, in examining the Scottish contribution to steamship building before 1850. As part of the History of British Shipbuilding project John Raper, working with Ian Buxton of the University of Newcastle-upon-Tyne, has compiled a computerized twenty percent annual sample of all tonnage registered in Britain from 1810. A preliminary analysis indicates that between 1810 and 1819, two-thirds of steam tonnage emanated from the Clyde. The Thames delivered 14.5%, southwest ports 13.1%, and the northwest of England 4.9%. Thereafter, however, the Clyde's pioneering lead was quickly overtaken (see table 3). In the 1820s the Thames built thirty-seven percent of steam tonnage, followed by the northwest of England with twenty-three percent, while the Clyde held third position with twenty-one percent. In

---

[4]John Strang, "Progress, Extent and Value of Steamboat Building and Marine Engine Making on the Clyde," *Economic and Social Statistics of Glasgow* (Glasgow, 1852).

the 1830s and 1840s the Thames maintained this lead, and together with south coast ports contributed half of all steam tonnage. In the 1830s the Clyde began to reassert its position, edging back to second place; by the 1840s it was nearly on a par with the Thames in total output. Over the entire period, Raper's data suggests that Clyde builders contributed twenty-six percent of steam tonnage, with the Thames the main builder with over thirty-seven percent.

Raper's data also allow us to go further in analysing the Scottish output of steamers before 1851. Based on his sample it is clear that Greenock and Port Glasgow were the dominant centres of steamship building in Scotland: Greenock alone contributed sixty-one percent and Port Glasgow twenty percent. Across the river Dumbarton added another four percent. Over eighty-five percent of all steamboat building on the Clyde was concentrated along its lower reaches, with the yards upriver at Glasgow contributing another ten percent. Less than five percent of these early steamers cannot be specifically attributed to Clyde builders. Indeed, we know that very little steam tonnage was built elsewhere in this period. The Tay experimented with a small steam ferry launched in 1814,[5] but Aberdeen's first steamship did not appear until John Duffus launched his *Queen of Scotland* in 1829.[6] All the east coast builders essentially clung to traditional building rather than turning early to the new experiments in steamboats in which Clyde builders clearly played a pioneering role and laid the basis for the establishment of the new shipbuilding in the west of Scotland.

Iron Shipbuilding in Scotland before 1850

The official data on ships built and first registered in the UK only began to differentiate construction material from 1850. Before that we have to rely upon significant milestones to chart the introduction of iron. While John Wilkinson demonstrated in 1787 that his iron barge would float, fifty years passed before Lloyds' accepted Fairbairn's *Sirius* as the first iron ship on the register.

---

[5]S.G.E. Lythe, "Shipbuilding at Dundee Down to 1914," *Scottish Journal of Political Economy*, IX (1963), 219-233.

[6]Thomas Donnelly, "Shipbuilding in Aberdeen, 1750-1914," *Northern Scotland*, IV (1981), 23-42.

Yet there were some previous experiments with iron. In England Aaron Manby launched his first iron ship in 1822, and his second, *Marquis of Wellesly*, in 1825. On the Mersey, William Laird built his first iron vessel in 1829, followed by John Vernon in 1833. In Scotland Thomas Wilson sailed his horse-drawn iron barge, *Vulcan*, in 1819 on the Monkland Canal. This was followed in 1827 by David Napier's *Aglaia*, a thirty-ton iron steamer which sailed on Loch Eck. In 1831 John Neilson's *Fairy Queen* operated on the Forth and Clyde canal.

All the evidence indicates that iron was a novelty until the 1830s, and was only used seriously in the 1840s. Raper's sample supports this view. He located only one iron-hulled vessel in the 1820s and a mere ten in the 1830s. In the 1840s this rose to seventy-eight vessels of 26,154 tons. Prior to 1849, the sample shows that the Thames, Mersey and Clyde were pioneers in iron construction, with twenty-one, twenty-four and thirty-seven percent shares, respectively. Scotland's lead in iron was even more marked than its dominance in steam before 1850.

Indeed, Raper's data allows us to identify the main Scottish pioneers in iron. While steamboat building had been dominated by Greenock and Port Glasgow, building with iron was pioneered in Glasgow. Govan built over thirty-eight percent of all Scottish iron tonnage before 1849, followed by Scotstoun on the opposite bank of the Clyde with twenty-three percent. The Glasgow yards contributed sixty-five percent of the total, while Greenock and Port Glasgow delivered only twelve percent. Across the firth at Dumbarton, iron building was more significant, with twenty percent of the Scottish total.

Outside the Clyde there was limited iron building. Carmichael's yard at Dundee is reported to have launched three small iron steamers in 1837,[7] while Aberdeen and Kirkcaldy had also built iron vessels before 1850.[8] Nevertheless, as in steam it was the Clyde which took the lead. This is again shown clearly by John Strang's compilations. Between 1846 and 1850, Clyde builders launched 123 iron vessels of 54,235 tons at a time that other rivers were still only experimenting with the material.[9]

---

[7]Lythe, "Shipbuilding at Dundee."

[8]Donnelly, "Shipbuilding in Aberdeen."

[9]Strang, "Progress."

Consolidation, 1850-1870

By the beginning of the 1850s, wood had virtually disappeared in ship
construction on the Clyde. In 1852, for example, only 3229 tons of
wooden steamers were built out of a total of 52,945 tons of new steam
vessels. Strang's data indicate that the Clyde built and launched 285,000
tons of iron vessels between 1851 and 1855.[10] That, however, is the
same figure recorded in the official statistics for all iron tonnage built
and first registered in the UK, implying that the Clyde supplied all the
iron tonnage in Britain in this five-year period, which was not the case.
Indeed, Strang only claimed that Clyde builders provided seventy-six
percent of all iron tonnage launched between 1856 and 1860 and sixty-
two percent from 1861 to 1865. The Clyde certainly led the way, but the
other great shipbuilding rivers soon followed.

Table 4
UK Shipbuilding: District Tonnage, 1871
(Tonnage Completed, Net Tons)

District	Total Tons	%Wood Sail	%Wood Steam	%Iron Sail	%Iron Steam	% Composite
UK	390,838	10.04	0.6	5.1	83.8	0.4
Thames/SE	13,038	33.1	2.7	4.5	57.7	1.9
Humber	28,410	12.7	-	-	87.2	0.1
Tyne	55,398	1.3	1.3	0.4	96.9	-
Wear	73,196	10.2	-	3.4	85.4	1.1
Tees	37,034	1.3	-	3.4	95.2	-
Mersey/NW	28,837	4.7	0.3	12.4	82.5	-
Clyde	115,136	1.8	-	8.5	89.7	-
Forth	1,557	35.8	-	-	64.0	-
Tay	6,090	10.4	11.6	-	78.0	-
Aberdeen/NE	7,314	40.4	4.2	23.7	31.7	-

Source: *BPP* (1872), "Return of the Number and Tonnage of Vessels the Building of
which was Completed in the Year 1871."

By 1871 the Clyde built and launched one-third of all iron
tonnage in the UK and was by far the most important iron shipbuilding
river in Britain. The Wear came next with nearly nineteen percent, the

---

[10]*Ibid.*

Tyne supplied over fifteen percent, and the Tees delivered ten percent. Collectively the three northeast rivers built forty-five percent of UK iron tonnage, exploiting the advantages of local iron suppliers from the expanding Cleveland iron district (see table 4).

The balance between sail and steam tonnage also changed the face of shipbuilding in the main districts by 1871. On the Clyde, ninety percent of output was iron steam, 8.5% iron sail, and only 1.8% was wooden sail. Only the Tees rivalled the Clyde in its virtually complete elimination of wood, while the Wear still had ten percent of its output in wooden sail. While both the Tyne and Tees exceeded the Clyde's proportion of iron and steam construction, by this time the differences were marginal. Steam and iron dominated British shipbuilding.

This generalisation did not apply to Scotland as a whole. On the River Forth thirty-six percent of tonnage built in 1871 was wooden sail, while the figure was 10.4% on the Tay (plus another 11.6% in wooden steamboats). In Aberdeen and the northeast of Scotland nearly forty-five percent of tonnage was still wood and forty percent was sail. The divide was broadly between east and west: the heartland of traditional Scottish building still engaged in considerable wood and sail construction, while on the Clyde steam and iron dominated.[11]

Into the Era of Steel, 1870-1914

The years 1870-1914 represent the peak of Clyde output and leadership. This period was remarkable for three developments: the rapid transition to steel (see table 5); the remarkable resurgence in sail construction on a river that was the cradle of steam; and the introduction of naval building on a river previously dominated by merchant construction.

Steel was used in ship construction from around 1860, but interest developed strongly in the 1870s when the Siemens process assured reliably good-quality steel plate. As the *Dumbarton Herald* observed in November 1880, "the application of steel to shipbuilding purposes has of late commanded a large amount of consideration. It may now be safely asserted that steel is the ship-building material of the future."

---

[11]These data are shown in maps in A. Slaven, "Shipbuilding," in J. Langton and R.J. Morris (eds.), *Atlas of Industrialising Britain* (London, 1986), 132-135.

In the previous year, 1879, the Clyde yards had launched 18,000 tons of steel vessels, 10.3% of the river's output. The UK statistics record only 21,000 tons of steel shipping built that year. By 1884 Clyde steel tonnage was forty-five percent of its output, 133,670 tons, more than the 109,400 tons shown as built and first registered in the UK.[12] Five years later over ninety-seven percent of Clyde output was steel-hulled (about 320,000 tons). By then about ninety percent of new tonnage registered in the UK was steel. The pace of adaptation was remarkable, and was not initially a response to cost, since steel plates were more expensive than iron in the first few years of transition. The superior quality of steel, and the savings in space and weight it enabled, appear to have been the factors which attracted Clyde builders, who specialised in higher quality, high-speed vessels.

Table 5
Summary of Hull Material of Vessels Built
At Scottish Ports, 1850-1909

Percent of Total Tonnage

	West Coast			East Coast		
	Iron %	Wood %	Steel %	Iron %	Wood %	Steel %
1850-59	78.7	20.8	-	3.8	96.2	-
1860-69	91.5	2.5	-	20.4	70.0	-
1870-79	97.8	0.3	1.5	80.1	19.6	-
1880-89	49.0	0.05	50.7	88.8	1.2	10.0
1890-99	-	-	98.5	4.6	0.5	88.7
1900-09	-	-	100.0	0.2	0.9	98.9

Source: See table 3.

But as steel displaced iron, the steel sailing ship made a remarkable recovery on the Clyde, where it was not only a specialty of yards like Russell and Co. and Connell but also an alternative form of building in depressed market conditions.[13] For example, in 1891, when first-class steel steamers were priced between £24-£28 per ton on the

---

[12]B.R. Mitchell and Phyllis Dean (comps.), *Abstract of British Historical Statistics* (Cambridge, 1962), chapter 8.

[13]See A.M. Robb, "Shipbuilding and Marine Engineering," in J. Cunnison and J.B.S. Gilfillan, *Glasgow; Third Statistical Account of Scotland* (Glasgow, 1958), figure 14.

Clyde, steel sailing vessels were priced at £11-£13 per ton.[14] Not surprisingly, in the depression of 1891-1893 steel sail reached peaks of 102,000 tons in 1891 (thirty-one percent of output), 161,000 tons in 1892 (forty-eight percent) and 99,000 tons (thirty-five percent) in 1893. Similar peaks of 40.5% of tonnage were achieved between 1875-1877, and over one-third of tonnage in 1886. Yet after the prodigious outpouring of steel sailing vessels in the early 1890s, this type of production virtually vanished. By 1900 only three percent of Clyde-built tonnage was steel sail, a level maintained until 1914 (see table 6).

Table 6
Share of Sail/Steam Tonnage in Construction

	West of Scotland %		East of Scotland %		Scotland %		UK %	
	Sail	Steam	Sail	Steam	Sail	Steam	Sail	Steam
1850-59	25.1	74.8	97.9	2.1	42.8	57.2	77.6	22.4
1860-69	35.3	63.9	84.1	15.9	43.2	56.2	54.1	45.9
1870-79	29.1	70.4	36.9	63.0	30.0	70.0	31.9	68.1
1880-89	18.2	80.2	10.0	89.9	17.3	81.3	22.0	78.0
1890-99	20.8	78.6	16.9	83.1	20.4	79.6	16.1	83.9
1900-09	3.4	96.6	-	100.0	3.1	96.9	5.5	94.5

Source: *Statistical Abstract of the United Kingdom*; Raper, "Register."

The third factor which characterised the period of Clyde ascendancy was the increasing share of warshipbuilding undertaken by the larger yards. Before the 1890s, the Royal Dockyards supplied the largest part of the tonnage required by the Royal Navy, but thereafter the growing desire for defence and the dreadnought competition with Germany pushed Admiralty orders increasingly into private yards. Between 1859 and 1889 private yards built 237 vessels of 861,237 tons for the Admiralty; the Clyde built fifty of 124,169 tons (14.4%), a mere two percent of merchant output on the river in these years. But between 1890 and 1914 naval building assumed greater importance. The Clyde built 162 naval vessels of 793,500 tons for the Admiralty, about twenty-six percent of all the work placed in private yards and equivalent to 7.6% of merchant tonnage delivered by the Clyde yards. The pace of

---

[14]*Dumbarton Herald*, 6 May 1891.

production fluctuated widely, but in 1910-1913 naval construction represented around ten percent of all Clyde output, and even more by value.[15]

In 1913 the Clyde launched 370 ships of 756,976 gross tons, an average of just over 2000 tons per vessel; in the 1870s the average was somewhat less than 1000 tons. Total output had grown from 180,000 tons, more than a four-fold increase in forty years. Within that period the east coast yards had been overwhelmed by the Clyde and now contributed less than ten percent--often less than five percent--of Scottish output. These remarkable achievements reflect the enterprise and inventiveness of the shipbuilders and marine engineers. It is to that contribution that we now turn.

Figure 1: The *Greenock* iron steam-frigate.

Source: *Illustrated London News*, 12 May 1849.

Enterprise and Innovation in Scottish Shipbuilding

Scotland's fame in shipbuilding is dominated by the reputation of the Clyde builders and engineers, and it is certainly in marine engineering in engines and boilers that the Scots made highly significant contributions to the development of modern shipbuilding. But the resilience of the sailing ship, and its continued importance, especially in the east coast

---

[15]Hugh B. Peebles, "Warshipbuilding on the Clyde, 1889-1939: A Financial Study" (Unpublished PhD thesis, University of Stirling, 1986), appendix E.

yards, was also based on notable Scottish contributions to the design of the traditional sailing vessel.

It is well known that the Tonnage Laws of 1772 and 1775 contributed to conservatism in the design of British sailing vessels. With the exclusion of depth from the calculations, and the significance of tonnage to port dues, British shipowners and builders concentrated on slow, narrow and deep craft. As a result, design and construction fell increasingly behind French and North American builders. But a revision to the laws in 1835, and a tidying up of registration in the new *Lloyds Register* from 1834, encouraged new approaches. Increasing competition also pressured owners to seek larger and faster vessels from British yards.

The most significant contribution by Scottish builders to this search for new lines came from Alexander Hall of Aberdeen, who redesigned his vessels with a fine sharp bow, known generally as the "Aberdeen bow," first introduced the *Scottish Maid* in 1839.[16] By the 1840s his ideas were being copied by other Aberdeen builders, such as Walter Hood and John Duthie. Soon the Stephen family introduced the idea at their Arbroath and Dundee yards.[17] It was quickly noted that Hall's schooners did well in competition with American rivals, and following the repeal of the Navigation Acts their reputation attracted orders for clippers from London and Liverpool. The Aberdeen and Dundee builders then entered upon a golden phase of wood and sail building in the great era of the clippers from the 1850s to about 1870.

Even on the Clyde, where steam was the main interest, there were important refinements in clippers in the 1850s and 1860s. Scott of Greenock, established in 1711 and the oldest shipbuilding firm in the world, built fine sailing vessels, but the most noted yard belonged to Robert Steele of Greenock, along with others like Henderson, Russell, Reid and Rodger. At the end of the clipper era, the short-lived Scott and Lynton of Dumbarton (1868-70) designed and built the *Cutty Sark*, which with the Aberdeen-built *Thermopylae*, was among the clippers that challenged time and endurance records on long-haul routes.[18]

---

[16]H.M. Carnegie, "Aberdeen Ships & Shipbuilders, 1839-1980," *Aberdeen University Review*, LVII (1977-1978).

[17]Donnelly, "Shipbuilding in Aberdeen."

[18]See F.M. Walker, *Song of the Clyde* (Cambridge, 1984), chapter 5.

Figure 2: The composite clipper ship *Cutty Sark*, a product of Clyde shipbuilding.

Source: Courtesy of the Trustees of the National Museums and Galleries on Merseyside.

Figure 3: Torchlight Launch of the iron screw-steamer *Azoff* in the Clyde.

Source: *Illustrated London News*, 11 August 1855.

The same skills that produced the great schooners--first in wood and then in iron--were quickly transferred to building large four-masted steel sailing barques in the 1880s and 1890s. Here Russell and Co. and Charles Connel and Co. were supreme, bringing to the Clyde a belated but well-deserved reputation for the design and building of great sailing vessels. Important as these contributions were, they were essentially a declining side show to the main activity in metal and steam, and it was there that the "Clyde-built" reputation was forged by the marine engineers.

Innovation and Enterprise in Marine Engineering

The Clyde, and Scotland's, contribution to nineteenth-century building in steam essentially focuses on three main innovations from which flowed innumerable refinements. The first was the commercial application of steam to power vessels, first exemplified in the *Comet*; the second was the commercial exploitation and technical development of compound expansion with its consequences for economy; and the third was the steady improvement in boiler design, best exemplified in Howden's Scotch boiler.

Although Henry Bell's *Comet* marked the true beginning of steamship building on the Clyde, William Symington and Patrick Miller were reported to have sailed a double-hulled paddle steamer on Dalswinton Loch in 1788.[19] Moreover, the *Charlotte Dundas*, also engineered and designed by Symington, steamed on the Forth and Clyde Canal in March 1803, but was rejected by the Canal proprietors who feared that the wake would damage the banks. Consequently, the commercial inception of steam navigation was delayed until Bell commissioned John and Charles Wood of Port Glasgow to build his *Comet*, the engines being supplied by John Robertson from Glasgow and the boiler by David Napier.[20] What these men demonstrated was that a successful steamboat could be assembled by combining the expertise of engineers, boiler-makers, and traditional wooden shipbuilders. What they did, others imitated and improved. Between 1812 and 1814 steamers were con-

---

[19]*Ibid.*, chapter 2; John Shields, *Clydebuilt, A History of Shipbuilding on the Clyde* (Glasgow, 1949), 25.

[20]Shields, *Clydebuilt*, 27.

structed at Leeds, Manchester and Bristol, as well as on the Humber and
the Thames. In Scotland, early steamboat building spread to the Tay,
where James Smart launched *Tay* and *Caledonia* in 1814.[21]

On the Clyde, imitation and improvement was very rapid.
Between 1812 and 1820 no fewer than forty-two steamers totalling 3200
tons were constructed.[22] The main builders were John and Charles
Wood and John Hunter of Port Glasgow; Archibald MacLachlan and
William Denny at Dumbarton; and James Munn at Greenock. The
engines were supplied principally by D. MacArthur, James Cook,
George Dobie, John Thomson, and John Robertson, together with the
Greenhead Foundry Company. Without exception these engineers were
located in the Tradeston and Camlachie districts in Glasgow, close to the
expanding textile factories which provided most of their market.

Most boilers came from the Napier Works. Indeed, the Napiers
proved to be an extraordinarily innovative family in the early years of
marine engineering and steam shipbuilding on the Clyde.[23] David
Napier was in fact the first to integrate engine making and hull construction in a single firm. He had several hulls built to take his own engines,
including *Active* and *Despatch* in 1817 and *Rob Roy* in 1818. Built by
Denny at Dumbarton, it was the first steamer to cross the open sea from
the Clyde to Belfast. In 1821 Napier established his own yard at
Lancefield, where he soon confronted the problems of the low efficiency
and reliability of early marine steam engines.

Napier's first design contribution was a wedge-shaped bow, first
incorporated in *Rob Roy*. Then, when confronted by the fuel hunger of
the early engines, which operated with boiler pressures of two lbs. per
square inch (psi) or less, he patented an improved version of James
Watt's surface condenser in 1821. But this was not used extensively
because of its complexity and expense. A more significant improvement
came in 1830 when David Napier's cousin, James, introduced his
haystack tubular boiler, which saved space and cut coal consumption by
about twenty-five percent; this became a popular engine for river
steamers. Five years later, David Napier introduced his steeple engine,

---

[21]Lythe, "Shipbuilding at Dundee."

[22]John Strang, *Economic and Social Statistics of Glasgow* (Glasgow, 1855).

[23]Shields, *Clydebuilt*, 35-52.

which improved upon the old side-levered type by dispensing with the spurred cogs.

Although David Napier moved to London the following year, the family's innovative role was continued by his cousins Robert and James. The various Napier engine shops and shipyard became the training grounds for many of the Clyde's most noted engineers and shipbuilders. The Lancefield works were managed by David Tod and John McGregor before they set up as independent engineers in 1834 and shipbuilders from 1836. Robert Napier's Camlachie works were managed by James Thomson, later joined by his brother George; they later set up as the shipbuilders J. and G. Thomson at Mavisbank in 1847. When the Napiers acquired the Parkhead Forge in the 1840s, one of the managers imported from London was William Beardmore. The Elders, father David and son John, also trained with the Napiers, as did Charles Randolph, William Pearce and A.C. Kirk. Robert Napier also diversified into shipowning and was involved in founding the forerunner of Cunard in 1839; he also designed and built the line's first four steamers.[24]

Although the Napiers began the search for economy in engines and boilers, the crucial advance came from two men who had worked for them for a time, Charles Randolph and John Elder. The principle of expanding steam successively in two cylinders had been applied to land-based engines since the early nineteenth century. Arthur Woolf had demonstrated an early form of compound expansion in 1804 and marine versions had been tried in Europe and America. But it was Randolph and Elder who patented a marine compound expansion engine in 1853 and fitted out *Brandon* with the new engine the following year. Randolph and Elder claimed that their new engine reduced coal consumption by up to forty percent, cutting the normal consumption of 4.5 lbs. per horsepower hour to about three pounds. Trial notes indicated that *Brandon* consumed 3.25 lbs. of coal per horsepower hour, a saving of around thirty percent.[25] Even though this was less than predicted, it was sufficient to establish the men's reputations. The demand for their engine encouraged

---

[24]The network of talent emanating from the Napiers was duplicated by the contribution made by the Scotts of Greenock and the Dennys of Dumbarton, and is illustrative of the multiplier effect of innovations and enterprise that characterised shipbuilding and marine engineering on the Clyde in the nineteenth century.

[25]Stephen of Linthouse Papers, University of Glasgow Business Record Collection (UGBRC), Stephen to Randolph Elder and Company, 8 February 1859, UGD 4/1/1.

them to found their own yard in 1860 and they quickly became a major force in Clyde shipbuilding. The Pacific Steam Navigation Co. was quick to appreciate the potential of the compound engine and established a long connection with the new firm.

The full benefits of the compound engine needed higher operating pressures than existing boilers could deliver. In 1862 a Glasgow engineer, James Howden, introduced his tank or cylindrical boiler, which with iron plates could deliver forty lbs. psi and soon achieved eighty lbs., thus enabling the engine to achieve the full economies sought by Randolph and Elder.[26] The "Scotch" boiler, together with the compound engine, was rapidly fitted to steamers plying routes to the Far East and Australia after the opening of the Suez Canal in 1869. About one-third of British merchant vessels were powered by compound engines in 1871; by 1875 three-fourths relied on engines based upon Randolph and Elder's innovation.[27]

The logical step to triple and quadruple-expansion engines also occupied the energies of Clyde engineers. The first successful triple-expansion engine was designed by A.C. Kirk at Elder and Co. and installed in *Propontis* in 1874. This was linked not to a Scotch boiler but to the more temperamental water tube boiler which operated at up to 150 psi as opposed to the eighty common in compound engines. Nearly a decade passed, however, before Kirk linked his triple-expansion engine to a modified Scotch boiler employing steel plates and a forced draught. This delivered higher pressures more reliably than water tube boilers and was installed in 1882 in *Aberdeen*. This was a dramatic breakthrough, cutting consumption by another twenty percent, and Kirk's triple-expansion engine linked to the improved Scotch boiler rapidly became the standard engine and boiler arrangement for merchant ships, further securing the Clyde's reputation. A quadruple-expansion engine was patented by Walter Brock at Denny in 1888, but was employed in only the largest cargo vessels.[28]

---

[26]J. Ravenhill, "Twenty Minutes with Our Commercial Steam Fleet in 1877," *Transactions of the Institute of Naval Architects*, XVIII (1877), 283.

[27]*Ibid.*, 281, 284.

[28]A. Slaven, *The Economic Development of the West of Scotland* (London, 1975), 178-180.

The other significant marine engine inventions in the period were the turbine and the diesel.[29] Neither originated on the Clyde, but both were quickly produced under licence and in the normal manner of marine engineering adapted and improved. Charles Parsons patented his direct-acting steam turbine in 1884, but did not set up his own company until 1894. The earliest applications were for naval vessels, but in an attempt to penetrate the merchant market Parsons turned to the Clyde. In 1901 he joined with William Denny and Bros. of Dumbarton and a Clyde steamship owner, Captain John Williamson, to establish the Turbine Steamer Syndicate to finance a turbine-driven steamer. The result was Denny's *King Edward*, which in 1901 became the world's first turbine-powered merchantman. Denny's early enterprise paid rich dividends, the company building no fewer than seventeen turbine-powered ships between 1901 and 1906.

Clydeside enterprise was also quick off the mark with the new diesel engine, patented in 1892 by Rudolph Diesel. The first marine application came in 1910 when two small vessels were built in Holland and Italy, but it was not applied to larger ocean-going ships until 1911, when the East Asiatic Co. of Copenhagen commissioned sister ships from Burmeister and Wain in Copenhagen and Barclay Curle and Co. on the Clyde. The *Selandia* was launched by Burmeister and Wain in 1911, quickly followed by *Jutlandia* in 1912 from Barclay Curle. After a century of steam, the motorship had come to the Clyde. But this did not open a new century of leadership as had the *Comet* in 1812.

The Clyde builders were first in the field with the steamship, and with compound expansion. They were not first with iron, nor with the screw; they did not make the breakthrough with the turbine or the diesel, but they were without exception in the vanguard of innovation throughout the nineteenth century, and it was this quick enterprise as much as initial invention which cultivated the Clyde's leadership in developing modern shipbuilding in Scotland, and in Britain generally. The consequent explosion in production had profound consequences for the structure of the industry and its firms.

---

[29]A. Slaven, "Modern British Shipbuilding," in L.A. Ritchie (ed.), *The Shipbuilding Industry: A Guide to Historical Records* (Manchester, 1992), 7-8. See also Walker, *Song of the Clyde*, chapters 11 and 16.

The Structure of the Industry

At the beginning of the nineteenth century Scottish shipbuilding was small-scale, with many short-lived enterprises entering and exiting with the cycles of local demand for small wooden vessels. The capital equipment in the early yards would commonly have included rudimentary slipways, basic timber "poles" or scaffolding, some large saws, saw pits and steam boxes, bolt cutters and augers, and perhaps in larger establishments shear legs.

At the end of the Napoleonic Wars Scottish output was around 11,000 net tons and average vessel size would have been around 100 tons. We have no clear evidence on the number of yards in operation, but on the Clyde there were about seventeen builders in operation by 1820 with an average staff of under fifty men.[30] Aberdeen had seven firms of similar size, Dundee three, and on the Forth there were yards at Leith, Grangemouth and Perth, as well as at smaller ports on the Angus and Fife coasts.[31] Few of the yards were of long-standing. Scott in Greenock was exceptional in its continuity.

What we know about the capitalisation of these early yards is largely conjecture. When Alexander Stephen acquired his dead brother's Arbroath establishment in 1830, it had twenty-seven employees and was valued at £505.[32] This scale was typical of the early single proprietor, family, and partnership firms.

It was possible for the small yards to operate with limited capital because of the nature of the industry. The yards and slipways were not normally owned, but rented on short leases. Timber was purchased by bills of exchange or sometimes supplied by the shipowner. Cash flow depended on commercial credit and on payments from the shipowner during construction. These instalments varied widely from place to place and with the condition of the market. In buoyant markets the builder could expect an advance of one-third of the contract price when the ship was framed; a second equal instalment was due when the vessel was launched; and the final payment was generally made at variable periods

---

[30]Walker, *Song of the Clyde*, appendix 3.

[31]Donnelly, "Shipbuilding in Aberdeen;" Lythe, "Shipbuilding at Dundee."

[32]UGBRC, Stephen Papers, 14 January 1820, UGD 4/16/1.

of three to nine months after the launch. When trade was less buoyant cash payments were often replaced by bills or combinations of bills and cash. It was not unknown for a builder to accept an old vessel in partial payment for a new one, the builder then being left with the problem of realising the capital value of the asset by selling it. In extreme cases, builders were forced to operate such vessels on charter.

In this type of environment it was common for shipbuilders to decline to the status of shipwright or advance to the position of ship-owner. Building "on speculation" was also not uncommon as builders sought to keep slipways busy. This was not as risky as it might seem, for in the first half of the century shipbuilders catered largely for a local market whose elements were well understood. Moreover, many early builders were highly mobile, visiting ports throughout the nation in search of innovations in design and construction and market information.

When steam arrived on the scene, it at first made little impact on these traditional and well-established arrangements. The engine and boiler were simply more parts to be assembled by the experienced ship-wrights. The functional separation of shipyard, engine work and boilership, and integration of these specialties into a single more complex firm came only slowly. However, there were a number of large integrated establishments on the Clyde by the 1850s. Robert Napier, Tod and McGregor, and William Denny and Bros. all combined engine works and shipyards, and were already large employers; so also were J. and G. Thomson and Caird and Co. Tod and McGregor employed up to 1900 men; Robert Napier and Co., 1600; and J. and G. Thomson, 1700.[33] By then there were no fewer than twenty iron shipyards on the Clyde and another dozen still building in wood. For those yards, the majority, which did not supply their own engines, specialist suppliers like Napier and Caird, and Elder, had emerged by the 1850s.

While the Clyde shipbuilders were increasingly turning to iron and steam in the 1850s, the Dundee yards turned their attention to wood and sail catering to the shipping needs of the local companies importing jute and increasingly catering to the developing whaling industry.[34] The

---

[33]*Dumbarton Herald*, 23 September 1858.

[34]Lythe, "Shipbuilding at Dundee."

Stephens set up in Dundee in 1843,[35] and the Gourlays established themselves first in the iron founding business in 1841, and added marine engineering in 1853 and shipbuilding a year later. They quickly became the largest yard in Dundee and pioneered steel and steam on the Tay. In Aberdeen the well-established firms, such as Hall, John Duffus, John Vernon and Walter Hood, continued to dominate shipbuilding. Judging from the tonnage levels produced on the Tay and Dee, where the main yards were capable of building vessels up to 1000 tons in the 1850s, the larger yards might by then have been employing in excess of 200 men.[36]

As iron became the main construction material from the 1850s, the yards that were determined to grow had to face quite new levels of capital requirement. When the Stephen family decided to embark on iron and steam building in 1850, and to open a yard on the Clyde by leasing premises at Kelvinhaugh, their initial outlay, according to a valuation in 1857, was around £9000.[37] The landlord had also just completed extensions and improvements to the slipways totalling another £9000. Consequently the capital investment for the yard was around £18,000, together with an annual rental of £1244. This was in fact a relatively modest establishment. In 1855 John Scott offered to sell his iron shipyard and timber pond to the Greenock Harbour Trust, which was keen to enhance its growing dock and ship facilities. The offer price was £30,000, but the deal fell through because of problems regarding some title deeds. A little later, when John Scott and Sons was in liquidation in 1861, its iron shipyard was sold for £15,000 and its wood shipyard and drydock for £30,000. The yards and engineering works then employed about 480 men. Across the river at Dumbarton, William Denny valued his establishment in 1859 at £50,000, with a further £87,000 invested in shipping.[38] It seems likely that larger Clyde yards were valued at around £50,000 in the 1850s, medium yards at £20-30,000, and smaller establishments at half that level again.

---

[35]UGBRC, Stephen Papers, "Remarks for 1842," UGD 4/16/2; "Commenced first new vessel in Dundee," 1 June 1843, UGD 4/16/2.

[36]Lythe, "Shipbuilding at Dundee;" Donnelly, "Shipbuilding in Aberdeen."

[37]UGBRC, Stephen Papers, 1 September 1857, UGD 4/18/7.

[38]UGBRC, Denny Papers, Journal, 1 June 1859, UGD 3.

By the 1870s the investment required for the largest iron shipyards was on the order of £200-300,000. Tod and MacGregor's Meadowside yard was purchased in 1872 by the shipowners Handyside and Henderson for £200,000.[39] In 1878, in the depths of a depression, Robert Napier's great yard and engine works was purchased by A.C. Kirk and J.S. Hamilton for £270,000.[40] Since these were the largest establishments, linking their sale prices to their average production levels and comparing them with other Clyde yards in the 1870s indicates that about ten must have been worth more than £150,000; a further eight would have been in the £60-£100,000 range; and the remaining twenty were probably valued in the range of £30,000-£50,000. The total capital investment in Clyde yards was about £3 million in the early 1870s.

By the end of the century the growth in scale and complexity of the industry had extended values four or five-fold. When John Brown of Sheffield acquired the Clydebank shipyard formerly operated by J. and G. Thomson in 1899, the purchase price was £923,255.[41] In 1902 the Scotts employed capital of £389,000 at Greenock, while at Port Glasgow the Lithgow/Russell yards had capital assets in excess of £700,000 and the Fairfield Shipbuilding Company was capitalised at £500,000.[42] At the same time William Beardmore acquired the old Napier yard and then established an entirely new naval and liner yard at Dalmuir, next to John Brown's. When completed in 1907 the total cost of Dalmuir was £923,036.

The most highly capitalised yards were clearly the great liner and warship building establishments, and it was the need for large capitals to enter the market that profoundly changed the character of Scottish shipyards, especially on the Clyde, from the 1880s. The family and partnership basis of the industry was greatly changed as large public limited companies came into being. Elder and Co. became the Fairfield Shipbuilding and Engineering Co. Robert Napier also took public status shortly before being acquired by Beardmore, which in turn took a public

---

[39]*Glasgow Herald*, 20 January 1872.

[40]S. Pollard, "The Economic History of British Shipbuilding 1870-1914" (Unpublished PhD thesis, University of London, 1950), 214.

[41]UGBRC, John Brown and Co. Papers, UCS 1/3/6.

[42]Peebles, "Warshipbuilding on the Clyde," appendix G.

company form in 1902. More significantly, the dominantly local control and ownership was penetrated by English-controlled armaments combines. John Brown and Co. of Sheffield acquired the Clydebank yard in 1899, making it essentially the shipbuilding division of a vertically-integrated coal, metal, engineering and armaments combine. William Beardmore engaged in the same process in acquiring Robert Napier's yard and then embarking on the Dalmuir venture. Beardmore was only able to pursue this course by having half its assets acquired by Vickers Sons and Maxim. By 1904 the Fairfield Company had linked with Cammell Laird and Co. and John Brown and Co. to establish the Coventry Ordnance Works, a syndicate to promote naval sales to foreign governments. Attracted to the new armaments complex developing on Clydeside, Alfred Yarrow and Co. removed from Poplar to Scotstoun, setting up its new yard there between 1906 and 1908.

Outside the armaments sector, merger was also in the air. Swan Hunter and Wigham Richardson and Co., itself the outcome of a merger in 1903, acquired the Clyde yard of Barclay Curle and Co. in 1912; the same year Harland and Wolff spread its wings from Belfast to acquire the London and Glasgow Engineering and Iron Shipbuilding Company. On the east coast some of the much smaller companies had also become public. By 1900 all three Dundee yards--Caledon, Gourlay and Dundee Shipbuilders Co.--had gone public. By contrast, at Aberdeen all four companies--Russell and Co., Alexander Hall and Co., John Duthie and Co., and John Duthie of Torry and Co.--remained unincorporated. Similarly, on the Forth partnerships prevailed at the five main yards, the largest of which was Ramage and Ferguson of Leith.

On the eve of the First World War, the great family dynasties still remained prominent in Scottish shipbuilding, generally as partnerships or single-proprietorships. These included Scott of Greenock, Lithgow of Port Glasgow, Denny of Dumbarton, Stephens of Linthouse, A. and J. Ingles of Pointhouse, and the smaller companies on the Forth and Dee. But the old pattern had been transformed by public companies like Fairfield, John Brown, Beardmore, Barclay Curle, and smaller firms on the Tay. The structure and scale of the industry had clearly changed, but irrespective of scale, all the companies were marked by strong individualism, aggressive competitiveness, and a conviction that each was the keeper of Scotland's reputation for quality and excellence.

Shipbuilding in Ireland in the Nineteenth Century

Michael S. Moss[1]

Ship and boatbuilding around the Irish coasts have long histories. Nearly every harbour had shipwrights, who constructed curraghs, brigantines, schooners, smacks, barques and galliots from local wood. As in other parts of the United Kingdom, each region of Ireland had distinctive craft: Donegal, Galway and Kinsale hookers, gleotogs and poucans; Wexford cots; Greencastle yawls; Dublin herring boats; and a variety of sloops, cutters and yawls. These vessels, typically between twenty-eight and forty tons, were used for fishing, coasting and Irish Sea trades. By the beginning of the nineteenth century there were shipbuilding or repair yards at Ballyrain, Baltimore, Belfast, Clare, Coleraine, Cork, Donagha-dee, Dublin, Dundalk, Galway, Killibeg, Kinsale, Larne, Limerick, Londonderry, Newport, Newry, Ross, Sligo, Strangford, Tralee, Waterford, Wexford, Wicklow, and Youghall. A few were well-established, such as the Waterford yard founded by Ambrose Congreve in 1737. Several were operated by shipbuilder/shipowners, like Devereux of Wexford, Mahony of Dungarven, McCarthy (later O'Keeffe) of Youghall, Russell of Limerick and Daniel Sweeney of Galway.[2]

In UK terms the Irish shipbuilding industry was small. Between 1788 and 1811 the number and tonnage of vessels constructed scarcely changed; if anything, the trend was downward (see table 1). In 1788 thirty-eight vessels totalling 1670 tons were built; in 1811 there were twenty-one with a total tonnage of 1331. Some years had greater activity, such as 1789-1792 (the opening years of the French Revolution) and

[1]The author would like to thank Rodney McCullough of Harland and Wolff and Michael McCaughan of the Ulster Folk and Transport Museum for their assistance in the preparation of this essay.

[2]Roger Finch, *Sailing Craft of the British Isles* (Glasgow, 1976), 118; Ernest B. Anderson, *Sailing Ships of Ireland* (reprint, Dublin, 1986), 257, 277, 278; Great Britain, Parliament, House of Commons, *Parliamentary Papers* (*BPP*), XIII (1806), 729.

Research in Maritime History, No. 4 (June 1993), 177-195.

1803-1804 (the resumption of war with France after the short-lived Peace of Amiens). The number of craft owned in Ireland rose by just 110, from 1016 in 1788 to 1126 in 1810, while total tonnage actually fell, from 60,776 to 58,646.

Table 1
Number and Tonnage of Ships Built and Owned
in Ireland, 1788-1811

Date	Built		Owned	
	Number	Tonnage	Number	Tonnage
1788	38	1670	1016	60776
1789	72	2760	1080	64361
1790	73	3163	1134	68236
1791	50	2334	1176	69230
1792	51	2464	1193	69567
1793	42	1629	1181	67791
1794	35	1659	1166	65164
1795	32	1441	1099	58778
1796	33	1654	1078	56575
1797	32	1802	1048	53181
1798	19	797	1025	49987
1799	20	1072	999	49825
1800	18	1105	1003	54262
1801	22	1680	1004	54242
1802	21	1385	1030	56510
1803	37	2324	1065	58871
1804	42	2418	1061	58060
1805	38	1611	1067	55755
1806	28	1212	1076	55545
1807	41	1687	1098	56902
1808	33	1838	1104	58958
1809	32	1235	1119	61150
1810	31	1643	1126	58646
1811	21	1331		

Source: United Kingdom, Parliament, House of Commons, *Parliamentary Papers (BPP)*, V (1810-1811), 229.

Yet these bald statistics disguise the success of the Belfast Ballast Board, which was responsible for the River Lagan waterway, in encouraging shipbuilding on the river. In 1791 the Board invited William

Ritchie, a shipbuilder from Saltcoats in Ayrshire, to open a yard at Auld Lime Kiln dock. The business equalled expectations and in 1807 his brother Hugh opened his own yard nearby.[3] In 1810 William Ritchie wrote that "since the commencement I have built thirty-two vessels and my brother eight, besides several lighters and small ones. The vessels I have built were from fifty to 450 tons burthen, the greatest part about 220 tons."[4] Almost certainly it was these larger vessels that explained the higher output in 1803-1804.

Irish builders, like those elsewhere in the UK, were quick to begin experimenting with steam power, following Henry Bell's successful innovation on the Clyde. The first steamer built in Ireland was constructed by Andrew and Michael Hennessy at Passage, County Cork, in 1815-1816, with engines supplied by Boulton and Watt of Birmingham. The second steamboat, built at Passage the following year, was engined by T.A. Barney of Cork. Yet it was not for another five years before the first steamer was built in Belfast, with an engine supplied by the local firm of Coates and Young of the Lagan Foundry. Despite this early interest in steam, shipbuilding remained small-scale, largely because Ireland lacked the raw materials to sustain advances in marine engineering. In 1832 twenty-five vessels of over fifty tons were built, totalling 1909 gross tons, and fifteen of less than fifty tons. By this time a number of larger yards had been established. In Belfast William Ritchie's yard was sold in 1820 to a fellow Scot, Charles Connell, and renamed Charles Connell and Sons in 1824. After a similar takeover four years later the other Ritchie yard was rechristened Alexander McLaine and Sons. Among the vessels over fifty tons built in 1832 was the 310-ton tea clipper *Fairy*, launched from the Connell yard. At Cork George Robinson and Co. established the Waterside Dockyards in 1830 and built the steamer *Cork Screw* in 1835 for the Cork-Liverpool service. At Londonderry in 1830 Pitt Skipton invested £4000 in a patent slip, which was taken over in 1835 by Captain William Coppin. Under his direction the yard specialized in sailing ships for the London and China trades. At about the same time a Waterford yard was established by Pope and Co.,

---

[3]Michael Moss and John R. Hume, *Shipbuilders to the World--125 Years of Harland and Wolff, Belfast 1861-1986* (Belfast, 1986), 1-5.

[4]Quoted in Denis Rebbeck, *Presidential Address on Belfast Shipyards 1791-1947* (Belfast, 1947), 5-6.

shipowners and merchants, to build sailing vessels for its trade to continental Europe.[5]

Following the lead of the Clyde, Irish builders began to diversify into iron in the 1840s. Lecky and Beale built the first iron steamer at Cork in 1845. Malcomsen and Son opened the Neptune Iron Works at Waterford in 1847, the same year launching its first vessel, *Neptune*, which inaugurated the steamer service between London and St. Petersburg. Three years later Ebenezer Pike founded the Cork Steamship Company to build iron ships. Despite these developments the number and tonnage of vessels remained small: twenty-four ships of 2695 tons in 1853. That year, however, marked a turning point in Irish shipbuilding with the opening of an iron shipyard in Belfast by Robert Hickson on the newly-constructed Queen's Island, following the deepening and straightening of the Lagan by the Ballast Board. Hickson was a Liverpool merchant with close links to that city's shipowning community. His first contract was for a 1289-ton wooden sailing ship for Edward Bates of Liverpool. In 1854 Edward James Harland, a Yorkshireman trained on the Tyne, was appointed shipyard manager. The following year Hickson's Belfast Iron Works collapsed and he was only allowed to retain control of the yard with the agreement of his creditors. Edward Harland engaged Gustav Wilhelm Wolff as his personal assistant in 1857.[6]

Harland took over control of the yard in 1858, trading under the name of Edward James Harland and Co. He was encouraged to take this decision by Wolff's uncle, Gustav Schwabe, to whom he was also distantly related. Schwabe was a partner in the Liverpool firm of John Bibby and Sons, which at once placed an order for three iron steamers which incorporated a theory developed by Harland since his time as a journeyman with the firm of J. and G. Thomson on the Clyde. These vessels would take advantage of:

---

[5]Letter from Robert J. Lecky, 19 December 1894, in *Journal of the Cork Historical & Archaeological Society* (1895); Anderson, *Sailing Ships of Ireland*, 236, 240, 246-247, 257-258; *Belfast Newsletter*, 21 March 1820; *BPP*, XXXIII (1833), 501; Moss and Hume, *Shipbuilders to the World*, 4.

[6]Moss and Hume, *Shipbuilders to the World*, 12-17; Anderson, *Sailing Ships of Ireland*, 236-238, 262; *BPP*, LII (1854-1855).

the greater carrying power and accommodation, both for cargo and passengers, that would be given by constructing the new vessels of increased length without any increase in the beam...The result was that I was allowed to settle the dimensions and the following were decided upon, length 310 feet, beam 34 feet, depth of hold 24 feet 9 inches, all of which were fully compensated for by making the upper deck entirely of iron. In this way the hull of the ship was converted into a box girder of increased strength.

Their rigging was equally unique, with pole masts, fore-and-aft rigs, and steam winches and braces for all the bearing lifts to reduce crew size. They were nicknamed "coffin ships" because of their distinctive shape. The connection with Schwabe played a significant role in the development and expansion of the business, which from the outset specialized in cargo/passenger liners.[7]

Table 2
Steamships Built in Ireland, 1853-1861

	Number	Tonnage
1853	24	2695
1854	53	9512
1855	42	10123
1856	44	7564
1857	39	6178
1858	46	4409
1859	43	7326
1860	42	11582
1861	31	9629

Source: *BPP*, XCVIII (1852-1853); LII (1854-1855); LI (1854-1855); LVI (1856); XXXV (1857); LIV (1857-1858); XXVIII (1859); LXIV (1860); LXI (1861); LVI (1862).

---

[7]E.J. Harland, "Shipbuilding in Belfast—Its Origins and Progress," in S.G. Smiles (ed.), *Men of Invention and Industry* (London, 1884), 288-290; Moss and Hume, *Shipbuilders to the World*, 11-18.

Figure 1: Harland and Wolff *Olympic* and *Titanic* under construction.

Source: Courtesy of Ulster Folk and Transport Museum.

Figure 2: Launch of *Olympic* at Harland and Wolff's yard.

Source: See figure 1.

Elsewhere in Ireland the industry was also expanding. By 1854 Ebenezer Pike employed 370 men at Cork, building in that year two steamers of 754 and 412 tons. In the same year William Brown and Co., which opened at Passage in 1850, constructed two full-rigged ships of 456 and 451 tons. Brown operated two large graving docks which had cost a reported £100,000. Robinson and Co.'s Waterside Dockyards began building the first iron barques in Ireland in 1855. At Waterford Albert White and Co. installed a patent slip in 1853, building a series of full-rigged ships before collapsing in 1856. Malcolmsen's Neptune Iron Works employed over 100 men by the end of the decade and had won contracts from continental Europe. By contrast, shipbuilding on the Foyle ceased with the closure of the Coppin yard in 1846.[8] The smaller yards, scattered around the coast, continued to build wooden fishing and coasting vessels. As a result of the welter of activity, output of steamers soared to 10,123 tons in 1855 and never fell below 4409 tons for the remainder of the decade (table 2).

From 1859 Harland and Wolff challenged Cork's dominant position by constructing two ships totalling 3000 tons--forty percent of Irish steamer production (see figure 3). Within a year the firm employed "one thousand workmen in the various branches of the fast expanding business." In 1863 it delivered seven vessels totalling 4554 tons out of a total Irish output of nine iron ships of 5987 tons. George Robinson at Cork shared in the boom of the early 1860s with a series of fast paddle steamers and tugs. Strong demand encouraged Walpole and Webb in 1864 to open Dublin's first large yard for iron sailing ships and paddle steamers. The recession after the American Civil War hit Irish shipbuilding hard. Harland and Wolff traded at a loss in 1865 and was only rescued by an order from John Bibby and Sons for three 3000-ton "coffin" steamers, based on its success with the first order. But the downturn was fatal for many of those which lacked a close family relationship with a large customer. George Robinson and Co. stopped building in 1869, converting its facilities to ship repair. In Dublin, Walpole and Webb was restructured as Bewley Webb and Co. before withdrawing from building in 1871. Although Malcolmsen's Neptune

[8]Anderson, *Sailing Ships of Ireland*, 238-239, 241, 249, 259-260, 262.

Iron Works at Waterford remained open, it built only small steamers, leaving Harland and Wolff as the only large yard in Ireland.[9]

Figure 3
Output of Harland and Wolff and Workman Clark

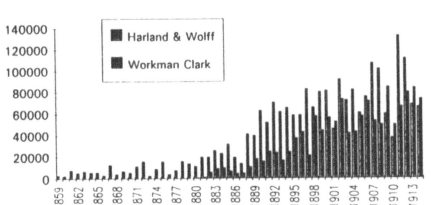

Source: Michael Moss and John R. Hume, *Shipbuilders to the World—125 Years of Harland and Wolff, Belfast 1861-1986* (Belfast, 1986), 506-565, and Workman Clark (1928) Ltd., *Shipbuilding at Belfast* (Belfast 1934).

In the late 1860s Harland and Wolff's facilities were greatly improved by the construction of the Abercorn basin and a graving dock by the Belfast Harbour Commissioners, which had superseded the Ballast Board. A further order from Bibby in 1869 prevented the yard from suffering the fate of most of its competitors. That same year Gustav Schwabe conceived a new venture to challenge Cunard and Inman on the north Atlantic. Christened the Oceanic Steam Navigation Co. and trading as the White Star Line, its ships were built by Harland and Wolff, managed by Ismay Imrie and Co., and financed by Schwabe. Under the direction of Thomas Ismay, White Star was an immediate success. The first six 3700-ton vessels were delivered in 1871 and 1872. Modelled on the "coffin" design, they had totally novel passenger accommodation. The next orders for two 455-foot, 5000-ton liners required the lengthening of berths and the installation of new equipment.[10]

---

[9]Moss and Hume, *Shipbuilders to the World*, 26-27, 507; Anderson, *Sailing Ships of Ireland*, 241-242, 262, 266-267.

[10]Moss and Hume, *Shipbuilders to the World*, 26-33.

The Harland and Wolff partnership was extended in 1875 to include three of the firm's managers, William J. Pirrie, Walter H. Wilson and Alexander B. Wilson. With shipbuilding in the doldrums and Bibby and Oceanic having sufficient tonnage to meet their requirements, the firm had to build sailing vessels and barges. Until 1877 the business scarcely made a profit. The following year Edward Harland again collaborated with Thomas Ismay and Gustav Schwabe to establish the Asiatic Steam Navigation Co. to serve the Far East. Contracts for four vessels were placed immediately with Harland and Wolff. Despite this order, in its first twenty years Harland and Wolff had not been by UK standards a spectacular success, building an average of 10,000 tons per year (figures 4a and b). The firm's output was dominated by the Schwabe connection, which accounted for over fifty percent of tonnage (see figure 5). Nevertheless, the yard dominated shipbuilding in Ireland, with six slipways by 1875 and no major competitors.[11]

By the late 1870s Harland and Wolff urgently needed its own engine works to maintain its position in the expanding UK industry. As a result, in 1878 it acquired the shipbuilding and marine engineering business of Alexander McLaine and Sons across the Lagan. The firm was spurred into expansion by the announcement that the marine engineers McIlwaine and Lewis, proprietors of the Ulster Iron Works on Queen's Island, were to begin shipbuilding on an adjacent site. Equally worrying was the construction of another yard on the north side of the river by Frank Workman and William Campbell, who had both served apprenticeships with Harland and Wolff and graduated to junior management positions. They were joined in 1880 by George Clark to form Workman Clark and Co. The Workman family had many connections with shipowners in Ireland and Scotland, while the Clark family was enmeshed in the Scottish and Ulster textile industry. With these strong ties, the new enterprise was well-placed to capture some of Harland and Wolff's custom. The new firm was an immediate success, and output climbed to over 10,000 tons in the third year of business (see figure 3).[12]

---

[11]*Ibid.*, 41-43.

[12]*Ibid.*, 43; Workman Clark (1928) Ltd., *Shipbuilding at Belfast* (Belfast, 1934); Liam Kennedy and P. Ollerenshaw, *An Economic History of Ulster 1820-1939* (Manchester, 1985), 94.

Figure 4a
UK and Irish Merchant Tonnage Constructed
1862-1900

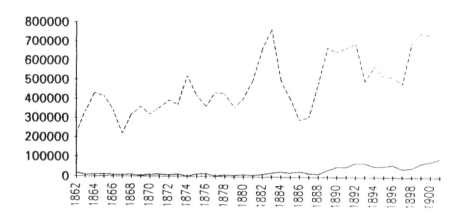

Source: Abstracted from Great Britain, Parliament, House of Commons, *Parliamentary Papers* (*BPP*), "Annual Statements of the Navigation and Shipping of the United Kingdom," 1862-1900.

Figure 4b
Percentage of UK Tonnage Built in Ireland

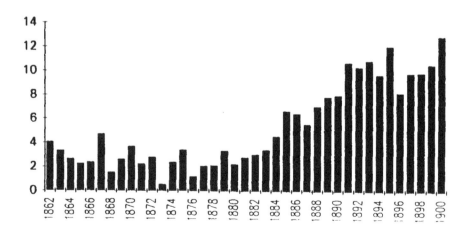

Source: See figure 4a.

Figure 5
Output of Harland & Wolff from 1859 to 1879

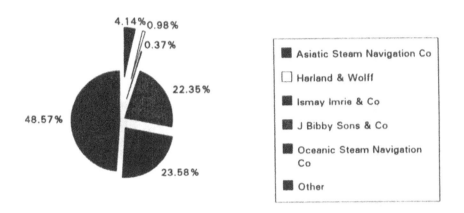

Source: Moss and Hume, *Shipbuilders to the World*, 506-565.

Figure 6a
Number of Sailing Ships Built in Ireland

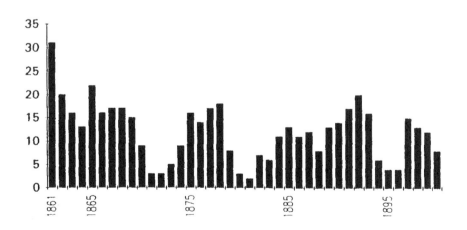

Source: See figure 4a.

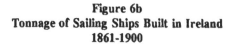

**Figure 6b
Tonnage of Sailing Ships Built in Ireland
1861-1900**

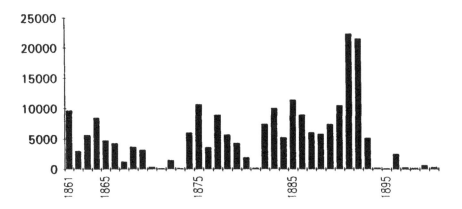

Source: See figure 4a.

Developments elsewhere in Ireland were on a lesser scale. At Carrickfergus on Belfast Lough, Paul Rodgers took over Johnson's small boatyard in 1874 and began to build iron schooners for the coastal trade, chiefly for J. Fisher and Sons of Barrow-in-Furness. On the Foyle plans were made to revive building with the support of the Londonderry Harbour Commissioners; Biggar and Co.'s Foyle Shipyards opened in 1882. John Comick opened the Dundalk Patent Slip and Shipbuilding Co. in 1876 to construct schooners and fishing boats. John Tyrrel and Sons, founded in Arklow in 1864, and Devereux's Dockyard Company at Wexford built and repaired coastal schooners. In 1878, at the nadir of the depression, eighteen sailing vessels of 5644 tons were constructed in Ireland. Numbers dropped in 1880 and 1881, but revived from 1883 (figures 6a and b). Yet none of the small yards needed a flow of new orders to remain solvent, since they could stay afloat through a steady stream of repair and refits. For this reason Malcolmsen's Neptune Iron Works stopped building in 1880 and, like Robinson at Cork a decade earlier, turned to repair.[13]

---

[13]Anderson, *Sailing Ships of Ireland*, 249-250, 262, 271, 278-280.

Apart from improving its facilities Harland and Wolff, influenced by Pirrie, sought to protect its market by making large advances and offering to build ships on four or five percent commission for a number of select customers. Those who received such favourable terms were required to place all their repair business with the company. At first this privilege was confined to the family network but was extended in 1882 to include the Liverpool-based African Steamship Co., and later T. and J. Brocklebank and D. and C. MacIver. Despite these concessions, the percentage of tonnage built for tied customers between 1879 and 1889 declined to 41.5% (see figure 7). Nevertheless, tied customers continued to be the main vehicle of Harland and Wolff's expansion, placing orders for the largest and most technically-advanced ships that incorporated novel features patented by the partners. After the resolution of the Home Rule issue in 1885, Harland and Wolff embarked on an ambitious plan to construct a new yard to the northeast of its existing berth to accommodate two 10,000-ton vessels for White Star. This investment allowed annual production to reach 40,000 tons per year in 1887 and to stay above that level for the remainder of the century. To ensure this demand, favourable terms for financing, including building on commission, were extended to several more clients, including the Baltimore Storage and Lighterage Co. in 1888 and the Union Steamship Co. in 1893. In addition, the firm was able to undercut its British competitors because Belfast's wages and cost of living were marginally lower.[14]

William Pirrie, now virtually in control of the company, was aware that building on commission was attractive only if costs were kept low. The best way to achieve this was to keep the shipyard fully booked. He thus refused Admiralty contracts, which from bitter experience he knew disrupted production and tied up facilities for long periods. He was also willing to build below cost during crises. This philosophy puzzled competitors; in 1890 representatives of the Clyde firm J. and G. Thomson, sent to examine the Harland and Wolff yard, concluded that

From the general information obtained and considering the somewhat extravagant expenditure in many of the departments compared with what is here, it does appear

---

[14]Moss and Hume, *Shipbuilders to the World*, 46-50, 57, 70-71; Sidney Pollard and Paul Robertson, *The British Shipbuilding Industry 1870-1914* (Cambridge, MA, 1979), 66-67.

somewhat curious how they can work so cheaply as to
procure such an enormous amount of freight carrying
tonnage, as, with the exception of their iron department
we consider that your establishment is all over as well
equipped as theirs and in many respects superior.[15]

Quite deliberately, Thomson's spies had not been allowed to see the
counting house, where the commission arrangements would have been all
too apparent. As a result of such deals, between 1889 and 1899 the
percentage of tonnage built for tied customers revived to over fifty
percent (figure 8). This recovery was accompanied by a continued
growth in throughput. Between 1890/91 and 1893/94 Harland and Wolff
built more vessels than any shipyard in the United Kingdom, due entirely
to tied business. A number of vessels constructed in these years included
innovative features. For example, four ships for the Union Steamship
Co. were fitted with overlapping twin screws and designed with a
shallow draft, enabling them to enter harbours on the west coast of South
Africa, especially Durban.[16]

Figure 7
Harland and Wolff Output By Major Customer 1879-89

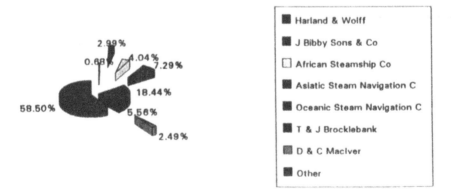

Source: See figure 5.

---

[15]Glasgow University Archives, UCS1/3/5, Report from James and George Thomson
Ltd. on operations of Harland and Wolff Ltd., Belfast, 1890.

[16]Moss and Hume, *Shipbuilders to the World*, 67-68.

Figure 8
Harland and Wolff Output by Major Customer, 1889-1899

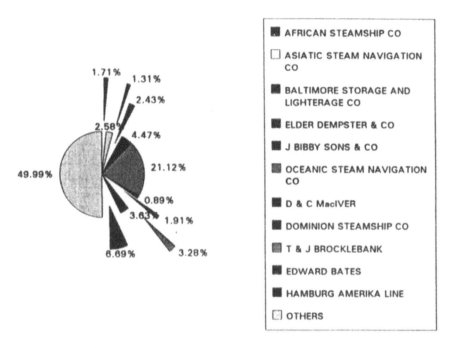

Source: See figure 5.

Production was disrupted by the next Home Rule crisis in 1893 and a serious fire in the summer of 1896, which damaged both the Harland and Wolff and Workman Clark yards and engine works. But by the end of 1896 Harland and Wolff's order book was filled, including a White Star contract for three 17,000-ton, 700-foot liners, "the largest and most elaborately and luxuriously finished vessels in the world." In order to build these vessels a giant gantry was installed over the ways, carrying mobile hydraulic cranes to lift the rivetting machines for the double bottoms and tank tops. The gantry was a novelty in the United Kingdom, probably based on one at Newport News in the United States; it attracted much comment in the technical press. The engine works were also re-equipped with labour-saving machine tools, also drawing on American practices much admired by William Pirrie.

Workman Clark's business, like Harland and Wolff's, suffered during the Home Rule crisis in the mid-1880s and recovered at the end of the decade. With the partners' family backgrounds in shipping and textiles, it was natural for the firm to specialize in cargo liners rather than the premier vessels built by Harland and Wolff. Charles Allan, whose family owned the Glasgow-based Allan Line, joined the firm in 1891 to open an engine and boiler works on Queen's Island adjacent to Harland and Wolff. Two years later Workman Clark took over the shipbuilding yard and engine and boilerworks on Queen's Island owned by McIlwaine and MacColl, previously McIlwaine and Lewis. The company at once began to reconstruct the yard to provide five berths. Increased capacity allowed Workman Clark to expand production so that by 1898 output was only a little behind Harland and Wolff. Yet unlike the latter, Workman Clark were much less dependent on contracts generated through family links (see figure 9).[17]

From the late 1880s Harland and Wolff and Workman Clark accounted for well over ninety percent of all the tonnage constructed in Ireland.[18] Between 1883 and 1893 the percentage of UK tonnage constructed in Ireland rose from just over four percent to more than ten percent (figure 4b above). This level was sustained for much of the rest of the decade, reflecting the remarkable achievements of Harland and Wolff and Workman Clark in establishing large shipbuilding businesses in a country without raw materials. All the iron, steel, metals, wood, and other materials had to be imported. In overcoming this obstacle, both firms were helped by the Belfast Harbour Commission, which continually upgraded facilities to meet the expanding needs of tenants on both sides of the Lagan. Despite a recession in the early years of the twentieth century, both continued to win large custom and to invest heavily in new plant and equipment. Workman Clark constructed the *Victorian* in 1904 for the Allan Line, the first turbine liner on the north Atlantic.[19] In 1911 Harland and Wolff, now integrated into Owen Cosby Philipps' Royal Mail Group, launched over 130,000 tons of new ships.[20] On the

---

[17]Kennedy and Ollerenshaw, *An Economic History of Ulster*, 94-95; Workman Clark, *Shipbuilding at Belfast*.

[18]It is impossible to produce accurate figures since the official production totals are less than for the two firms combined. This is because they exclude foreign orders.

[19]"Shipbuilders of Other Days," *Shipbuilding and Shipping Record* (29 December 1949), 786.

[20]Moss and Hume, *Shipbuilders to the World*, chapters 5 and 6.

eve of the First World War, Workman Clark overtook Harland and Wolff for the first time. Although the Clyde dominated UK shipbuilding in the late nineteenth and twentieth centuries, no two yards consistently built such a large proportion of the nation's total output.

Figure 9
Workman Clark Output by Major Customer, 1879-1900

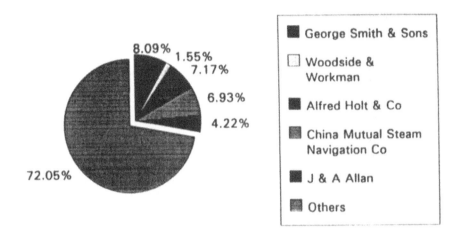

Source: Based on the ship list in Workman Clark, *Shipbuilding at Belfast.*

Elsewhere in Ireland shipbuilding continued to be more chequered. Biggar's Foyle shipyards built twenty-six sailing ships and six tramp steamers from 1882 to 1892. The sailing vessels were full-rigged steel ships of 1200-1800 tons. The business collapsed in 1892 and the plant was taken over on a care and maintenance basis by the Londonderry Harbour Commission. Re-opened in 1899 by the Londonderry Shipbuilding and Engineering Company to construct cargo liners and ferries, the new business was short-lived and the yard closed again in 1904.[21] In Dublin, shipbuilding, which had ceased in 1869, was not revived until December 1901 when on the initiative of the Dublin Port and Docks Board the Dublin Dockyard Company was established by Walter Scott and John Smellie, both from the Clyde. A completely new shipyard with five berths and repair works was established at the

---

[21]Anderson, *Sailing Ships of Ireland*, 250-253.

northwest corner of the Alexandra Basin. From the outset the Dockyard Company specialized in coasters of about 300 feet, supplemented by yachts and motor launches.[22] The building of wooden schooners by the smaller shipyards began to dwindle after 1894. The vessels became smaller--mostly fishing boats, as steamers began to replace sail even in the coastal trades (figures 6a and b above).

Figure 10: Harland Wolff engine works, Belfast, 1898.

Source: See figure 1.

The history of shipbuilding in Ireland presents some similarities with other parts of the United Kingdom. Traditional boat building persisted to serve local needs (coastal trades and fishing) and eventually declined. Large-scale shipbuilding was concentrated in large towns where there was adequate deep water and with sufficient infrastructure and labour to support them. What is remarkable about Ireland is the development of two large shipyards of the Lagan in Belfast with no

---

[22]J. Smellie, *Shipbuilding and Repairing in Dublin--A Record of Work Carried out by Dublin Dockyard Co. 1901-1923* (Glasgow, 1923), 51-60.

indigenous raw material resources in an environment of considerable political uncertainty and not elsewhere; for example, at Cork or Dublin. Part of the explanation must be the proximity of the Lagan to the Mersey and to a lesser extent the Clyde. More important must be the entrepreneurial and technical skill of Edward Harland and his partners, particularly William J. Pirrie, assisted by their Liverpool connections with the shipping trades. They, along with the partners in Workman Clark whom they had educated, were able to use these links to build and extend their businesses, while at the same time exploiting the political uncertainties to persuade or bully the Belfast Harbour Commissioners to provide space for expansion at very reasonable rates. The reason there was no development at Cork was almost certainly because there was sufficient repair work available from the transatlantic lines to satisfy the firms which had found the experience of shipbuilding unprofitable. Dublin and Londonderry are more perplexing. The absence of shipbuilding at Londonderry was probably due to the strength of Belfast, whereas Dublin's lack of participation may have been due to the lack of adequate management of the Lagan until the end of the century.